THE END

THE BOOK

PART SEVEN

THE NINTH OF AV

J. L. ROBB

Energy Concepts Productions books may be ordered through booksellers or by contacting:

Energy Concepts Productions
A Division of Energy Concepts
3328 E Whippoorwill Drive
Duluth, Georgia 30096

Because of the dynamic nature of the Internet, any web addresses or links contained in this book may have changed since publication and may no longer be valid. The views expressed in this work are solely those of the author and do not necessarily reflect the views of the publisher, and the publisher hereby disclaims any responsibility for them.

Bible scriptures are New International Version unless otherwise noted.

ISBN: 978-1-5323-9406-5 soft cover
ISBN: 978-1-5323-9405-8 hard cover
ISBN: 978-1-5323-9407-2 digital copy

Printed in the United States of America

Other books by JL Robb:

Preface

"This know also, that in the last days perilous times shall come. For men shall be lovers of their own selves, covetous, boasters, proud, blasphemers, disobedient to parents, unthankful, unholy, without natural affection, trucebreakers, false accusers, incontinent, fierce, despisers of those that are good, traitors, heady, high-minded, lovers of pleasures more than lovers of God; having a form of godliness, but denying the power thereof: from such turn away."

2 Timothy 3:1-5 (AKJV)

In the New Testament, Paul talks of events and moods in the Last Days of Earth as we now know it. The description above gives some indication of what people will be like in those days.

Are there terrible times, now? Throughout history, there has always been terrible times of suffering. Tragedy and disaster. Small pox and Black Death raised their ugly heads and have killed millions. History is dotted with "natural" disasters: earthquakes, tsunamis, tornadoes and hurricanes, volcanic eruptions and giant sinkholes.

In the past however, narcissism was kept in check for the most part, except for royalty. The common man remained mostly humble because he did not have the financing to be narcissistic.

That is hardly the case today. An hour in front of the TV or social media gives one a good idea of how very special so many feel they are today. Expensive cars, homes and smart phones seem to be available readily to much of the population. Common sense tells us that this is good, not bad; but is it? Porn shops in the palm of your hand. The devil is not stupid.

Are children more disobedient to parents than in past generations? Are they more disrespectful? What about ungrateful? Lovers of money?

Social media has become a Garden of Slander, and natural affection has become unnatural affection.

Paul's message was similar to Isaiah's message seven centuries earlier:

"Woe to those who call evil good, and good evil, who put darkness for light and light for darkness, who put bitter for sweet and sweet for bitter."

These descriptions of the Last Days are happening now, more than any other time in history. Pick up a newspaper or view a news site and make note of all the *unprecedented* weather and climatic events.

John's vision, described in Revelation, indicates that the climate will get much warmer. It was not Al Gore's idea. But the cause is solar activity, not mankind.

"The fourth angel poured out his bowl on the sun, and the sun was allowed to scorch people with fire. They were seared by the intense heat and they cursed the name of God, who had control over these plagues, but they refused to repent and glorify him."

Revelation 16:8-9

Isaiah also mentions increased solar activity when referring to the Last Days:

"The moon will shine like the sun, and the sunlight will be seven times brighter, like the light of seven full days, when the Lord binds up the bruises of his people and heals the wounds he inflicted."

Isaiah 30:26

As each day passes it seems there is more hatred in the world. Not dissatisfaction and not disappointment. Hatred seems to be raging. One needs to look no further than Washington, DC and European capitals.

The Ninth of Av is the seventh and final book in the *The End: The Book* series. The ninth of Av is the ninth day of the fifth month of the Jewish Calendar and usually occurs late July.

The date has a tragic history for the Jewish people, including the date that the First Temple was destroyed and the date of the destruction of the Second Temple.

It is also the day of the antichrist.

Note from the Author

The Ninth of Av

THE END: THE BOOK Series is a fictional account of the predicted apocalypse as outlined in the prophetic books of the Bible. Several readers have asked me, "Is this book true?"

It is true that the Biblical end will happen, but I have written this series as a counter-weight to the apocalyptic fiction coming out of Hollywood, like *Armageddon* and *2012*, that fail to include God and His role in this approaching war of good vs. evil that was predicted 2,700 years ago.

Any similarities between things that are occurring now and things written in this series are purely coincidental. It would be impossible to write a *true* account of the Biblically described End Times.

The Ninth of Av is the seventh book of the seven-book series and represents a day in the month of Av, the fifth month of the Jewish Calendar. The month of Av is also the Month of Mourning.

"Why do the nations conspire and the peoples plot in vain?
The kings of the earth rise up and the rulers band together
against the Lord and against his anointed…"

Psalms 2:1-2

J.L. Robb is an author and writer with a Bachelor of Science in Zoology, North Carolina State University. A U.S. Navy Veteran, Robb lives in the Bible Belt with his Great Dane and a kitty named Glock. Robb is a member of Civitan International, Friends of Gideons and The American Legion.

We support our Veterans!

Dedication

I dedicate *The End: The Book: Series* to Yahweh and His Holy Son, Jesus, who saved my life. He will save anyone who asks.

Thank you God for helping me write this series.

A special Thank You to daughter Erica who designed all seven book covers, web page and videos, etc.

www.TheEndTheBook.com

When asked why he had given up the synagogue for the church, Zolli replied, "I have not given it up. Christianity is the completion of the synagogue, for the synagogue was a promise; and Christianity is the fulfillment of that promise."

"Once a Jew always a Jew."
Israel Zolli, Chief Rabbi of Rome 1943

List of Main Characters

Abc the Bartender: General Manager and bartender at *The Divide Disco & Café*.

Aboud Rehza: aka Vinny. In charge of U.S. Operations for Jihad's Warriors. Twin brother of Mohammed Rehza who is in charge of European operations.

Aludra: Sister of Muhammed Khalid, Jihad's Warrior in charge of Afghanistan and Pakistan. She and her brother live in the Korengal Valley of Death, Afghanistan-Pakistan border.

"Wild Willy" Briggs: Master of Nanotechnology. Ex-Navy, CIA and Homeland Security. Works closely with Israel's Mossad.

Chad "Chadbo" Myers: Assistant Director, Near Earth Object and Heliospheric Laboratory, Goddard Space Flight Center, Greenbelt, MD.

Chuck Hutz: a.k.a. Hutz the Putz. After auto accident, speaks fluent Hebrew and witnesses to others while in a trance.

Condi Zimmerman: Independent news anchor/reporter and host of The Condi Zimmerman Show.

Edgar Allan Poe: Homeless veteran who discovers terrorist plot. Becomes terrorism expert with Homeland Security.

Gray and Andi Dorey: Friends of Jeff Ross, philanthropists and owners of *Dine for Dollars*, a restaurant for the homeless or just the hungry.

Jeffrey Ross: Avid atheist and ex-husband of Melissa. Father of three daughters, Jami and Jenni (twins) and Audry, his youngest.

Kari Vermi: News anchor with OLNN, Omega Letter Network News. Columnist with omegaletter.com

Kipper T and Missy T: Angels who appear to Jeff in dreams.

Melissa Ross: Divorced from Jeff Ross, mother of twins, Jami and Jenni, and adopted daughter, Audry.

Samarra Russell: Married to Senator Jack Russell. Past Director, Communicable Diseases Research Center, CDC. Responsible for theft of Spanish Flu virus.

Scott Johnson: Assistant manager of *The Divide Disco & Café*.

Sheryl Lasseter: Director of United States Public Relations Liaison. Works directly for the U.S. President.

The Admiral: Justin P. McLemore. A graduate of the U.S. Naval Academy and retired four-star Admiral. Director of Near-Earth Object and Heliospheric Laboratory, Goddard Space Flight Center, Maryland.

Vinny: Aboud Rehza, a product of wealthy Saudi parents. He and his twin brother, Mohammed, had been child prodigies; and both spoke several languages fluently. A man of many aliases.

What has happened so far?

For our struggle is not against flesh and blood, but against the rulers, against the authorities, against the powers of this dark world and against the spiritual forces of evil in the heavenly realms.

Ephesians 6:12

Part One: And Then the End Will Come

Jeffrey Ross is Duluth, Georgia's most eligible bachelor; but not by choice. Retired Navy SEAL and successful entrepreneur, he had been married to Melissa almost 25 years; and he thought everything was hunky-dory. They had beautiful twin daughters and adopted daughter, Audry and a nice home in a country club community, nice cars and toys, what could be wrong.

Melissa asked for the divorce, begrudgingly. She loved Jeff, but he didn't believe in God, never had; but what was worse was his ridiculing of believers. Over the years, her faith grew stronger and she enjoyed her church community; but she and the daughters enjoyed it alone. No way was Jeff going to step foot in a church.

The divorce and Melissa's subsequent remarriage had taken its toll; and while Jeff wasn't a broken man, he remained in the dumps for the next four years. The most eligible bachelor wasn't available. He was hoping his wife would come back.

Jeff made new friends and maintained most of their old friendships too, as did Melissa, including The Admiral, Sheryl, Chadbo, Wild Willy and Abe the Bartender.

Nine thousand miles away, along the border of Pakistan and Afghanistan, the Korengal Valley of Death festered with various jihadist groups, Muslims with a common cause: Kill the infidels. That would be everyone except them.

Jihad's Warriors, virtually unknown, unlike al Qaeda, had infiltrated the borders of Europe and the United States for years, decades. The U.S. border with Mexico was as porous as Swiss cheese; and jihadists had taken advantage with bribery and murder.

The Chechen jihadists from Eastern Europe looked, talked and acted as American as mom's apple pie. The Arab jihadists passed easily for Latino immigrant laborers, but these were not laborers.

The Divine Plan was to run America and Europe out of money. The warriors knew the West couldn't protect every single nursery school, church, synagogue, campground, shopping center, hospital and highway. It would be easy. Once economically destitute, the Islamic takeover of the world would finalize.

While Manhattan and Chicago remained the desired targets, security was tight. The Islamists would concentrate on the Bible Belt, more Christians that turn the other cheek rather than fight.

Jihad's Warriors were financed, not by Muslims so much as by a group of wealthy Japanese businessmen bent on revenge for the nuclear bombings of Nagasaki and Hiroshima during World War II. They were the grandsons and granddaughters of those burnt alive in December, 1945, the Baby Bombers. Money was no problem.

Jeffrey continues his pursuit of Melissa, now widowed, and can't help but notice all the people carrying The End Is Near signs. They seemed to be everywhere. Then there were the disappearing people, and Jeff remembered his mom's lectures.

"In the last days, sonny boy, people gonna be disappearin', yes they are. You start seeing folks vanishin' in thin air, you better find God. That's all I can say."

A creature of habit, Jeff had a routine that included the Dunwoody Starbucks every morning for coffee and the Atlanta newspaper. He was a news junkie. The Mayan Apocalypse was just around the corner, and people worldwide were preparing for The End. Ridiculous.

One warmer than usual spring morning, record heat the words of the day, Jeff enjoys his latte and paper when suddenly his world changes... again.

The brown cargo van circling the small shopping center explodes with vigor as America's first suicide bomber begins a wave of terror like the nation has never seen. Two minutes later another explosion several blocks away blows up a Dunwoody day care center. Forty-seven dead in a split second.

Jeff's Navy buddies, Chad Myers and The Admiral, work with the Goddard Space Flight Center in Maryland. Astronomy buffs, their primary concern was space objects on a collision course with planet Earth. Near-Earth objects, mostly small asteroids, had become more commonplace.

Unfortunately, news of the object most recently discovered would now have to be shared with the world as it made its way past Jupiter on a course that would hit Earth in less than a year. The object, still invisible to most telescopes, was dark, massive and unavoidable.

Sixty-five million years earlier, the dinosaurs and most living creatures had been wiped out by an asteroid only six miles in diameter. The Dark Comet was more than a hundred.

As the world reacts to the coming devastation, many begin to believe that the end really is near this time; and there was nothing anyone could do about it. There was little panic.

When Jeff's friend, Samarra receives a strange call, she returns home as instructed. She would follow the instructions as directed, or she would receive her son's head in a box instead of the finger she stared at in desperation. And she did.

Samarra's access to Atlanta's CDC biological disease labs made her job simple and soon the Spanish Flu, one of the great killers of all time, is loosed into an unsuspecting world. It was inevitable, millions would die.

In the Indian Ocean, a hijacked nuclear attack sub vanishes. The only remnants were an oil slick, clothing and assorted debris but not enough to indicate the submarine was at the bottom of the Marianas Trench.

As New Year's Eve approaches, Jeff and Melissa visit Grand Cayman Island to celebrate memories and await the coming comet. To most it seemed the Earth would end months before the predicted Mayan prophecy.

A few hundred miles east of Grand Cayman, on the island of Montserrat, the Soufriére Hills volcano erupts and is blown into the Caribbean Sea. The massive tsunami that is generated speeds across the ocean toward Puerto Rico, Jamaica and… Grand Cayman.

Part Two: You Have Been Warned

Jeff returns from Grand Cayman Island alone. He and Melissa tried to escape the giant wave but were washed off the 4-story roof of their beachfront hotel. Melissa's body was never found, and Jeff mourns his loss. He had prayed they would reconcile, his first prayer since a child; and it looked like it might happen.

The New Year started off with a bang, literally, when the U.S. suffered its first nuclear strikes, one at the Diego Garcia island chain in the Indian Ocean that destroyed most of America's B-52 bomber force. The second destroyed the Buford Dam, Atlanta's fresh water supply.

The Dark Comet continued its journey toward Earth, two weeks until impact. Attempts to destroy the comet with the world's nuclear weapons supply failed to deter the coming tragedy.

The world became unified for the first time in history in their effort to stop the comet, and joyous applause erupted globally when the comet slammed into the moon instead of Earth. Unfortunately, the resulting debris from the lunar collision meant waves of meteor showers for Earth, many of which made it through the atmosphere, destroying numerous communities, including the Three Gorges Dam in China.

Thankful that the world was still intact, Jeff flies to California to buy his million-dollar dream car, a one of a kind 1954 Cadillac Pininfarina Cabriolet. Maybe that, he hoped, would occupy his mind a while. Shopping was great for depression.

Upon arrival at the La Jolla Jetport, Jeff's tragic misfortune continues as he is struck with the deadly and pervasive Spanish Flu. During his hospitalization, he begins to have a series of strange dreams, dreams of small white churches in fields of blooming daffodils. Dreams of a tiny Arizona town named Lukeville. The

European riots had become infectious, and America's cities did the same as gasoline reached $8.00 a gallon. The police forces, hampered by budget cuts and not enough employees, became brutal; and rioters were killed mercilessly.

The jihadists coordinated closely with a well-organized Christian militia under the philosophy of *The enemy of my enemy is my friend*. Their common enemy was the U.S. government.

The Admiral's romance with Sheryl blossoms cautiously, at least until the kidnapping. That's when he discovered his real feelings, the ones he had sheltered for sixty years.

Recalling their private conversation, he wasn't really surprised that the President had sold out Israel; only, it wasn't Israel's God that was trying to kill everyone in America, it was Islam's God.

What was surprising, and shocking, was the rumor that there were thousands of infiltrators living and working in the nation's infrastructure: nuclear power plants, water treatment facilities, food distribution warehouses.

Vinny, a.k.a. Aboud, hasn't gotten any nicer as he continues to meet with his deputies at the concrete plant in Lukeville. The meetings, though brief, usually occurred on the Mexican side of the deep, underground tunnel connecting the concrete facility in Lukeville with the beer distributor on the other side of the border. Plans were made, plans of terror, death and destruction; and the stored weapons and nerve agents were the vehicles Allah would use.

Wild Willy continues his work with Mossad and Senator Jack Russell, Samarra's husband. The nanotech spybots were no longer experimental and looked like assorted bugs, but Will was especially fond of the dragonfly style. Looked just like the real thing.

Samarra's case goes to the U.S. Federal Court in Atlanta. The charges are numerous, including international homicide charges for the tens of millions killed because of the Spanish Flu. During the trial, Samarra's senator husband is arrested in a San Francisco shower house with a young boy and charged with possession of child porn and sex with a minor. Senator Russell stated that he thought the boy was 12, the new legal age of consent in the United States.

After Jeff's recovery from the Spanish Flu, he continues to have the strange dreams about a couple named Missy T and Kipper T, reggae music and disco lights; and the room, the one with the dark door. You don't want to go through that door. Missy T made the comment numerous times.

Jeff's life, a life that's never dull, continues to change suddenly and often. He finds himself having second thoughts about the whole religion thing, at least sometimes. He really couldn't explain how the Gideons Bible kept showing up.

One day Jeff gets a call from Samarra. Her trial was over quickly, temporary insanity; and her penalty was light. She asked if she could visit, they had been friends for many years.

During her visit to Jeff's Sugarloaf estate, yet another megacryometeorite storm hits North Atlanta. Jeff's home is spared, but a young girl in a Porsche is killed in his neighbor's driveway. The large ice bomb that hit the new Porsche Spyder was estimated to weigh 120 to 150 pounds, larger than a beach ball.

Samarra informs Jeff that she and Senator Russell are now divorced; and over the next few months, a new romance blossoms. There had always been something there.

The months passed swiftly, and soon Jeff plans a visit to his dive shop in Negril. Before going to Jamaica to check on the business, Jeff and Samarra become engaged, though a date is not set.

Jeff's journey to Jamaica is plagued with thoughts and confusion, not about his profound love for Samarra but about all the natural disasters going on. It was downright scary.

The Admiral told him about the large rock that appeared to be leaving the Moon's orbit, and he finds himself hoping to God that it wouldn't. He fell asleep and dreamed, dreams of earthquakes and volcanos, roaring seas and asteroids, drought and poisoned waters… and Melissa. He prayed in his dream, a prayer that Melissa hadn't suffered in the tsunami, that she had been killed instantly in the fall.

Part Three: Visions and Dreams

Hailstorms are the talk of every news station it seems, as Jeff cruises the highways with his new Cadillac, listening to Al-Jazeera News. Millions of acres have been destroyed in Europe, and Northern California's crops are not spared. Homeless and Starving in the U.S.A. has become the chant of protesters as the hail batters crops and wildlife into the ground.

Two years after Melissa's death, Jeff finds love with a friend from the past; and his kids are receptive to the romance, amazingly. Amazing because Samara has been acquitted of stealing the Spanish Flu virus from CDC due to temporary insanity. That theft, now in the hands of the blackmailing Jihadist Warriors is doing its job well with estimated global fatalities now in excess of fifty million.

Vinny's (a.k.a Aboud) jihadist terror group continues to wreak havoc in the United States as his twin, Mohammed, known in the small French town as The Preacher, wreaks the same in Europe. The penetration of France's largest nuclear power plant's automated facility management system was simple, and access to the plant infrastructure now rested in the hands of Mohammed.

Mohammed has a following of gullible Christians who bought his fakery; but then, he is a good actor. The basement of the small, stone church tells another story as he collects more and more propane tanks, one at a time from different locations. The church is a sitting bomb, but Mohammed loved explosions. It ran in his family. Soon enough he would meet with Dmitry to secure the procurement, now paid for in full by the secretive Japanese group, the Select. They hate Americans even more than the Muslims hate the Jews. Two billion U.S. dollars for five high-yield, thermonuclear weapons.

Jihad's Warriors have penetrated the Mexican border for several years, usually with the help of the drug cartels. Now that had all changed, and the border was more porous than Swiss cheese. The

U.S. administration continues to be oblivious to the religion of Islam and seems to think all Muslims are Arabs. That's good for Vinny.

As the earliest hurricane in Atlantic history bears down on Florida, news from Goddard Space Flight Center and NASA is no better. The dark comet's collision with the moon at first seems like a silver lining, since it would have ended all life on Earth had it not been for the moon. The moon was now pink instead of white, and the surrounding rings of debris has a divine beauty of sorts.

The beauty quickly becomes a beast as Earth begins to be bombarded by debris, and meteorites hitting Earth become common news as flights throughout the world are in disarray with many airports closing intermittently. Some reports from China suggest the possibility that the lunar debris may be poisoning fresh water supplies.

Just north of Clemson, South Carolina, a cotton farmer's crop duster is stolen with plans to dust Atlanta's new football stadium during the Super Bowl. The dual-winged crop duster is one of a kind. Powered by Daimler-Benz, the Italian Fiat CR42B engine powers the plane to the horse farm north of Marietta in less than thirty minutes. There the banner will be attached advertising free beer at Jamaica Joe's.

Jeff's romance with Samarra blossoms quickly. The chemistry had always been there, even during her marriage to Senator Russell. When the good Senator is caught in compromising positions with young boys in bathhouses, Samarra's divorce follows. Jeff feels it is meant to be.

Excited about his wedding plans, for the first time in a long while Jeff finds himself deliriously happy. He leaves for Jamaica to check on his declining SCUBA business with plans to return during Christmas when he and Samarra will marry on the beach. The flight to Negril is non-eventful, other than a few meteors in the distant sky; and he checks into the Ross Suite at the Charela Inn. A message from Rosalie, the maid he had grown to know well, is disturbing.

Jeff's flight back to Atlanta does not ease his emotional conflict. How will he tell the kids? How will he explain to Samarra that Melissa is alive and well, rescued after the Cayman tsunami by Jamaican fishermen? How will he let them know that Melissa has no memory of them, or him and is preaching Jesus to a bunch of Voodoos or whatever you call them, in the rainforests of Jamaica?

It seems to Jeff that just as things finally start going good, God throws in a monkey wrench just to keep you on your toes. Only he still cannot get his arms around the concept of a god who is invisible but created everything. That story was unbelievable, but then a lot of his life is becoming unbelievable. If he could only see a sign.

Chadbo and The Admiral continue to carefully monitor all the things flying around Earth, dismayed that it was only a matter of time before a big one hit the planet. There have been numerous close encounters with asteroids a couple of football fields long, but they are small compared to many they have discovered. Plus there is the unprecedented solar activity and stars that seem to be disappearing. The two men recognized that all stars eventually burn out, only stellar theory suggests that takes billions of years. Why would so many be disappearing at the same time?

The Mother's Day Massacre, as it is now called has caught everyone off guard. Random sniper attacks and bombings on Mother's Day claim hundreds of lives, mostly women and their children. A bombing by a Christian Militia group completely destroys Atlanta's Five Points Marta station and most of the travelers and MARTA staff inside.

As Jeff and Samarra continue to plan their New Year's Eve wedding in Jamaica, at the suggestion of Melissa, Dmitry Ustinov waits in a small Monaco café for The Preacher. The French military guarded the streets of Paris and other affected cities because of the failure of the Civaux Nuclear power plants. Israel is blamed for the intrusion into the plants' security systems, and anti-Semitism is out of control in all of Europe.

Dmitry warns Mohammed that the five thermonuclear weapons are extremely dangerous and much more destructive than the bombs of Nagasaki and Hiroshima.

"When these babies go off, Mohammed," Dmitry whispered, "You need to be at least thirty miles away."

Of course, as Russia's number one illicit arms supplier, Dmitry planned to be far, far away when St. Petersburg was reduced to cinders and ash. He loved the motherland, but he loved dinars more.

Though Dmitry knows little of Jihad's Warriors' plans, he does know that New Year's Eve in Times Square will be one to remember.

New Year's Eve on a beach in Jamaica turns out to be as surprising as the soon to be Manhattan Event, at least in Jeff's mind. The marriage is perfect, the guests are perfect, even the Voodoo priest who accompanied Melissa is perfect, her latest conversion conquest.

Melissa's memories have returned for the most part, and she stands on the beach by the quiet surf, talking with her three daughters and pointing upward to a bright star in the clear, Jamaica night sky. Jeff glances upward at the star and was certain he saw slight movement. Maybe it was a plane.

In Manhattan, eight large, black Mylar balloons are attached to two, 2-kiloton briefcase nuclear bombs, a play being acted out in three other high-rise buildings surrounding Times Square. The suicide bombers high-five each other as the balloons are released from the Penthouse and into the dark night sky above New York City. When the eight bombs go off, they will be in the warm bosoms of seventy-two virgins.

Melissa gives the kids a big hug, turns and walks over to Samarra and Jeff. It is nearly midnight, and her head suddenly feels light. Her skin tingles and tiny goose bumps appear. She truly is happy for the newlyweds. She glances skyward, searching for the star and is startled to see how much closer it is. Maybe it's an airplane, she thought quietly.

As midnight approaches, less than five seconds away, Melissa kisses Jeffrey Ross on the cheek and squeezes his hand gently. The white light in the sky grows in intensity and moves high above the beaches of Jamaica's south shore; and the crowd stared, mesmerized or too frightened to move. Melissa's parting words will forever stay in Jeff's mind.

"Here's a sign, Jeffrey," and with that she rises into the air, quickly toward the white light, now more like the midday sun, and disappeared. The star quickly dimmed and then it too disappeared, and silence lingered with the small crowd. The Voodoo priest who spent the evening talking with anyone who would listen about "de Lady of de Sea" and how she saved him, vanished in an instant.

Part Four: The Disappearance

As a group of large, Mylar balloons float over Times Square, the New Year's Eve celebration never turns chaotic as the nearly one million celebrants in the crowd below are vaporized in an instant, not the result of the Rapture but the detonation of several low-yield nuclear weapons, hanging below the large, helium filled balloons. Wall Street will never be the same, and ATMs across the country cease to operate.

A minute prior to the detonation and seen by only a few, some people in the crowd disappear, simply vanish; and this disappearance of people occurs all over the world. It is the beginning.

Heat records are broken daily and environmentalists continue to scream and demand more funding to prevent the warming caused by mankind. Only there is no more funding. The free world is in financial disarray, as Jihad's Warriors continue their battle to run the West out of money.

The continuing Islamic attacks have terrorized the nation and the world; and every three months, like clockwork, the death toll dedicated to Allah, rises.

Iranian nuclear sites come under nuclear attack from an unknown source somewhere in the Mediterranean Sea, only to learn that the sites were exotically constructed decoys.

If man's attempts at destroying civilization are not enough, nature's fury raises the human and animal death toll exponentially. Unprecedented hailstorms flatten entire villages, killing people and livestock, pets and plants as leaves and branches are stripped from trees.

Chadbo and The Admiral closely monitor numerous incoming meteors, one of which the world must destroy or be destroyed by the massive, arsenic laden rock. The strike is successful; and thousands of miles above Earth, the incoming asteroid is destroyed. A large cloud of arsenic dust slowly descends on Earth, pulled by gravity.

Vinny and his Islamist gang plan small nuclear attacks along the West Coast but have no idea the West Coast will soon be no more, at least no more life.

A small asteroid makes its way from the moon's rings toward Earth but is given little priority. It is heading for the Antarctic with virtually no potential for damage.

Chadbo, concerned with possibilities, monitors the small space object and his fears are recognized. The asteroid explodes high above the Ross Ice Shelf, slamming a five-mile stretch of the shelf into the ocean. A large surface wave, a wave the size of no other, rushes northward toward New Zealand, Hawaii and the West Coast of the United States.

At 2,700 feet in height, the wave sinks a third of the world's navies and thousands of pleasure craft. Skirting along the California

Coast, the skyscrapers of San Diego and Los Angeles are no match and collapse to what had been ground below.

In less than ten hours, millions have died along the coasts of California, Oregon, Washington and Alaska. The death toll in Japan, China, Indonesia, India, Australia and New Zealand top ten million and continues to climb. There are no longer Mexican resorts along the Pacific coast.

Jeffrey Ross and Samarra, now married, have had little honeymoon so far; and Samarra continues to recover from the strange bite. A physical toll has been taken, and she wonders if she will ever have her strength back.

Jeff rediscovers an EPROM that a homeless man gave him a couple of years earlier and finds there is a Christian extremist group in the mountains of North Georgia that appears to be working with the jihadists.

Well aware that he should take someone with him, Jeff heads to the mountains alone. His million-dollar sports car is later found in several pieces at the bottom of Tallulah Gorge.

Part Five: The Two Witnesses

With the nuclear annihilation of Manhattan, the financial hub is no more. Though ATM issues are gradually repaired, getting cash is iffy at best; but life goes on. It must.

The strange disappearance of people slows dramatically, though more of the vanishings have made their way to social media outlets. Youtube and Vimeo are awash in live videos of folk disappearing at dinners, weddings, funerals and underground churches.

President Morsi, a Shi'a Muslim of Iranian heritage, is the leader of the world it seems as more and more nations join the New World Order Federation and turn over control of their militaries. The United Nations is extinct.

Climate change is more than the talk of the town these days, and temperatures continue their upward trend. The extreme winds feel more like a blast furnace than a fresh, summer breeze.

The death and destruction caused by the collapse of the Ross Ice Shelf is realized. The West Coast of the Americas, as well as the eastern edges of Asia are not recognizable; and millions are drowned. In the process, most of the world's navies sink to the bottom of the sea.

Hailstorms are epidemic in parts of the world, even worse than the raining lunar asteroids.

In Jerusalem, two strange and tall men appear on the ancient Temple Mount, dressed in dark, burlap-looking clothes and begin to preach to the Israelis.

"You missed the Messiah," they proclaim, day after day with the same, consistent message: God brought you back to Israel, and you have betrayed Him again. You cannot keep enough of The Law to make it to the next life. Only through recognizing the Christ will you achieve that glorious goal.

Time passes and the two preachers continue their daily rants, condemning Israel for rejecting the Messiah and the entire world for their decadent ways. As months become years, the people of Israel and the world begin to hate and despise the two men who now proclaim they are the Two Witnesses of Revelation 11.

Assassination attempts become routine but to no avail as the Two Witnesses call down the wrath of the God of Heaven, and the world catches fire. Anyone who tries to harm the Two Witnesses are engulfed in flame, what science is now calling cases of Spontaneous Human Combustion.

Extreme drought encompasses Earth, and the Middle East has no rain for nearly three years. The only sources of fresh water are the frequent and horrific hailstorms. Millions of livestock and thousands of people are killed by the Hail from Hell.

The Two Witnesses, because the people do not repent from evil, call down fire from Heaven; and the world suffers her worst lightning storms in history.

Fires rage from the Appalachian Mountains to the Rockies, from the Pyrenees to the Alps; and smoke and toxins fill the air. Those with respiratory problems have no chance.

Jeffrey Ross and his group of senior citizen friends seek meaning in a world of anarchy. Vinny, a.k.a. Aboud, and the Jihad's Warriors continue their reign of terror on the United States while his twin brother does the same in Europe.

President Morsi stuns the world with miraculous acts, some not seen since the days Jesus walked the earth; and the Children of Israel become convinced Morsi is the Messiah.

Part Six: The Third Woe

Chuck Hutz, now an international star, appears on TV often, uncannily predicting unprecedented weather events. Like the Two Witnesses, he becomes more hated with his accuracy. During an interview with Condi Zimmerman, he vanishes in the middle of a conversation. While this disappearance on live TV would usually be considered a miracle, in the new and improved America, anything-God could get one in big trouble. Morality police, pushed by ultraorthodox Islamic immigrants, are on every corner.

Nuclear attacks from a Saudi-based Red Crescent ship two-hundred miles off the coast of Virginia, devastate United States Navy stations in Norfolk and St. Marys, Georgia.

Vinny kidnaps Jeff's family, threatening to kill Audry; and Jeff's obsession with Vinny grows. With help from Wild Willy, the search is on; and Will works magic with his Israeli-designed drones.

When the Two Witnesses are killed in Jerusalem, the entire globe rejoices; and the bodies are left lying in the street for three-and-a-half days. The celebration comes to a sudden halt when the Two Witnesses begin to stir and are raptured into the heavens for all to see.

A video is released though Al Jazeera News, and the Catholic world is shocked as they watch Jihad's Warriors crucify the kidnapped Pope. It seems the long awaited world domination by Islam's most prolific killers, described in the Iranian story of the Twelfth Imam, is upon them.

Militant Islam continues to spread throughout the Caribbean, and the passageway into America remains simple. Trinidad to Belize to Mexico. An unexpected event for the migrants was the plague of rabid animals, and simple bites turned fatal after thirty days of torment.

Life on Earth is quickly becoming misery on Earth, and the sun is no one's friend. Every day seems hotter and brighter, scientists now blaming the sun instead of man. Lunaroids falling from the dark-red moon continue to scatter microscopic arsenic across the planet; and water sources turn into pools of blood, caused by the hemorrhaging of all underwater animal life.

Abe the Bartender, after a near-death experience, begins to have wild dreams of a future world he hopes is only a dream: An earth on fire, a barren planet void of trees, ash-filled air, darkness and disease. Then he meets Condi Zimmerman when she books a news report series in Duluth, and they become instant friends. She tells him of reports out of Israel about the third and final woe, described in Revelation; and Abe describes the prophecy. Seven final events will come upon the world, and each is worse that the predecessor. These Seven Bowl Judgments bring much of the remaining world population to its knees. Remarkably, few repent and most curse God and anyone who believes. Christianity is nearly nonexistent.

Jeff is introduced to a pastor from England, B.J. Stagner, while searching for Vinny. B.J. and Jeff discuss the fishing around Dalton's beautiful lakes; and B.J. tells him about a new fishing buddy he met, a guy named Vinny.

Samarra, sick of Jeff's obsession with Vinny, informs him that she is filing for divorce. On the other side of the Atlantic, a large part of La Palma is collapsing into the sea, but Jeff heard neither Samarra nor the News Alert.

"There is an emergency tsunami warning for the entire East Coast of Canada, the United States, Mex..."

Prologue

Flight to Israel

Jeff ran in the house; and the smell of smoke permeated the hot, still morning air. In a flash, he had his belongings thrown onto a U.S. Navy burlap bag from things past. They were waiting, and expediency was most important.

He took one last look at what was once a beautiful home, before the gangs, wild animals and giant pieces of ice falling from the sky. He felt like crying but had no time for that display of emotion. He would miss Duluth, but not as much as he missed Jami and Jenni. He threw the bag in the back, and Scarlette let out a yelp. She was such a coward.

Jeff and Great Dane Scarlette rode quietly in the Land Rover toward Briscoe field and Wild Willy's B36J Peacemaker. Hopefully they would make it before the runway was swallowed by the ever-growing field of sinkholes.

"OLN News," he said to the audio system; and in an instant, he was listening to his obsession. It was like a never-ending movie.

"…record heat in the Holy Land, except in Jerusalem where the temperature is a mild ninety-two Fahrenheit. The dedication of the Third Temple is less than four hours away, and the Jews and Christians in Israel are celebrating zealously. There are few

security people for this dedication, and Israeli officials are duly concerned. Today is the Ninth of Av, the fifth month of the Jewish Calendar and has a history of terrific tragedies. Hopefully this will not be the case today.

"The United States, Europe and South America continue to burn, adding to the haze and darkness. With 3 major eruptions in the past week, including Yellowstone, gases and ash are killing people and wildlife as the sky grows darker with each day. England is calling the unprecedented disaster, the Days of Darkness. The eruptions are being blamed by meteorologists for all the devastating hailstorms around the world. An estimated twelve-thousand people were killed yesterday in Sydney as Australia reels from yet another unprecedented disaster.

"The Eastern Mediterranean Sea is now the world's greatest warship traffic jam in history, as the militaries continue to surround Israel. While the new temple is being dedicated, the military cordon around the country, tightens. There are reportedly more military weapons in an area no greater than Delaware than at any time in history.

"Is the sun getting brighter? Scientists think..."

The sun did seem especially bright, but Chadbo had warned of such. His research and latest book, *The Temperament of the Sun*, claims that the sun is seven-times brighter than when it formed on the fourth day of creation, a belief he held until he disappeared that day. The man was brilliant.

Jeff dodged a small sinkhole, but there was little traffic. Everyone was afraid and stayed home these days, armed and ready; and it seemed a civil war was just around the corner. Already, Christian militias were bombing Islamic temples and synagogues while Islamic jihadists waged holy war against anything Christian, Jewish and atheist. It was only a matter of time before the great war of good versus evil would begin.

Glancing left, the landscape that was once filled with green, hundred-foot oaks and tall, slender pines was now a Field of Nightmares. Tall vertical, black stubs stood at attention, a salute to Satan maybe. He figured the ground would smoke forever. Twenty to thirty wild dogs and coyotes fought among the stoic statues of once green trees, chasing something.

His mood became melancholy as he drove toward the airport. He missed the world the way it *had* been. He missed the bright yellow daffodils and the hummingbirds, the occasional snow and rainbows, the white sands of Florida beaches and majestic Smoky Mountains. It had changed fast, and he was beginning to wonder if he would make the cut, the Final Cut. *The road to perdition is wide*, he recalled; and his mother, rest her soul, had reminded him way too often.

"...mass grave discovered in Israel containing the remains of more than 4,000 Jews, all beheaded. Initial reports claim the bodies are those of the missing Messianic Jews, killed for claiming Jesus is the Jewish Messiah. Orthodox extremists are the suspected perpetrators.

"Now to the mysterious light in the sky called Blip. It is getting closer, approaching at a speed that scientists once thought was impossible. If Blip continues on the current trajectory, it will collide with Earth somewhere close to Turkey. That would be a bad day for all the military surrounding..."

He turned into Briscoe Field North Parking Lot and drove directly to the runway. The behemoth of a plane sat on the widest runway in the Atlanta area, with all ten engines idling. His left front wheel dropped into a small depression but did not tilt. He ran to the plane, trying to keep up with Scarlette as she leapt up the portable stairway. Audry greeted her at the door.

"Hurry, we gotta go," Wild Willy shouted. "Or we won't be going anywhere. Never seen anything like the invasion of the sinkhole monster."

"I am so glad you made it," Audry said, giggling.

"Well, thank you," Jeff replied, assuming.

"I was talking to Scarlette, Dad," the teenager said. "But I am glad you made it too."

Jeff, Audry, Samarra and Scarlette took seats in the Video Previewing area of the modernized bomber. Scarlette jumped onto a recliner and yelped in fear as it began to electronically recline. Wild Willy and The Admiral occupied the tight cockpit up front and revved the engine RPMs for takeoff as soon as everyone was seated.

"We have to take off!" Will shouted again, over the sound system. "Fasten up, Buttercup!"

Will was certain the ground shook beneath the wheels. He had flown the plane since his purchase, many times. He knew the feel of the bomber when preparing for takeoff. He slammed the throttles to full and finally released the brakes. The plane accelerated slowly, gaining speed at what seemed a snail's pace; and Will said another silent prayer. He had said a bunch of silent prayers lately.

Fifteen-thousand feet to the east, a growing sinkhole collapsed under the runway and the reinforced concrete path began to slowly sink. The B36J lumbered down the runway, unaware.

Chapter One

"The world is a dangerous place to live; not because of the people who are evil, but because of the people who don't do anything about it."

Albert Einstein

"Mr. Ross?"

"...retaliated against Pyongyang. The submarine fired multiple rockets. We do not know whose submarine, but suspicions are the United States. Reports are that Pyongyang will glow for many years to come."

"Yeah?" Jeff said, answering his phone.

A pause.

"My name is Vinny."

Vinny, a.k.a. Aboud Rehza. Wanted Dead or Alive.

The man was notorious in the intelligence community and important enough to warrant a twenty-five-million-dollar bounty. The man responsible for blowing up the Buford Dam and thousands of deaths in Atlanta. He was also connected to the New Year's Eve bombing of Manhattan, now a radioactive wasteland.

"Vinny?" Jeff said, holding his breath. This man made him nervous.

Hearing the name of her husband's obsession and world's nemesis, as well as her kidnapper, she followed Jeff out the French doors and onto the patio.

The wind was picking up, and the hail melted quickly. Across the backyard, in what had been a garden before the drought and hailstorms hit, a black bear munched on peaches from the lone

Georgia peach tree. She did not know that bear liked peaches and watched the bear, pensively. Drool dripped thickly from the animal's mouth.

"Have you heard of red mercury?"

Jeff's heart raced with the question, a question concerning a rumored catalyst, at least the Defense Department claimed it was a rumor.

"I have not," Jeff lied, loading his GPS app to trace Vinny's whereabouts.

"There is no need to load your apps, Mr. Ross," Vinny anticipated. "This phone is way beyond *secure*. Please do not attempt to outwit me. I am trying to save your life, and many others."

Jeff scribbled a note on a napkin and handed it to Samarra. Ten minutes earlier, Samarra threatened divorce if he did not give up his obsession with Vinny; and now here he was, on the phone.

Samarra read the note: *Google: red mercury explosive.*

Samarra grabbed her iPad-12A from the charging station and typed. She could not believe what she found; and fortunately, most credible sites claimed it was fake news. She opened a link and began to read an article about Sam Cohen, the man who developed the neutron bomb.

"You are trying to save my life?" Jeff smirked. "You have attacked my family twice; and reports are, you were responsible for wiping Manhattan off the map. And now you wish to save my life."

Jeff checked the GPS app, and it appeared Vinny was in Lahore, Pakistan. That couldn't be, Jeff thought. Lahore had just been nuked by India. He glanced over his shoulder toward Samarra who was reading studiously.

Samarra learned about the effects of a neutron bomb while in medical school at Emory University. Basically, it was a nuclear explosion without so much explosion but much more neutron radiation. Buildings, cars and other inanimate structures were not so readily blown away in the case of a neutron bomb, but anything plant or animal would die almost instantly from radiation poison.

"That is true, Mr. Ross," Vinny answered.

Jeff checked the GPS app again, and now Vinny's location was London. Audry walked into the kitchen, grabbed a Krispy Kreme doughnut and sat at the table with her dad. Jeff gave her the look, but Audry paid no attention. She grabbed the pen from the table and jotted something onto an index card. She handed it to Jeff; and he read, puzzled, though puzzling was not unusual for Audry. She was a complicated young lady.

I gave Vinny one of your wafers.

"Mr. Ross, I cannot change the things I have done in the past; but be assured, I did these things because I thought it was what God wanted me to do."

Jeff looked at Audry, more puzzled. He had never mentioned the wafers to Audry, had he?

"Your daughter saved my life from an eternity in Hell, Mr. Ross. When I took your wife and children, I did not plan to let them live; but I did. Audry is… different. I think Allah must love her very much. I think God must love her very much.

"She spoke to me about the magnificent forgiveness of Jesus, explaining that he would forgive any sin of the person who would only ask him and believe, including me."

Jeff checked the app. Now Vinny was in Tokyo.

"Before I dropped your family off near Dalton, I told Audry I was sure that Jesus could never forgive me for all the lives I had taken, all the families I had destroyed."

Samarra continued to read while Jeff was glued to the phone. Audry, with chocolate cream on her chin, stared lovingly at Jeff.

"Then she did the oddest thing, Mr. Ross."

Samarra was intrigued. Red mercury, though non-existent according to the CIA and Department of Defense, was the WMD choice of the day with Islamic terror organizations. They had been chasing it globally, ready to pay big bucks, ever since the Russians made it available to the world after the end of the Cold War. Without red mercury, according to these articles, Russia would not have been able to produce hundreds, maybe thousands, of briefcase nukes. Interesting that those briefcase nukes had never been found, she thought.

"What was that?" Jeff asked, checking the GPS again. Paris. Odd things were the norm for Audry.

Samara was deep in thought. One report in September, 2004, stated that British police arrested a group of four who were intent on purchasing the supposedly non-existent compound and were offering $550,000 per kilogram.

Samarra did a quick mental calculation. A quarter million for a pound of mercury antimony oxide. Why? Why was it so valuable? She continued to read the article.

Developed in Russia during the Cold War, mercury antimony oxide is said to triple the yield of a nuclear explosive and led to the development of the once rumored briefcase nukes. We now know it was not a rumor.

Another advantage of red mercury nukes rather than uranium and plutonium nukes, is its undetectability. It is speculated that thousands of softball-sized Red Mercury bombs have been stolen from Russia and shipped around the globe.

According to Dr. Beverly Gregson, a British weapons expert, and I quote, "The small size of a Red Mercury nuclear weapon, the inability to detect it and the long shelf life makes it the most desired weapon of mass destruction on the terrorist wish list. There could, theoretically, be hundreds of cities across the globe with one or more melon-sized RM bombs hidden and waiting for a signal. A lad with a backpack or lunch box could annihilate several city blocks or even a small village. If the rumors of this turn out to be true, terrorism could blackmail the governments of the world."

"Audry gave me a wafer and her Bible, Mr. Ross. She said if I let the wafer dissolve in my mouth, I would be eager to learn the truth. She said it worked for you."

Samarra absorbed the information. For every credible article she found claiming that red mercury was a myth, she found other credible articles claiming it was not. Sam Cohen had become an obsessed proponent.

After the first Gulf War, the International Atomic Energy Agency stated that boxes of red mercury information were found with offers to develop the compound and sell it to whoever Saddam Hussein wished. Samarra wondered why she had never seen these reports.

"I asked her where you got the wafer, I was thinking it might be poison; but she seemed honest. She said your guardian angels gave it to you, because you believed in the *Money God* at that time.

"I waited two months before eating the wafer. When I did, I suddenly had a great thirst to know the God of Abraham and how Jesus got to be his son. That is a difficult story to fathom, wouldn't you agree, Mr. Ross?

"I started reading her Bible at page one and never stopped. It is much different than the Quran, but when I read the last chapter in Revelation, I understood. Jesus gave John this incredible vision and told him this, this Revelation story, was the *end* of the story. Then I knew the Quran could not be true."

As Samarra studied the information concerning red mercury, it reminded her of the lost continent of Atlantis. Those in the know say Atlantis was a myth; but many who lived in 350 B.C., believed otherwise. Kind of like this mercury antimony oxide.

"Mr. Ross, are you there?"

Now Vinny was in Istanbul.

"Yeah, I'm here."

"When I finished reading the young girl's Bible, I was most impressed with Revelation. I was born to believe Muhammad was a prophet, but the Apostle John was the last prophet. The more that I read in Revelation and cross-referenced the footnotes, the more I began to recognize *real* prophecy. I devoured scripture, like I had a 3-track mind and can only believe it was that wafer."

While the old Soviet Union developed red mercury as a venue for almost invisible, amazingly deadly weapons, Dr. Cohen saw its potential in the realm of the neutron bomb. A softball-sized nuclear weapon, catalyzed with mercury antimony oxide, that could kill every person within two miles and leave the buildings intact, for the most part. You would win a war while minimizing the rebuilding costs.

"So I guess you're now a Christian?" Jeff mocked. "Maybe a preacher? Evangelist Vinny Penny, a perfect moniker for you."

The hatred in Jeff's voice was evident, and Vinny thought the old man might have a heart attack. He wondered why a young, beautiful woman would have ever married such an old man.

"Mr. Ross, I understand your anger and hatred toward me. I hate myself. I have killed many, believing in my heart that it was for God. Hasn't that gone on since Adam and Eve were kicked out of the Garden of Eden? People have been killing for God for six-thousand years.

"Here is the deal. The United States and Europe, what is left, will suffer a drone attack, *Project Drone Swarm*.

"There are hundreds of these red mercury bombs planted in cities and towns all over the world. The drone swarms will not be seen in the night sky as they fly over the targets and initiate a digital signal.

"These are very powerful weapons; and they are not mythical, Mr. Ross. I am giving you warning. This cannot be stopped, unless Jesus Christ intervenes; but it may be possible to save millions of lives. You know people that can make it happen."

"Why don't you turn yourself in, Vinny?"

Jeff found himself agreeing momentarily with the notorious Vinny. The world needed a Jesus intervention, but he didn't think that was going to happen. At least not yet.

"That will not happen, monsieur," Vinny answered with a perfect French accent. "I will help from a distance. I already have helped."

"In what way?" Jeff asked.

Samarra continued to read, and a smile crossed her face. The United States CIA claimed the mythological substance was a ruse to set up terrorist networks. The CIA and other agencies would stage a fake sale of red mercury; and terrorists would flock to the location, willing to pay tremendous amounts of cash for the compound. When they showed up, they were captured or killed.

"I killed my boss. He was the creator of the drone swarm project."

"Mahmud?" Jeff asked.

Vinny was surprised that Ross knew Bubba by his real name. Hardly anyone did. Mahmud looked like a Bubba if there ever was one.

"Yes," Vinny answered. "He met his fate in an IHOP parking lot."

Jeff recalled the story. A van exploded, and a homeless man came to riches.

"I know all about you, Mr. Ross; maybe as much as you know about me. I can help you. We have two weeks until Labor Day. After that, it will begin.

"If I am arrested, I will be of no help. Millions will die. These bombs are sitting on shelves, disguised as art. They are mounted in street lights and fake fire hydrants. They are planted in city gardens and hidden in air conditioning ducts."

Twenty minutes passed, and Samarra had absorbed much knowledge about $Hg_6Sb_2O_8$ and its unbelievable power, should red mercury exist. She glanced outside where Audry and Jeffrey sat pensively at the patio table.

Cohen made the claim to an anonymous news source that possibly a hundred RM mini-nukes were already in the hands of terrorists. He also claimed that Saddam Hussein, leader of Iraq at the time, had taken delivery of fifty; though none had ever been found, or reported found.

The news droned on.

"… La Palma. The death toll is unknown, but we do know the eruption destroyed the entire western flank of the island. Morocco and East African coasts have been slammed with waves estimated at thirty to forty feet.

"The giant wave, one of many the world has suffered the past few years, should hit the Atlantic coasts of the Americas in less than six hours. Some estimates of wave height when it comes ashore as 'in excess of' one hundred feet.

"In other news, a pandemic…"

"Okay, Vinny. What do you suggest?

"The diseases spread, unbeknownst…. as parents all over the world rebel against vaccinations. Now outbreaks of once lost diseases are raising their heads. Polio is again killing children; but this time around, the elderly were vaccinated long ago and have avoided the resurgence.

"A large sinkhole has swallowed the Burj Tower in Dubai, and…"

"Be at *The Divide* in one hour."

Jeff glanced at Samarra, studious and reading away.

"You mean *The Divide* in Duluth?" Jeff asked, incredulous.

"That is the one, Mr. Ross. A friend, a preacher, will meet you there on the second level. He is well aware of his risks but his desire is to help. Please be alone. As I said, if I am dead, I cannot help. I have confessed, Mr. Ross, to this preacher. Armageddon is upon us."

Chapter Two

The Admiral and Sheryl landed uneventfully in Lawrenceville. There had been no meteor showers for the pilot to dodge and no inadvertent hailstones knocking a wing off or something else exciting.

The private jet taxied to a halt, but a large aircraft parked near a shelter off the East Runway caught The Admiral's attention.

"What is it?" Sheryl asked, her arm looped in his as they exited the small jet. The Admiral nodded toward the World War II era-looking plane.

"Looks sort of like Wild Willy's B-36."

"I think he keeps it at Warner Robbins Air Force Base," Sheryl said. "It's his Ferrari."

They laughed and joined the two pilots in the shuttle bus. The 15-passenger bus took the access road to the private jet quarters, passing within a quarter-mile of the large, gray plane.

"What's that?" Sheryl asked the pilot, pointing toward the behemoth.

"That, ma'am, is a B-36-J Peacemaker, once the largest plane in the world."

"I'm surprised it could land here," The Admiral said, almost certain it was Will's plane. "Whose is it?"

"Landed on the new runway, fifteen-thousand feet," the co-pilot said. "Supposedly flew in from Warner Robbins. Seems to be a big secret."

The Admiral drove the bright-red, Jeep Commander along Duluth-Lawrenceville highway and was surprised by all the abandoned properties. Surely this many people had not simply disappeared. Wild dogs or coyotes were everywhere. Sheryl held his hand tightly as they rode down the trafficless highway toward

Duluth. The American Flag at the American Legion Post waved horizontally and tall pines leaned in the wind.

"Did you get Jeff?"

"Nope," The Admiral said. "He will be happy for us though. Wind sure has picked up."

"Think he's at home?" Sheryl asked.

"No one answered, and I called three times. Probably having lunch at Piatto on Main Street. He loves that place."

The Admiral turned left on Buford Boulevard, and it was like they were in a different land. Families were eating and walking dogs, the roadside barbeque house was packed and music flowed from the Town Green.

"Looks like revitalization has worked well," Sheryl said, amazed at the progress. "Guess they don't know."

After Buford Dam had been nuked, Duluth and other small towns along the Buford Highway corridor built their own reservoir and supply system. While some towns dried up, literally; the Buford Corridor only got better. Then the fires came to the mountains.

As the fires moved southward, burning one town after another, many residents began to move; and housing prices dropped accordingly. When the fires stopped a year later, the low housing prices brought a small population boom.

"Yeah," The Admiral said, understanding. "People don't seem to know or care that the world is ending."

Sheryl agreed. More people than ever thought the Bible was myth. Pakistan and India were in a nuclear standoff. North Korea nuked South Korea. Initial, unsubstantiated reports were that North Korea had suffered nuclear retaliation from someone, probably a U.S. Nuclear sub. This surely must be the beginnings of the War at Armageddon, or Gog of Magog; and she found herself depressed on a day she should have been happy.

"Maybe they don't know," Sheryl quipped, longing for the days of non-nuclear wars, no asteroid strikes and a normal climate, "because they don't *want* to know. Like someone not going to the doctor, because they are afraid they might have cancer."

A sudden gust blew a large wastebasket across the Green, and signs from a group of *Pedophile Rights* demonstrators flew across the parking lot.

Pedophile rights? What was the world coming to, she wondered, knowing in her mind exactly what the world was coming to: The End, at least the end as we now know it. Man, it was hot, she thought. Maybe Earth was becoming Hell itself.

"What if no one comes?" she asked, thinking about their surprise wedding.

They had discussed where the wedding should be, maybe Cape Cod; but she had cold feet about anything beachy or too close to the coast. It seemed to her that the coasts of the world had become dangerous places.

He parked the red Jeep in the City Hall parking lot, and they meandered across the Town Green toward *The Divide*, hand in hand.

The Fountain on the Green was the center of activity and water blew sideways in the stiff breeze. They walked up the steps and into *The Divide*, crowded with news junkies gathered around the many flatscreens.

The Admiral scanned the room, but Jeff was nowhere to be found. A table of eight celebrated a birthday on the second level and a couple of men sat in the corner.

They walked to the bar where Abe the Bartender adjusted the volume on one of the TVs. He spotted The Admiral and Sheryl immediately.

"Well, well. A surprise," Abe greeted. "Jeff didn't mention that you were coming to town."

"It is spur-of-the-moment," Sheryl said. "We're getting married," she whispered.

"Really?" Abe said. "It's about time."

He winked at The Admiral and gave Sheryl a hug.

"Want a fresh lemonade?"

J.L. Robb

Sheryl nodded in the affirmative, and The Admiral asked that a bit of vodka be added to his.

Abe knew The Admiral and Sheryl well and had for several years. It seemed they had been engaged forever, but the past few years had been anything but normal.

"Never saw you partake until after five. Getting nervous about the marriage?" Abe asked, arching his eyebrow and smiling at Sheryl.

In the dark corner of the second level, two men conversed quietly; and Jeff still could not believe who the preacher turned out to be. None other than the guy he met in Dalton, B.J. Stagner from England. B.J. was the guy who taught Vinny how to fish, and he might introduce him to the man who nuked Manhattan.

Jeff knew he could spend the rest of his life in a federal prison, or worse, for not arranging the immediate capture of B.J.; but he had a gut-feeling. Plus, did he trust the government?

"Where is Jeff?" Sheryl asked Abe.

She could hardly wait to tell him and Samarra. She was as excited as a school girl at the prom.

"He's upstairs talking to some guy I've never seen before, some tall guy," Abe said as he spiked The Admiral's lemonade.

The Admiral read the trailer across the OLNN newsfeed, and Sheryl knew right away that something was going on. The Admiral's eyes were wide and glued to the trailer.

"What's wrong, Justin?" she asked.

The two men walked silently down the stairs, as Jeff escorted B.J. to the front door. They did not shake hands or slap each other on the back in friendship, and Abe made note. Jeff did not look happy.

"More bad news," The Admiral said, nodding at the TV over the bar tuned to BBC. "Isn't that Leanne Jones, the British gal who rescued a Muslim immigrant from drowning last week in Runnymede?"

12

"... should hit the East Coast in about two hours. Cape Cod and Boston have begun evacuation, as have other cities to the south."

"Yes," Sheryl said, listening intently, "That is her or her twin. The reports said she was a news commentator. BBC is big stuff."

"A large part of La Palma Island collapsed into the Atlantic Ocean, which has been predicted for years, when the Cumbre Vieja volcano erupted. Canary Islands monitoring buoys detected a small rise in sea level at 6:12 AM, Eastern Standard Time. At this point, there is no indication how massive the wave will be when it hits the United States. It could be minimal, or not.

"Let's go to Tim Andrews in Casablanca. Tim, you have been based in North Africa since you moved from Vidor, Texas. Have you ever seen this much activity? Has Morocco had any effects from the eruption?"

Jeff spotted The Admiral and Sheryl and was surprised. Their visit came with no notice, and he wondered what was up. He felt sick.

"Man," Sheryl said, looking at Jeff. "You are as pale as Justin's skinny, white legs. Are you okay?"

"My legs are not skinny," The Admiral said, laughing.

Abe glanced at Jeff and was concerned. He looked like he was going into shock, gray and clammy.

"No, I'm fine," Jeff lied. "Let's get a table."

"Leanne," Tim said, *"Much of Casablanca is under a state of emergency, as is the entire coastline of Africa. This eruption had been anticipated for a number of years."*

Abe motioned the new hostess-manager, Jacqueline Potts. The tall woman with black hair with a blue streak grabbed a few menus and made her way through the growing crowd.

"Jackie," Abe said, "this is Sheryl and her hubby-to-be, The Admiral. You will see them wander in from time-to-time, when they're in town. Everything is on the house today."

Jackie shook hands with the couple, a glint of curiosity in her smile. They seemed pretty old to be getting married.

Jackie Potts, at 32 years of age, was one thing if she was no other. She was a great judge of character, and she liked these two. Still, she wondered how love could be on anyone's mind these days. She had read the complete Bible nine times, cover-to-cover; and the world was definitely headed for a bad day. Why would anyone want to get married?

"Ya'll are so cute!" Jackie said, leading them toward a table for four. "Follow me."

"*The tsunami hit the coast about an hour ago and has been followed by three more waves. The third wave was the largest,*" Tim continued, reporting from a hilltop safe zone, wiping beads of sweat from his forehead. The heatwave was even worse than the dreaded Texas heatwaves.

"When are ya'll gettin' married?"

"Tomorrow," Sheryl said, nonchalantly, as though marriage was a daily activity. She strained to hear the latest tragedy playout on the news. Another tsunami, and she thanked God for intervening. They had planned to go to the coast to get married.

"Really?" Jackie said, and stopped in her tracks. Tears of joy now flowed from her eyes. "I want to hug your necks," and she did. "Bless your hearts. Ya'll look so happy. How long ago did you meet?"

"*Casualties are high, with some estimates in the tens of thousands. It is very populated along the coast, Leanne.*"

"Last century," The Admiral said with a smile.

"*Leanne,*" reporter Tim Andrews continued, "*The talk of the town is not the tsunami or the windstorms but something called Red Mercury. Ever heard of that?*"

The hostess laughed and thought the old guy was funny. He reminded her of her grandpa. She started to seat them; and Jeff asked if they could have a corner booth, something away from the crowd when he heard the red mercury comment. He stopped.

"*Yes,*" Leanne said, "*I have.*"

Leanne Jones had heard of red mercury. It was also the talk of London. Her best friend, Dr. Beverly Gregson, lived in Manchester and was a nuclear weapons expert; and that was all she talked about lately, the devastation that was associated with the compound.

"*So, what is the talk, Tim?*" she asked.

Jackie escorted the three to a corner booth, wondering why they wanted to be so isolated; but when she turned to seat them, they all stood watching the news. She had never seen so many newsaholics until she got the new gig at *The Divide*.

She placed three menus and a wine list on the table; and Jacqueline the hostess rejoined the group watching the news alert but not knowing why.

"*Leanne*," Tim said, glancing out to sea from the hilltop, "*I had never heard of red mercury until this morning when I arrived in Morocco. Apparently, it is sort of a catalyst of some kind that makes a nuclear weapon tens, maybe hundreds of times, more destructive.*

"*There is a lady in England, maybe you have heard of her, who is the world's expert on red mercury. Most governments say the substance does not exist; she says otherwise.*"

"*Dr. Gregson*," Leanne said. "*She is my closest friend. We went to college together.*"

Sheryl watched Jeff. He was acting bizarre, he was pale and he was sweating. The wedding news seemed to pass right over his head.

"We need to talk," Jeff said, and they took a seat at the table with three menus.

"I've heard of Red Mercury," The Admiral said. "Supposedly does not exist, according to the CIA."

Jeff glanced quizzically at the man dressed in the dark, purple suit. He looked familiar.

"Well then, you guys are not going to believe this story," Jeff began, spreading the black, linen napkin in his lap.

Two hours and a pitcher of lemonade later, the story had been shared. Sheryl agreed not to contact the President or Homeland Security, a risky move at best. She could spend the rest of her life in a federal prison instead of in marital bliss; but according to Vinny, the Senate and heads of the intelligence agencies were a part of the plan. The plan was to be the destruction of the most powerful country ever to grace planet Earth, which would open the world to conquest by the forces of the New World Order and President Morsi.

"Apparently, the intention is not to convert the United States to Islam but to destroy it. Let's go to the house," Jeff suggested. "Samarra should be home by now."

"I can't comprehend how this catalyst could work," The Admiral said, walking toward the front doors. Outside the late afternoon sky darkened. "By the way, why is Wild Willy's B-36 sitting at the airport in Lawrenceville?"

"He told me," Jeff laughed for the first time this day, "that it was for our evacuation to Israel. He thinks an EMP will take out all the power any day now, and the plane is shielded heavily. Will had the plane refurbished but used the old tube-type electronics, minimal micro-circuits."

The three said their goodbyes to Abe the Bartender, and Abe closed their tabs, scanning the fake buy-sell barcode.

The sun was setting, and soon the dark red moon would rise, barely visible. The last bit of news Jeff heard on one of the TVs as he exited the café, stopped him in his tracks for the second time that day. To Jeff, it seemed some sort of climax was about to take place.

"Blip is back."

Chapter Three

It also forced all people, great and small, rich and poor, free and slave, to receive a mark on their right hands or on their foreheads, so that they could not buy or sell unless they had the mark, which is the name of the beast or the number of its name.

Revelation 13:16-17

W hat is your first memory, Abe?" the doctor asked.

Abe cried quietly and tears flowed down his face. The hypnotic journey to this point had been quick and depressing; though in actuality, he was forty-minutes into the session.

Abe's morning appointment was at 9:00, and he arrived fifteen minutes early, as usual. He did not believe in *late*. He checked out the diploma hanging on the wall just inside the entry, *Dr. Dave Cook, Hypnotherapist*.

He checked in, met with Dr. Cook, relaxed in a comfy chair with headphones and was monotonized into a hypnotic stupor within ten minutes.

Dr. Cook, not a medical doctor but a Ph.D., met the man everyone called Abe the Bartender three years earlier while volunteering at *Dine for Dollars*, now rebuilt after the fire. They hit it off right away, because Abe had always had a curiosity in hypnotism and the benefits thereof. Though not best buddies, their paths had crossed several times. Dave had been surprised by Abe's call, an invitation to his wedding and a request to meet.

"Abe? What is your first memory? Can you recall?"

"My father beating the crap out of my mother with a belt," Abe said without pause.

"How old were you?" Tim asked.

Abe had invited Dr. Cook to *The Divide* for breakfast and conversation, which was a little odd in itself. They met the next morning; and Abe was full of questions, most about relationships. He explained that he had become very "smitten" for the first time in years, actually decades, and feared he wasn't relationship worthy. He had never had success.

"How old were you," Tim asked again.

"Four," Abe said with a sob. "Maybe three."

The breakfast meeting had lasted two hours, and Dave learned a lot about the man he met three years earlier.

Abe's father was physically abusive to both Abe and his mother but seemed to idolize Sarah, his older sister. That idolization did not last, because Abe's father was killed in yet another Israeli skirmish with Hezbollah. He explained that growing up in Israel had been difficult and was happy when his mother took them to New York to live with their uncle's family. He did not escape the fighting. Uncle Herschel was a mean man and was always giving Aunt Helen a smackdown.

"You said at breakfast that you loved your mother but was sure she did not love you. Why do you believe that?"

Abe recalled the painful memories, though he had not recalled the memories until he turned forty. Now the memories were plain as day.

"She didn't watch me," Abe replied.

The doctor listened as Abe told his story and was surprised at the detail.

"When I was about one-year old," Abe continued, "Mom left me in the bathroom sink. She was giving me a bath but left for a few minutes. I turned on the hot water and was scalded before she returned. I do not remember, thankfully; but I was in the hospital three days."

Abe did not remember the pain or the trip to the hospital but had heard the story many times over the years.

"Then there was the near-electrocution at age three when I stuck a metal fingernail file into an electrical outlet, once again left alone."

Abe's composure was now relaxed and there were no more tears. There was more anger if anything. Dave thought about his own childhood in the sixties. Parents didn't seem to worry so much back then. Giving a three-year-old a metal fingernail file today would be child abuse.

"And there was the falling incident," Abe said.

"How old were you then? Where did you fall?"

"I fell out of the car," Abe said. "A blue, 1962 Kaiser Carabela with white sidewall tires. I remember it like it was yesterday."

Dave listened and had never heard of a Kaiser Carabela as Abe explained how he simply opened the back door and rolled out into the street. He remembered the siren of an approaching ambulance and his head, wrapped in a big, white bandage.

"They were built in Argentina."

"Do you think your mother was negligent?"

"Yes," Abe said after a short pause. "She didn't fasten my seatbelt."

The session continued for twenty minutes before Dr. Cook awakened him from his hypnotic state.

"You okay?" Dave asked.

Abe rubbed his eyes and smiled. He felt amazingly happy and energized.

"I feel great."

"Abe, let's get together again next week if you have time," Dave suggested.

"Aren't you going to put me under?" Abe asked, looking at the doctor in utter seriousness.

"We've already been there, big guy," Dave said, patting him on the back. "You will recall in a while."

Another appointment was scheduled, and Dave walked Abe to the door, then hesitated.

"Abe, I have a question. You are here today because you are getting married to a woman you describe as 'an accomplished and beautiful woman.' You are a lucky man."

Dave paused, choosing his words carefully.

"So what's the question?" Abe asked.

"A couple of months ago, we were talking at *The Divide*. We both agreed that the end of the world as we know it is upon us. We discussed that blip of light you and a few others have seen, and you said that you believed it was one of the signs in the sky announcing the return of Christ."

"I remember," Abe said. "And I know where you're going."

"Where?" Dave asked.

"Because I said that anyone who would fall in love, with the world in the mess it's in, was an absolute nut."

"Yep. That's the question. Now you're in my office getting prepared for marriage."

Abe didn't say anything at first, squeezing his right wrist. He reckoned the pain could be from the buy-sell implant the week before. Many internet posts had protested the requirement, and a few said it was the mark mentioned in Revelation. He turned and shook Dave's hand.

"God weaves mysteries in our lives, don't you think? She came out of nowhere."

Abe walked out the door of the doctor's office and toward his 1965 red GTO, one of three GTOs that he owned. A brisk breeze held the office door open, and Tim walked out to the porch.

The sun was bright, brighter than it used to be, he thought; and he watched Abe as he strolled across the parking lot. He liked the man and would talk to him further about the *blip*. He also prayed silently that Abe would get over the hatred he had in his heart for his mother. Then he could have a relationship. And besides, if his memory was correct, 1962 cars did not even require seatbelts. If parents only knew what they do to their kids.

"Abe," Dave said, and Abe turned to face the hypnotist. The doctor's hair suddenly looked grayer. "I hope that you can find love in your heart for your mother. You know, seatbelts were not a requirement until 1966. Your mom could not have fastened your seatbelt if there was none."

Abe glanced skyward, as though in search of an answer; but he knew the answer. He did not know what the sound was but saw nothing unusual.

"The 1962 Kaiser Carabela was ahead of its time, I guess."

Dave turned to walk back in his office when he heard the sound, like a whoosh; and then the entire earth shook. He spun quickly around.

Abe was lying on the hot, asphalt parking lot, the black Cadillac Escalade a few feet away sat scrunched with four flat tires; and a huge chunk of crystal-clear ice shattered and spread across the parking lot. Then two more hit.

Dave rubbed his eyes and slapped the side of his head, as a shard of ice flew by and slammed into the building. He was certain he had not seen what he had just seen. A chunk of ice the size of a car could not fall out of the sky. He guestimated the mass at three, maybe four-hundred pounds. There wasn't a cloud in the sky.

People rushed out of the few office buildings that remained occupied after the fires, curious and frightened. Dave ran toward his newest patient, still stationary on the ground but suddenly turned and ran back to the building, as did all the others.

The otherwise quiet, Georgia day turned into a day of loud whooshes as a mega-hailstorm slammed the cities of Buford, Suwanee and Doraville with a near blizzard of huge hailstones the likes of which the world had never recorded in history. The same unprecedented atmospheric event happened throughout the world.

Seeking shelter inside his concrete and tempered glass building, Dave turned to check on disabled Abe. He searched the parking lot, but Abe was nowhere to be seen.

Chapter Four

"The morning light gave a view that was never to be forgotten. There was not a building in the entire city that escaped damage; most of them were just a pile of rubble."

Charleston Earthquake, 1886

Mt. Pleasant, South Carolina

"I will never give up my faith in Jesus," Kathi stated emphatically. *"Never!"*

"Same here," Marvin agreed.

"Kathi Monroe," Kathi said, introducing herself. "I lived in Mt. Pleasant… before they nuked the airport. Now it's a ghost town. This area has so much history."

"And radioactivity," Marvin said.

"The radioactivity levels are much less than predicted. Scientists say it is because the wind continued to blow for weeks."

No one in the small Bible study group had ever met. A secret meeting of believers, no longer spread through apps but word of mouth instead. Apps had proven to be easily hacked by the U.S. government; and the remaining churchgoers held secret meetings in small groups, always looking over their shoulders. While churches were still allowed, statues, crucifixes and crosses were not.

Charleston, once known as the City of Churches, had been quite faith-based; but not anymore. Since the disappearances began years earlier, most believers had either disappeared or moved elsewhere. Now most of the historic churches and synagogues had been vandalized.

"Tell us about it," Marvin said.

"About what?" Kathi replied, confused.

"About Charleston," Marvin answered. "I'm new to the area. So many churches are boarded up or vandalized."

"Or turned into a mosque," the girl named Jaimi Tindel said, a grimness crossing her face.

"Yeah," Kathi said. "That's for sure. Charleston's oldest synagogue, I think the fourth or fifth synagogue in the United States, is now a mosque, can you believe that?"

"I can," Marvin quipped. "They have done that throughout history. Muslim warrior-fanatics have always conquered and then converted churches and synagogues to mosques, a slap in the face of the Man upstairs, in my opinion. After all, look where al-Aqsa mosque sits in Jerusalem. The Jewish Temple Mount. Ever read any of the Jewish Prayer Book?"

"Not really," they all agreed. "Have you?"

"The al-Aqsa mosque is not sitting anywhere anymore," Jaimi said, "not since the earthquake."

Jaimi's alert-app went off, but the phone was in vibration mode. She glanced quickly, noting the Tsunami Alert. Surely it had nothing to do with Charleston. The floor of the abandoned church moved slightly, a small sort of roll. She prayed silently that the church would not collapse.

Outside the church, a ruckus; and the group held their clubs and baseball bats tightly, in fear of wild animals that now attacked rather than running.

"I have read it many times," Marvin said, concerning the prayer book. "And the Islamic takeover is about to be over, finis! Let me quote from one prayer, because the Jews of that time knew they were to blame, and many wondered if they had made a wrong judgment about Jesus. Not much good happened to them after his crucifixion.

"Because of our sins we were exiled from our country and banished from our land. We cannot go up as pilgrims to worship Thee, to perform our duties in Thy chosen house, the great and Holy Temple which was called by Thy name, on account of the hand that was let loose on Thy sanctuary. May it be Thy will, Lord our God and God of our fathers, merciful King, in Thy abundant love again

to have mercy on us and on Thy sanctuary; rebuild it speedily and magnify its glory."

"Wow," Kathi said, impressed with Marvin's knowledge. "Are you Jewish?"

"No," Marvin said. "Just interested in the end-times stuff."

"Then how about a little Jewish history of Charleston?" Kathi asked.

Kathi gave a brief history of the place she loved more than all others... Historic Charleston and North Charleston; and the group listened nervously with a chorus of growls and snarls of wild animals, only a few feet away.

"I think Charleston was founded about 1670 or 1671 and was considered 'Jewish-friendly' by 1695. By 1750, there were enough Jews to form a congregation, Kahal Kadosh Beth Elohim, synonymous with Holy Congregation House of God..."

"Yes, if I can interrupt," Marvin said, "the Coming Street Cemetery in Charleston is still the largest Jewish cemetery in the South. Isn't that right?"

"Yes, that is correct," Kathi continued. "And now, as Jaimi said, it has been converted to a mosque."

The floor began a slow undulation; but no one seemed to notice, sort of a semi-vibration. Vibrating terra firma had become the norm. Kathi held her scream as an absolutely, huge wharf rat meandered at the doorway. The rats were much larger than a couple of years before, and she attributed the mutation to the nuke that took out the airport.

"When the pilgrims and first settlers came to America, they were mostly Christians," Kathi continued, "trying to escape the wrath of Christianity. Sounds odd, doesn't it? Christians escaping Christians. Kind of like Muslims trying to escape the crazy ones, you know?

"There were few Jews and Muslims and even fewer Buddhists and Hindus. As John Jay, the first Supreme Court justice stated, the United States was considered a Christian nation.

"Anyway, back to the Jews and Charleston. The newly formed Jewish congregation of 1750 grew quickly; and in 1794, the largest synagogue in the U.S. was dedicated. It remains today."

"Only the name has changed," Jamie said.

"Yep, that is correct," Kathi continued. "Now it is the Mahdi Temple of Fire. Kahal Kadosh Beth Elohim was the oldest synagogue in continuous use before America suddenly became a Muslim country. Makes me wanna puke!"

The group of four sat uncomfortably in the dark basement meeting place. Hardly anyone went to regular churches anymore, Kathi knew for sure. They all taught man's word instead of God's word anyway, so what did it matter. And besides, even the big churches were being monitored by the government.

"Ever wonder why we were not raptured?" Kathi asked the small group. Her faith was strong and always had been, but this was a question that constantly nagged her soul.

No one commented but all had wondered. Why were there still people going to the huge Presbyterian church across the street? The crowds weren't what they used to be, but still… why weren't they raptured?

"I've wondered," Marvin said and introduced himself to the group. "Marvin Thiel."

"Marvin C. Thiel, Jr. of country music fame?" the young lady with dark hair said, sticking out her hand. "Jaimi Tindel."

They shook hands.

"You were so fantastic."

Marvin blushed, but no one would notice in the darkness of the meeting place. To the north, a siren began to wail.

"Were?" Kathi asked.

"Let me tell you about this guy," Jamie interrupted. "I was at the concert."

Marvin was dumbfounded.

"I went to Marvin's last concert in Nashville. Ten minutes into the concert, a trash can next to the stage blew up. Killed 37 people, and Marvin was in ICU for weeks."

"I remember that!" the fourth in the group said. "Blamed it on Muslims but turned out to be a Christian militia out of North Georgia. The trash can was filled with Islam stuff. By the way, my name's Charles Stribling. Call me Charlie."

"That's right," Marvin said. "Tried to set it up to look like it was another Islamist attack. Now the Christian militants and Islamists have their own war going."

"Why is that siren going off," Charles asked. "Sounds like a tornado warning."

"Mt. Pleasant," Kathi said. "Disaster warning. We better check it out."

The group made their way from the basement of the closed church and gathered by a broken window. The sky was clear and blue, and the sun shone brightly. There were no clouds in the sky. A lone black and white police SUV passed by slowly, announcing something. It was unclear.

"You must evacuate!" the loudspeaker sounded.

"Evacuate?" Charlie asked. He ran toward the patrolman as the black-and-white came to a halt. The policeman pulled his gun but did not show it.

"Sir, what's going on?"

The other three came out of the church and walked slowly toward the police car. They glanced skyward and saw nothing abnormal. The wind was gusty, but that was not unusual in Charleston. The outdoor digital thermometer on the deserted church read 104°.

"You haven't heard?" Officer Gus Longo asked, sizing up the man and his friends. He recognized Charlie but could not recall his name.

"No sir," Charlie said. "We heard the warning siren, but our phones are in-and-out, some kind of solar interference. We haven't been able to check the news."

"You kids got about thirty minutes to find high ground, and there ain't much of that around here. You got wheels?"

"High ground?" Kathi asked. "Why? What's going on?"

"Tidal wave's comin' from over there in Africa somewhere. S'posed to hit the Atlantic Coast in a half-hour." Gus glanced at his watch.

"I have a van," Marvin said.

"Then you guys… and gals, better get in it and head west. Elevation 'round here's about twelve feet. The wave's s'posed to be eighty feet high, maybe bigger."

"You look familiar, Gus," Charlie said, looking the man in the face. He could not place it, but Charlie never forgot a face.

"Yeah," Gus said. "You ever been to Birmingham?"

"Once was enough," Charlie laughed. "Hey, I remember."

"Yep," Gus said, "I gave you a speedin' ticket, I think. I was an Alabama Highway Patrolman. Small world."

Jaimi slapped at a mosquito and noted Kathi's concern as she scanned the water outside the Battery. The Battery, named after a military defense battery from the Civil War, was one of Charleston's grandest tourist destinations, before the bomb, and existed along the protective sea walls of the Charleston Peninsula. Old and magnificent, historic antebellum homes lined the waterway with unimaginable sunrises.

"What are you looking at?" Jaimi asked.

"The water level," Kathi answered. "If it starts dropping, we're in big trouble."

Far out at sea, the seemingly insignificant wave traveled toward the Atlantic Seaboard, a steady speed of four-hundred eighty miles per hour. The wave was two hundred miles from impact, huge but mostly invisible as most of the wave remained beneath the sea, causing turmoil and destruction of the seafloor below.

In the unseen wake of the wave, sea creatures large and small floated to the surface, dead from the underwater impact. Ocean water, pushed westward by the unprecedented Atlantic wave, began to rise; and Gus quickly noticed water slowly approaching up the slight incline of King Street.

"Oh bullfeathers," Gus said. "You kids better jump in. We gotta get the heck out of Dodge. Hurry," he shouted.

The water approached, now only a block away.

Gus hit the accelerator while sharply turning the steering wheel, and a second later they headed toward I-26 West. The water pursued the black-and-white like a highway patrolman chasing a speeder; and Gus flew through an intersection with siren blaring. There was hardly a car on the road.

"Turn that up," Jaimi said, and Marvin turned the radio volume up. Country music blared from the worn-out speakers. "And could you put it on the news?"

"How far are we from Saint Matthew's Lutheran Church?" Kathi asked.

"About a mile," Gus answered. "Why?"

"*...count in Europe is now up to three-hundred seventy-six homes mysteriously blown up yesterday. More than six hundred are dead and the toll is reportedly climbing by the hour,*" the commentator reported.

"We need to get there," Kathi said nervously, glancing out the rear window of the patrol car. They were not going to make it out of the city, she was sure, as the car sped through pools of water, already flooding the lower-lying streets.

"I thought we had thirty minutes," Jaimi cried.

"We need to get to the church if we can," Kathi repeated. "It's the highest building in Charleston. It is very sturdy too, made it through the Earthquake of 1886 and Hurricane Hugo."

Gus turned right on King Street. The evacuation proved to be successful, as there were no cars on the streets, including fire or rescue vehicles.

"I'm the last one," Gus shouted.

"The last one what?" Charlie yelled from the back seat of the black and white police SUV.

"The last cop in Charleston to evacuate. Think I waited too late."

In the rearview mirror, the new Marriott collapsed; and the SUV rolled and bounced down the now undulating street. Gus was certain they would not make it and said a silent prayer.

"If you guys are believers," Gus shouted above the sound of crumbling structures, "pray!"

Chapter Five

Chadbo studied the solar images from the Helios IV satellite and continued to scratch his wrist. His buy-sell implant had been removed because of severe pain; but so many stores would not let him buy anything, not even food or toilet paper, without the implant. So he succumbed. Almost everyone succumbed.

There were holdouts who said it was the Mark of the Beast, but they were starving to death. What was one to do? And besides, an implant could not even be seen, and *Revelation* plainly said that the mark would be visible. Everybody was a fanatic these days; and besides, the implant was not visible.

The split-screen exhibited unbelievable images of the sun and its changing corona on the left and the latest tsunami news from the Canary Islands on the right. A newsfeed ran across the bottom of the large monitor, allowing him to stay current on all the earthquake activity. It was interesting that recent images from Mars showed similar activity, multiple Marsquakes.

His phone rang, The Admiral's tone.

"What's up? And I apologize again for not making it to your wedding today. Glad you decided not to get married at Cape Cod."

Chad watched the screen on the right. In an hour, Cape Cod would be completely under water. Evacuations were ongoing and looked like everyone would make it, at least on the Cape, except maybe the diehards who refused to leave. They would certainly drown.

"Yellowstone's up," The Admiral said.

"Yeah, I just saw the newsfeed. A lot is going on."

"What about Tamu Massif?" The Admiral asked.

"Tamu Massif?"

"Yes."

"The newly discovered Tamu Massif?"

"That's the one," The Admiral said. "About a thousand miles or so east of Japan on the bottom of the Pacific Ocean. The size of New Mexico."

Chadbo remembered reading of the discovery, a volcano that rivaled the largest ever discovered in the solar system, Olympus Mons on Mars.

"What about it?" Chad asked. "If I recall, it has been inactive for many millennia."

"Not anymore. You know, it was named after Texas A&M University. TAMU. It's part of a giant, undersea mountain range. Last eruption was 60,000 years ago."

The Admiral paused, possibly distracted by something, Chad figured; because he had been talking a mile a minute.

"And?"

"And there were three substantial earthquakes in the area within the last thirty minutes, a 7.3, a 6.2 and the last was 8.0. There are many volcanologists that think they may be connected to the Jerusalem quake."

Chad reviewed the streamer but saw no mention yet of the seismic activity.

"How did you find out? I still see nothing from the U.S. Geological Survey site."

"New app, Chadbo. You need to keep up," The Admiral laughed. "Anything new with the sun?"

"I thought you had a wedding to celebrate? Are you guys still planning on getting married today?"

Chad sometimes wondered if The Admiral and Sheryl would ever get married. Things kept coming up, like comets colliding with the moon and moon rocks colliding with Earth. There were the arsenic-laden streams and lakes, water turning to blood…

"Decided to wait a week, Chad. Sheryl said it doesn't feel right to get married on the day a tsunami slams the coast and kills who knows how many."

"That makes sense," Chad said. "The news is reporting that New York and New Jersey have miles-long backups, even in the tunnels; and people are abandoning their vehicles and leaving them. Lincoln Tunnel is a disaster.

"You asked about the sun," Chad continued. "Surface temperature readings were rising for weeks and then there was a lull…"

"Yeah, we were hoping it was not a lull," The Admiral said.

"Well, it's not lulling anymore and has come back with a vengeance. The surface temperature is being monitored 24/7 and has risen from a nearly-constant 10,000-degrees to 11,000, a ten percent increase. That doesn't seem possible."

The Admiral quickly checked the price of *Trane*, and the air conditioning company's stock continued to rise. He silently thanked the Good Lord. He knew the air conditioning industry would be booming a few years ago when it really started heating up. In only three years, the stock increased from $150 to $882 per share. He should have purchased more.

"What are you doing?" Chad asked. "Checking those HVAC stocks?"

"Yep."

The two friends laughed when laughter seemed inappropriate. The Admiral started to end the call, but Chad interrupted. He had a hot date with Sheryl at Duluth Civitan Club's *Shuffle Board for Autism* fundraiser. The seniors had great fun, raising money for the kids.

"What do you think's going on with Yellowstone?" Chad asked. "You think this is the Big One?"

Chad glanced at the latest data-alert, and the sun was locked and loaded for a coronal mass ejection. It had been anticipated; and he prayed that when it happened, the CME would not hit Earth. He glanced at the newsfeed.

...sea floor continues to rumble under the Pacific, and temperature monitoring buoys indicate a rise in water temperature of four-degrees.

"Could be the Big One," The Admiral said. "Earthquake swarms are normal in Yellowstone, but the swarm that started in January is only getting more massive. The quakes are small, most less than 4.0; but there are so many. Thousands of dead animals from the gases since they closed the park. New Madrid in Missouri is also acting up."

... And now this: A report from the Vatican Observatory is stating that the strange Blip, that bright light that has been reported in the sky and now seen by many, was observed during many of the disappearances that have happened at night. New World Order government officials state the disappearances are pure mythology and are threatening arrest of anyone who proposes otherwise.

The Blip. That sucker just keeps on appearing. Chad thought it perplexing; but when Melissa disappeared that night, there had definitely been a strange light in the sky. What could it be? Astronomically, it made no sense.

...Stars are disappearing. Reports from the darkest places in the world report that stars continue to simply disappear.

"New Madrid," Chad mumbled.

"Yeah, Chadbo. Seems like the whole world is cracking up. Lynn Tomay, that geologist that's always on TV talking about Yellowstone, said this morning that all these geological events seem to be tied to the Jerusalem quake."

Chad watched the live feed from Folly Beach, a seaside community a few miles south of Charleston. A wave grew in the distance, a wall of gray; and then the camera was submerged. He wondered how high the camera had been mounted.

Chapter Six

Gus drove with abandon, and the black and white police SUV bounced down the cracking asphalt, toward Saint Matthew's Lutheran Church high ground. All around, it seemed that buildings were collapsing; and thick dust and crushed concrete filled the air. A hole appeared in the road, coming out of nowhere; and the SUV plowed ahead, now running on three tires, a quarter-mile to go.

"Are we going to make it?" Marvin yelled, trying to be heard over the sounds of the earthquake and falling debris.

Gus was glad they weren't in New York City, imagining how difficult it would be to maneuver through falling skyscrapers. He did not answer and concentrated on controlling the wobbly SUV.

"We have to run for it!" Gus yelled, pulling to the edge of King Street.

The ground rocked more than shook as the quake-that-would-never-end continued in its destruction of the once beautiful gem of the South. Fires broke out everywhere, and natural gas lines snapped like twigs in a California forest fire. Historic Charleston was ablaze.

The group ran like they had never run before; and Gus was surprised he could run so fast, considering the lung transplant the year before. The unknown bacteria had come out of the blue, and no antibiotic could control it for long. Thank God for the Kinsella Vaccine.

Jaime stumbled and fell to the ground and was sure her foot was fractured. Kathi grabbed her in a rush of adrenalin and a dab of fight-or-flight; and they ran as best as they could toward the church, now five-hundred feet away. The church tower swayed.

✡ ✡ ✡

Vinny sat silently and listened to B.J. as they fished at Lakeshores Lake, about six miles outside Dalton. The water appeared as glass, hardly a ripple; and the cool, mountain air made him wonder if this was what paradise was like, and if Jesus would forgive him on Judgment Day. B.J. assured him that, according to Jesus, only one sin was unforgivable… so maybe he had a chance.

A layer of white, early-morning fog hung from the limbs of the water oaks and long-leaf pines on one side of the lake. On the other side, the oaks and pines were nothing more than black, charred monuments, standing in defiance against the mountain fires the previous year, called down on Earth by the Two Witnesses.

Jeff's apprehension had been expected, but Vinny considered the meeting a success. B.J. had not been arrested. That would have ruined the entire plan; and since that day, there had been four other meetings. B.J. the Peacekeeper had become his best friend. How odd that seemed. How fast it had happened was the miracle.

Vinny pondered the innocence of the American mind, the almost blind trust Christians seemed to have for one another. In his Muslim homeland, no one trusted anyone. Instead of loving neighbors as themselves, they seemed hell-bent on killing each other. But he now knew why. The angel of Genesis had foretold the hatred among Muslims for each other. Seemed almost the opposite of Jesus' teachings.

"When does it begin?" B.J. asked.

"What?" Vinny asked, watching a small bass part the tranquil surface of the water, fifty-feet away, probably feasting on one of the many disease-ridden mosquitoes.

Vinny fiddled with the lure, careful not to prick his finger. A small tub of nightcrawlers sat in a cup holder. A hawk circled overhead, and Vinny wondered if Jeff was nearby.

"The swarm."

"I don't know," Vinny said. "Initially, it was to start in Europe on St. Stephen's Day last December 26. Do you know St. Stephen's Day, B.J.?"

"I do, Vinny. Boxing Day in Europe. But I am surprised you know?"

"St. Stephen's Day was not an accident," Vinny said. "My brother and I studied Christian holidays, planning carnage where the most Christians would be."

The study had been interesting to Vinny, but brother Mohammed considered all Christian holidays to be of the devil. In retrospect, that now seemed ludicrous.

"Stephen was the first martyr for Christ. They were all martyred eventually," Vinny said.

A sadness spread across Vinny's face, and B.J. studied the odd man. How could someone so peaceful have killed so many? Was he the devil, or was he redeemed and somehow a part of the final act in God's awesome play?

"All but John," B.J. said. "He lived on to write the Book of Revelation and die at an old age."

"I did not know that," Vinny said. "That's strange."

"Not really, Vinny. John was the only apostle of the twelve who went to Jesus' crucifixion. All the others scattered in fear. That is why God gifted him."

Gifted him… Vinny thought about that.

"In what way?"

"He gifted him by letting John live to an old age and allowing him to write the final story in the Bible, the Revelation of Jesus himself. Think about that."

Vinny had considered Revelation for more than a year, since seeing the video on an Arabic social media site. The scene had been the village dump, somewhere in Afghanistan, where villagers burned trash, much like the Jews had burned their children, a sacrifice to Moloch, and later their garbage in Gehenna, a valley south of Jerusalem.

The video focused on a single piece of paper, written in French, laying among the burned trash, a page from the Book of Revelation, a warning from Jesus. Vinny found it remarkable that the page had not burned.

Then the camera zoomed in on the page, and the verse changed Vinny's life.

"I warn everyone who hears the words of the prophecy of this scroll: If anyone adds anything to them, God will add to that person the plagues described in this scroll. And if anyone takes words away from this scroll of prophecy, God will take away from that person any share in the tree of life and in the Holy City, which are described in this scroll."

Among the trees on the bank that were not burned, large, mangy creatures stirred, hungry and hidden in the foliage. The sounds of the two men a few feet from the bank had attracted them from their exploration for anything edible. Three of the black bears foamed heavily at the mouth, and the scent of rabies was pervasive. Even the others in the group avoided the rabid animals.

"That's why I like you, B.J.," Vinny said, looking him straight in the eye. "You and Steven have made me rethink so many things I grew up learning."

"We all grow up learning stuff, Vinny. It's called programming in the digital world. You were programmed to be Muslim. I was programmed to be Christian. We are what we are. Then one day we start thinking about it, at least some of us."

"Thinking about what?" Vinny asked after a pause. He was sure he heard something that should not have been heard. He scanned the shores.

"Thinking about my beliefs. I went through stages of doubt as a kid. I was confused about some things I read in the Bible."

"Like what?"

Four of the black bears and two cubs descended slowly into the still waters, hidden by limbs and branches along the shore. The three with rabies stayed hidden and hungry, but their phobia of the water overwhelmed their reflex to eat.

The group cautiously headed toward the boat, silently.

✡ ✡ ✡

Gus, Kathi and her three friends made their way to the church doorway, jarred and splintered by the still rumbling earthquake. Jaime, covered in perspiration, winced in pain but maintained.

"Is this thing gonna ever stop?" Marvin yelled, and the ground kept undulating like a solid but wavy sea.

The seven Muslim immigrants taking refuge in Saint Matthew's heard the approaching footsteps and held tightly to their weapons. Since immigrating from Germany to the United States the previous year, Lutheran Christians had welcomed them to the German evangelical church.

The ground shook with sudden violence and the group of five fell hard to the ground. The impact shattered what remained of Jaime's leg, and Charles Stribling scooped her from the ground and ran toward the entrance. Jaime held on for life, and blood oozed from a compound fracture of the left femur.

The church steeple, the highest in the area, had adorned the church since 1872 but now teetered at a forty-five-degree angle, a fall to earth in its near future.

Founded by Johann Andreas Wagener and a few other German-speaking citizens, Wagener also founded Walhalla, South Carolina in 1849, a town of mostly German immigrants and was eventually elected mayor of Charleston in 1871.

Today, they hoped it would be safe-refuge for the group. Inside, seven waited quietly. The roar of the coming flood drowned the streets three blocks away and manholes in King Street began popping like corks in champagne bottles at a New Year's Eve party, large fountains of water pushing them forty feet in the air.

King Street bowed and finally collapsed, sinking into somewhere unknown; and Gus' police SUV disappeared in a flash. Out to sea, not far from the Charleston shore, South Carolina's most beautiful islands sank deep into the sea. Islands from Edisto to Hilton Head disappeared, and Marvin recalled the prophecy… *Every island fled away and the mountains could not be found.*

Running up the steps of the church as fast as possible, they made their way inward. All the walls were vandalized and broken glass littered the floors. Stained glass windows were now simply holes in the walls of the once pristine church; and Islamic symbols adorned nearly every surface.

Kathi heard something, a scrape or a click, and turned quickly, startled at what she saw.

✿ ✿ ✿

B.J. was the first to see the bears, nose and eyes barely above the water's surface but would have seen nothing had it not been for the red-tailed hawk. With a splash, the hawk smacked the water, scooping up the two-pound bass with minimal effort. The bears seemed to also be startled, and now made no attempt at stealth.

Vinny's heart nearly beat out of his chest, thinking at first they were coyotes. His coyote phobia was beyond comprehension.

B.J. pulled the cord but the engine did not catch. Why had he not changed the spark plug he wondered, as the six beasts closed quickly. The boat began to rock from the bear-generated waves. B.J. pulled again, and arthritis screamed across his mind.

"Let me have that!" Vinny shouted.

Vinny was certain he could smell the horrendous breath of the starving bears and grabbed the pullcord forcefully. One yank was all it took, and the twenty-horsepower motor whimpered to life.

Ten minutes later, B.J. and Vinny shared a beer, laughing at the close call. A large chunk bitten from the back of the small fishing boat was a reminder hard to forget. Finally, Vinny commented.

"After Labor Day."

B.J. closely surveyed the waters, and figured he would never look at the quiet lake quite the same.

"Labor Day?"

"Yes," Vinny said. "Sometime after Labor Day the drone swarm will take the world. There will be much death, and the collapse of governments should follow, at least that is the plan. Unless I can stop it... if I don't get caught first."

Only Jumpin' Johnny had the schedule of drone strikes in the United States. Vinny had confided in JJ, he liked him. But he knew right away that Johnny was skeptical of the B.J. relationship. They remained allies and friends, but Vinny noticed the coldness that had developed. He would get the information from JJ the next time they met. Then he would kill him.

In the forest along the lake shore, not far from the bear attack, the sniper lay still, breathing at a rate not far from death. He took aim, B.J. the infidel in his sight. The sniper fired and blew B.J. over the side of the boat and into a pool of blood-red water.

Vinny quickly glanced toward the sound of the shot, then rolled over the side of the boat, into the water, using the boat as protection. He reached behind his back and withdrew the 5-inch hunter's knife.

"Vinny, Vinny!"

The shout came from the woods not far away, the direction of the sniper fire. Vinny pulled B.J. to the side of the boat, careful to keep his head above water. He was breathing, but barely. Three rabid bears that stayed behind heard the human voice and sniffed the morning air. They liked what they smelled.

"Did I get him?" the voice yelled, and Vinny immediately recognized it. "I saved you from the devil, Vinny! Show some appreciation."

Jumpin' Johnny Hussein walked to water's edge, tightly holding the rifle.

"Vinny, Vinny," JJ shouted. "Come out wherever you were."

"Are!" Vinny shouted back. "You always get those sayings wrong. Why did you kill B.J.? He was giving me vital information."

Vinny stayed behind the small boat for protection, but the bullet passed through both sides easily. Neither man was hit. Unfortunately, Vinny dropped his only weapon, and the knife slowly descended to the bottom. B.J. moaned.

Chapter Seven

"See how numerous are my enemies and how fiercely they hate me!"

King David, Israel
980 BC (est.)

My priorities were screwed up."

"I coulda told you that, Jeff," The Admiral laughed. "I feel guilty for not being a better influence."

The Admiral laughed again, chuckling at his humor. He was certain Jeffrey Ross had priorities rearranged now. When they were in the Navy together? Probably not. A breaking news alert appeared on several screens at *The Divide*.

"This just in from Dalton, Georgia. The remains of…"

"You know what I mean," Jeff said, noticing Sheryl's new hairdoo for the first time. "Nice hairdoo, you hot mama."

"Thanks," Sheryl said, not feeling at all like a hot mama… maybe a cold mama.

The wedding was delayed again, and briefly she wondered if fate was against her. Maybe the Good Lord didn't want her married; but then that blew her theory, one of her many, as to why she was left behind- to help Justin strengthen his faith. The Admiral could be a stubborn man and was sometimes far too logical.

"What I mean," Jeff continued, "I used to always hang around intellectuals, it seemed so important to me."

"Pardon me?" Sheryl asked. "You *used* to hang out with intellectuals? Thank you."

Sheryl excused herself when her phone chimed with *God Bless the USA* and walked out to the beautiful Town Green for privacy. It was a secure call from the White House.

Most of the trees on the Green had few leaves this year, and many died after the fires in the north and the extreme drought. No leaves, no photosynthesis.

About fifty news junkies were in *The Divide Disco & Café*, all gathered around large flatscreens announcing the newest devastation to befall the United States, this one out of Dalton, Georgia. Jeff wondered what news from Dalton could possibly make international news channels.

"Three rabid bears were shot on the banks of Lakeshore Lake as they ravaged the body of a middle-aged, possibly 'Middle Eastern or Hispanic' male. A reporter at the scene claimed that the police found one of the dead bears with a notebook in its mouth. The police have denied that report, but the reporter's video has appeared on the Vimeo link and shows otherwise."

"Hello?" Sheryl answered.

It was the new president. She liked this one and hoped he didn't also succumb to the Spanish Flu. Her heart skipped a couple of beats.

"Sheryl, we have a PR issue. I want you to hear it before it makes the news."

This president had developed a trust with Sheryl right from the start. He told it like it was and did what he said. He was hated by the masses though. It reminded her of King David when he ruled over Israel, all twelve tribes. He was hated by many who wanted him dead. Hopefully… that would not happen.

"Mr. President," she said, hoping her knocking-knees would not give her nervousness away.

"You are going to hear a report out of your neck of the woods, Sheryl. It is about a man the police found being eaten by some bears…"

"In Dalton?" she interrupted.

A pause.

"You already heard?"

"Yes sir. It was on the news when you called. I didn't hear any details though. Why is this of national interest?"

"It's not of national interest. It is of *worldwide* interest."

Fifteen minutes later, Sheryl walked back to the front door and entered *The Divide*. Though the sun was high above in the clear, blue sky and anyone could tell it was brighter, Sheryl's world had suddenly turned dark, a world where reality was the standard, not reality TV.

"What a way to go," Jeff said, genuinely concerned about who was killed by the rabid bears. What if it was Vinny? He hoped not.

Sheryl pulled the high-top stool out from the table and took a seat. She did not comment and felt faint.

"Wonder what's with the notebook?" The Admiral asked, reaching over to take Sheryl's hand. It was as cold as ice.

The video from the *Dalton News* reporter clearly showed white but bloody paper in one bear's mouth. The police could deny all they wanted, but Jeff knew what he saw. The screen switched to a hospital room; and there lay Pastor B.J. Stagner, his confidant.

"Sheryl," Scott said, serving up some fresh lemonade and one mint julip, "You're as white as a ghost."

Scott Johnson, manager of *The Divide*, worried about Sheryl. He felt certain that she should have disappeared too, she was so Christian. He knew it could happen at any time, just like it did with Karen. He wasn't sure he would ever get over that. His first love.

As the others looked at Sheryl, she was clearly distressed. She was perspiring profusely and definitely had a case of the pales.

"Pastor B.J. Stagner made a statement this morning from his bed in the Trauma Recovery Center, admitting that his severe wounds were not the result of the bear attack and refusing to take the rabies vaccine."

"What's the matter, Hon?" The Admiral asked, squeezing Sheryl's hand more tightly, hoping to share his warmth.

"I have some discouraging news," she said.

The next fifteen minutes, Sheryl shared her story with the small group. She trusted their silence; and besides, what difference did it really make now?

"The police found a bloodied notebook in the mouth of one of the bears, just like we saw in the video. Ed Poe, with Homeland Security, contacted President Travis directly. Poe claimed the White House, Congress and Senate could not be trusted with the information."

She wiped her forehead with the black, linen napkin, wondering if the air conditioning was being all it could be.

"Mr. Poe told the President that the highly confidential find mapped out a plan of destruction and terror, not only for the United States and Canada, but Europe as well. Europe surely needs no more terror."

That was an understatement, she thought. London's Big Ben had been blown up and the Eiffel Tower, destroyed. In Russia, much of St. Petersburg and her beautiful churches had been wiped out with a 5-megaton nuke. Muslim immigrants, shown mercy by the Europeans, had turned much of the land into Shariah-inspired war zones. Greece's olive orchards were on fire, and another three-thousand Spaniards and Portuguese had burned to death while trapped in their cars, trying to escape the arson-fueled forest fires in their regions.

"*There is good news and bad news out of Charleston, South Carolina*," the OLNN commentator droned on.

"You've heard of Red Mercury?" Sheryl asked, looking at Jeff. It had been the subject of discussion the previous day.

The small group of friends and confidants shook their heads in the affirmative. Jeff glanced at the flat screen above the fireplace, and the people glued to the news. The news had become like a never-ending movie, a movie of tragedy rather than a love story.

"Only, recently," Jeff answered. "Like The Admiral said, it was supposedly a rumor."

"And not such good news out of Cape Cod and Washington, DC. What is now being called the La Palma Wave, washed ashore with great speed, the largest wave on record to hit New England and the Mid-Atlantic regions. Based on when the wave struck Charleston, the speed of approach topped five hundred miles per hour. Nearly all of Historic Charleston has been destroyed. As the wave hit, a 6.5 earthquake also struck three miles offshore. Some scientists are claiming there is a connection.

"At a church in North Charleston, several survivors have been found, including five Muslim immigrants. One of the immigrants actually had a baby girl as the disaster struck, but all are safe and sound. The baby is named Lutheran, after the church that gave them shelter.

"Now to Blip…"

"No, Red Mercury is not a rumor," Sheryl said. "The 'bloody papers' the police found in the bear's mouth was a carefully mapped out time-schedule of a series of events that are to happen in the United States the same time it happens in Europe. Some of the info is being described as a gold mine by Homeland."

"We have an astronomer as our guest, Dr. Juanita Garcia from Kitt Peak National Observatory in Arizona. Welcome."

"But much of the information is in some kind of a Kentucky Fried Chicken code. The interesting part is, Homeland Security has found this code in the past. The code is connected somehow with the nuclear attacks in Manhattan and Surprise, Arizona."

"Thank you for having me as a guest," Juanita said, rubbing her palms together. *"This Blip is…"*

"Let me interrupt for just a second if I may, Dr. Garcia, so the viewers will understand, what exactly is this light that people call Blip?"

"President Travis insinuated that there are references to some sort of Drone Swarm. These drones will be launched at night so not to be easily visible, from numerous sites around North America and Europe."

"Where did these goons get the drones?" The Admiral asked. "Amazon?"

"Yep," Sheryl said. "From Amazon, eBay, Alibaba and numerous other outlets. They are readily available, even from Walmart."

Jeff listened to Sheryl intently but overheard the word, even with his mind going in so many directions, a subconscious recognition. *Blip.*

He and Abe had been two of the first to see the light, brighter than an old Brownie camera flashbulb. The light would appear and disappear, often instantaneously. He held his hand up, a gesture to shush. The discussion stopped, and all eyes turned to the interview.

"This is a good question," Juanita started. *"We are not entirely sure what is the light, you know what I say? Often it approaches from the direction of Sun and cannot be seen until it is near Earth. The light was first reported about six years ago in West Georgia and Alabama and has been seen only a few times since, as far as we know.*

"However, I say this light we now call Blip because of its ability to appear and disappear in a flash, seems to be associated in some way to the disappearances that have occurred around the world."

"Okay, let me stop you there," Laura said. *"You are acknowledging the disappearances? President Morsi and the New World Order claim there have been no disappearances and that it is a conspiracy theory. The President of Israel recently said the same."*

Laura Blayton made her money by interviewing interesting people, and she was a believer in the rapture of the church. There was a prophecy that believers in God and His Christ would join Christ in Heaven; and it would happen instantly, in the *twinkling of an eye.* Only… she thought it would happen to everyone at the same time. She also knew that Morsi was a liar, and maybe the antichrist and silently hoped her time would be soon.

The subject of the strange, intense light had taken the world by storm as more and more people saw it; and then it simply disappeared. There were many eyewitnesses, no matter what World

Ruler Morsi had to say. Her next conquest, she decided, would be the two men in Georgia, the first reported observers of the phenomenon.

"*Dr. Garcia?*"

Juanita paused, contemplating her response. Crossing President Morsi was not a good idea, because he was surely the antichrist. She knew that for sure. The wrong answer could end her teaching career, as well as her very life.

"*Laura,*" Juanita said. "*I do not know politics, only know astronomy. This strange and intense light often appears where there are claims of people disappearing. I personally have not seen a disappearance.*"

Jeff looked at Sheryl; and she looked at him, a bingo-moment look. Blip had appeared when Melissa vanished from the beach in Jamaica, one of the first disappearances.

"*We have analyzed this light thoroughly,*" Juanita continued. "*It seems to have no trajectory, sort of a free spirit. Sometimes it even zigzags. Never has anything like this phenom been recorded.*"

"*Dr. Garcia, you are the head of Solar Research at Kitt Peak National Observatory. Is that correct?*"

"*Yes. I have been in that position for seventeen years.*"

"*You are also a proponent of the theory that many of the earthquakes suddenly occurring might be a result of the warming of earth's crust?*"

The crowd in *The Divide* seemed mesmerized by the interview. Since so many had disappeared the past few years, lots of the ancient pagan religions had taken hold. There were even rumors of human sacrifice rituals in New Mexico. With the rise of the Eastern religions, many had a growing and obsessive curiosity about Christianity and the rapture theory.

"*I do believe that the warming of the crust and mantle of Earth are some causes of the recent earthquake activity, possibly initiated by the Jerusalem Quake.*"

"*So you are an adherent of the global warming controversy?*"

Juanita paused, irritated.

"Global warming is not a controversy, Laura; it is a fact. The only thing not certain is whether man is causing the warming or is it occurring naturally? Or both."

Juanita gathered her thoughts. She was constantly questioned about climate change and global warming. The globe had been warming for thousands of years, and now the warming was causing more warming, like a perpetual motion machine. Warming begat warming, and there had been a lot of begetting the last few years.

"Beneath Antarctica, there is volcanic activity that has increased significantly the last five years. Ice is melting below the surface at an unprecedented rate. Man has nothing to do with this melting.

"At the bottom of the Marianas Trench, entire communities of sea chimneys have been discovered, pumping out seven-hundred-degree water. It is a virtual steam oven, constantly heating the surrounding water. The oceans are warming, and the byproduct is a warmer climate. Then there is the increase in solar activity, also not caused by human activity."

"Has anyone seen Abe?" Jeff asked, deciding that the news about the strange, bright light had concluded.

"Not me," Scott said while replenishing everyone's lemonade once again. The heat and humidity made for thirsty people.

Scott, too, had been fascinated with the interview and found the interviewer especially interesting. Laura Blayton. He was sure they had met somewhere in the past.

"You're staring at the girl, Scott," Sheryl said with a wink and nodded toward the TV. "I have seen that look before."

Scott blushed, like he always did.

"Okay, back to red mercury," Jeff said.

Sheryl continued the story, stating what President Travis told her in confidence. Much of the information gathered from the bloody notebook was in the KFC code, but the code should be easy to decipher. If the feds wanted to decipher, that is. It was truly uncomfortable, not trusting the government, her employer.

The drone war would consist of single-drone and multi-drone swarms, some containing hundreds of the small, intelligent aircraft.

"How dangerous could they be?" Scott asked. "I mean, they can only carry so much weight. They could not carry a heavy explosive."

"Wrongo," Sheryl said. "Drones on the market today are used in delivery systems and farming. Many can carry upward of a hundred pounds. However, according to President Travis, the drones will not be carrying explosives.

"Red Mercury," Sheryl continued, "acts much like a catalyst and increases the explosive yield of a conventional weapon. A nuclear weapon's yield is increased tens of times, maybe more. A small 2-kiloton nuke becomes a 20 to 50-kiloton weapon, a far greater force than either of the nukes dropped on Japan.

"Ed Poe at Homeland told the president that during the past five years, Islamists have infiltrated the southern border like never before. The new wall the U.S. was building had proven too little too late. Intelligence sources estimate that, with the aid of North Korea and their miniaturization skills, there could be as many as two hundred small-yield nuclear weapons, hidden in air conditioning ducts, street lights, monuments, military bases, and high-rise apartments. Anywhere and everywhere.

"The drones are fitted with electronic transmitters that trigger a timing mechanism within the red mercury device. When they fly over a site, the bomb timer is set by the drone's signal. Five minutes later... Boom."

"Big boom," Scott said.

"... *saying that Blip is actually a lifeform?*" Laura asked, astonished by Dr. Garcia's revelation.

"When does this swarm war start?" The Admiral asked.

"We don't know, Justin," Sheryl said, holding The Admiral's hand tightly. "Soon. We are counting on the codes to have that information, and maybe the targets."

"I am saying that the light is made up of many organic compounds, unlike asteroids. These compounds are the precursors of life on Earth. So yes, there could possibly be life on Blip. Certainly."

"If you can get me that info," Jeff said, "I am sure B.J. Stagner could have it decoded."

"The guy in the hospital?" Sheryl asked, remembering the name from the news blurb earlier. "The preacher?"

"Yep," Jeff said. "That would be him."

"What kind of life," the commentator asked Juanita.

Dr. Garcia said nothing but clutched a tiny Bible tightly in her hand, in spite of the danger. Tears swelled in her eyes as she contemplated her possible arrest.

"Jesus' army. He is coming to save us."

Chapter Eight

Abe and Condi sat in the booth at Calypso Jack's, each drinking a cold beer and holding hands. Condi felt like a schoolgirl for the first time in many years, and Abe was just glad to be there. She was very pleasant to the eyesight and personable too. What was not to like?

"What did you do, Abe?"

Abe explained his visit a few days earlier to Dave Cook, though he did not mention the hypnosis session. He would hold off on that bit of news for a while.

"I…" Abe paused. "I don't really remember, Condi."

Abe had been traumatized by the ice bomb storm, and Condi's concern was obvious. She was aware of the megacryometeorites that more-and-more often were falling from the sky and had even interviewed the guy who discovered the large chunks of falling ice and coined the name.

"I heard a sound. It was barely audible but within seconds, there was the loudest boom I ever heard. From that point, I remember nothing until I woke up in the middle of some bushes beside the parking lot. I stumbled to my car, which somehow made it through the storm without a scratch and drove to my doctor's office. I think I was shell-shocked. There were huge chunks of ice in the parking lot, and nearly every car was damaged."

"PTSD," Condi said. "Used to be called shell-shock, but now it is Post Traumatic Stress Disorder. Do you have ringing in your ears?"

Actually, Abe did have ringing in his ears; and it had never occurred until after the ice ball storm.

"Yeah," Abe said. "I do."

"That happens a lot with PTSD victims. I read an article about it last week. It will probably go away."

Condi read the streaming text along the bottom of the large screen over the bar. A soccer game was being played in South America, but the text-thread had nothing to do with the game.

"That can't be right," she said and excused herself. She walked closer to the soccer game, reading the thread, rubbed her eyes and reread. This was not good.

Abe joined her and now both saw the streaming News Alert. The bartender and the patrons were oblivious to the message, focused only on the game; and Condi wondered if the bartender could even read English. Israel was being invaded, like the prophets foretold; and the world watched soccer.

"Let's go," Abe said, grabbing Condi's phone and purse off the table. Abe left thirty dollars beside his nearly full beer glass to cover the cost of two beers and tip, hoping that Wild Willy and Aludra were not in Israel.

"I can't believe it," Condi said, breathless. Her heart was pounding away. "Where are we going?"

"*The Divide*," Abe said. "They have twenty TVs, all tuned to different news channels."

Heading south on Buford Highway at just below the speed limit, there was little traffic. They were surprised when they topped a hill and saw three Suwanee Police cars in a ditch. Just ahead, the traffic lights in the intersection all flashed yellow and then went out.

"Hold on," Abe yelled. "I'm going for it."

There was little choice. The signals seemed inoperable, and Abe prayed no one was coming. He slammed the accelerator to the floor as he downshifted to third, and the GTO screamed through the intersection of Sugarloaf Parkway and Buford Highway.

The crash between the tractor-trailer and the pickup truck that had been riding Abe's bumper for two miles, trying to get him to race, was loud and complete. The black pickup burst into flames as fenders, bumpers and F150 Ford bucket seats flew down Sugarloaf Parkway. The tractor-trailer came to a halt on a dirt hill beside the road, and Abe wondered again why so many wanted to race his GTO. It was no contest.

"All the traffic lights are out?" Condi said as they cautiously passed through another intersection. Several cars were stalled in the middle of the road while others tried to maneuver past. Some of the vehicles seemed totally out of control, and a neon-blue Corvette crashed into the laundromat on the corner.

"Wonder what's going on?" Abe asked, mostly to himself and noticed that the radio was only static. What happened to *The Condi Show*?

A TV-14 FOX helicopter flew low overhead, the sound of the self-rotating blades flapping in the wind. A near-silent helicopter did not register in Abe's mind, and then it crashed into the same laundromat as the Corvette, also bursting into flames. Several people ran from the building, most on fire but made it to the outdoor fountain where they jumped into the basin, all except one.

"Should we stop?" Condi asked, and black smoke filled the air.

"I don't think so," Abe said without pause. "Something is going on with the electrical grid it appears. Chadbo has been texting about some dangerous solar activity. I bet that is the answer to cars in the ditch and crashing helicopters."

"Might be more disappearances?" Condi asked. There had been numerous plane crashes when pilots and copilots vanished.

Abe considered Condi's comment. The disappearances seemed to have stopped, which he found disappointing.

"Maybe," he said with a glint of hope. He did not want to endure what was coming.

"Do you believe in the rapture?" Abe asked.

"Of course," Condi answered. "At least I do now. I grew up in the church, but the preachers never mentioned it. Then one day I came across Hal Lindsey on the radio. He was talking about the accuracy of the Jewish prophets, which I found very interesting. He explained the rapture theory, and it did not seem like a theory at all. Ever heard him?"

"Oh yeah. Most everyone interested in prophecy has heard of Hal. What church did you go to?" Abe asked.

"A tiny Presbyterian church in rural New York."

Entering the intersection of Old Peachtree and Buford Highway, the traffic signals were operating properly, no cars were swerving or helicopters crashing; and everything seemed perfectly normal, except the heat. Five minutes later, they entered *The Divide*; and it appeared everyone in Duluth decided to do the same. Abe had not seen a crowd like this in four years.

"Rural New York?" Abe questioned. He had grown up in rural New York. "I spent time in New York too."

The crowded restaurant was silent as people surrounded the TVs, seeking news on the nuclear war in Asia and the invasion of Israel by Iran, Syria and Turkey. This, Abe found, was the most troubling; and he was sure there was a Russian connection.

"Could this be the War of Gog of Magog?" he asked. "The one mentioned in Ezekiel?"

Condi said nothing. She had no clue about Gog and Magog.

"You can explain that later," she said and squeezed his hand.

They were surprised to see Chadbo on one of the news channels and drifted over to hear what he had to say. Most of the other large screens covered the war in Asia.

According to reports, North Korea was a wasteland for the most part; but their leader had planned well for such an event. For the privileged, an underground city had been built deep into the Kangnam Mountains along the Chinese border.

From the security of the underground city, sixty-six secret launching platforms were armed and under North Korean control. Their successful miniaturization of nuclear weapons combined with the red mercury catalyst, reeked devastation onto South Korea, Japan, Guam and U.S. Naval assets surrounding the peninsula. Two complete U.S. Aircraft Carrier fleets now rested on the bottom of the Sea of Japan, a result of a couple of perfectly placed nuclear missiles.

Abe and Condi grabbed a seat and had Chadbo to themselves as everyone else watched the world at war. Abe asked Scott for the remote, and soon they had a split screen. The Israel invasion was on the left and Chadbo, on the right, talking about the sun.

"The Queen City of the Hudson," Condi said. "That is where I was raised, about 35,000 people."

"Poughkeepsie?" Abe asked, incredulous.

"Yeah, how did you know?"

"Dr. Myers," the host asked Chad, *"How long will this effect, this EMP, be with us? Will it affect the entire world?"*

"No. Mostly the Southern Hemisphere, this go 'round. There will probably be some marginal effect as far north as Atlanta and as far south as Peru and Chile. The most pronounced effect is the area between."

"Here in Atlanta, what can we expect and how long will it last?"

"I have close friends who live north of Atlanta," Chad said, *"and have received reports of intermittent power-outages, flashing traffic signals, minor stuff. South Florida on the other hand and most of Central and South America, will suffer and are suffering. Electric grids will be fried, and transformers will explode. Some of those transformers take a year or more to build, and many have exploded or short-circuited by now. Any aircraft, or any modern aircraft, will probably crash or at least experience problems. Older aircraft and cars, say thirty to forty years old, might be unaffected."*

Abe's phone sounded but the screen pixelated and went blank. Probably the sun. He gave Condi a brief hug, looked directly into her eyes and said, "I was raised in Poughkeepsie, too. Jefferson Street."

"For those who lose grids," Chad continued, *"may God help them. There will be no running water, lights, food. Grocery stores have already been raided. South Africa has declared a strict form of Martial Law. Looting and rioting in parts of China is out of control, and their military is on alert."*

"How long will it last?"

Chad scratched his wrist, still sensitive from the implant.

"Maybe two or three days for those who have lost only transformer systems. By tomorrow, there should be no new effects; because the solar winds will have passed Earth. However, those who lose their grids could suffer for years."

"Could this lead to civil wars?" the host asked.

"It already has. Indonesia, the largest Muslim country in the world, broke out in war yesterday. Muslims killing Muslims."

Condi wondered if she had ever known Abe as a kid, since she lived a few blocks away from Jefferson Street; but the war talk led Condi's eyes to the left split screen. An hour earlier, she was sure there had been scenes of tanks and armored carriers going off to war in the Golan Heights. Now the scene was Jerusalem; and Jews danced in the streets, as if in celebration. How could that be?

"Can we turn that up?" she asked Abe, and he quickly complied.

"...celebrating in the streets after the miracle at Golan. Many Jewish biblical scholars are asking, 'Could this be the Gog of Magog event?'"

"What miracle?" Condi asked. She recalled no news of the attack on Israel. "What does the Gog-Magog thing have to do with this and what does it mean?"

Condi was not familiar with the term but had had plenty of opportunities in her life, because the subject had come up several times.

"Can you explain that to me, Abe? What is this war about?"

Chapter Nine

*"On the mountains of Israel you will fall, you and all your troops
and the nations with you. I will give you as food to all kinds of
carrion birds and to the wild animals."*

Ezekiel 39:4

The Admiral awaited breakfast at the Gwinnett Mall
IHOP, sipping a cup of steamy coffee and reading the
Gwinnett Gazette.

The lights occasionally blinked from intermittent power
outages; and each time, the air conditioner restart took five minutes,
thanks to a time-delay for safety. He was amazed at how warm the
restaurant could become in five minutes, and other patrons fanned
themselves with menus. Early afternoon temperature was a hair
above 110°, and the restaurant was mostly empty because of the
heat.

The wedding was once more planned, and the small chapel at
Berkeley Lake was again decorated. The wedding would be small,
maybe fifty or so. He was nervous. A conversation from the next
booth wafted into The Admiral's space, and he soon found himself
eavesdropping.

"Yep. I looked it up. Some ancient guy named Ezekiel talked
about a future war against Israel. The coalition against Israel is
described as an enemy from the north. Did you know Russia is
mentioned?"

The Admiral scanned the daily news, but he continued listening
to the two women in the next booth, Sally and Cathy, or maybe
Katie.

"No," Katie answered. "I did not."

The retired admiral considered the strength of his faith,
wondering how strong it could be. He knew nothing about Ezekiel?

"Yeah, he called them the people of Rosh or something like that. Those who study this stuff say that's modern-day Russia."

"Yes," Katie agreed. "But it seems the people who studied about this Gog and Magog war have mostly disappeared."

The two ladies paused and glanced around the restaurant, just to make sure. They could be in serious trouble if the wrong person overheard, but IHOP appeared nearly empty. New laws and codes restricted speaking of *any* religion in public areas and enforcement was strict.

The Admiral spotted Sheryl in the parking lot as she walked toward the entry. He admired her more than she knew, and her graying hair blew in the steady breeze. She was beautiful.

"Well, it doesn't really matter. Something happened, not sure what; but the Israelis are calling it the Miracle of Golan, whatever it was."

Katie sat silently for a moment as she tried to recall the story about Gog and Magog that her grandma used to tell every Easter when she prayed that Jesus would soon return. Apparently Jesus' return had something to do with this war.

"My grandmother used to tell this story every Easter, but I was little. Then grandma became one of the vanished. If this is *that* war, I think all the enemy troops went crazy or were miraculously destroyed by an earthquake or something. All the dead soldiers that were planning to attack Israel would be left on the battlefield and wild birds would eat the flesh off their bones."

"Gross!" Sally said. "I just had my lunch!"

"Sorry," Katie apologized. "That's what grandma said."

The Admiral stood to greet his bride-to-be when the two ladies spotted him, and fear crossed their faces. The Admiral smiled at them, confused at their expressions and said, "Today is my wedding day." Without saying a word of congratulations, the two ladies hurriedly paid their bill and exited.

"What was *that* about?" Sheryl said, a grim look upon her face, not the look of an almost newlywed.

"I have no idea. I overheard their conversation, at least part. They were discussing something about... I couldn't really understand... something about God and Magod?"

Sheryl took her seat, sliding across the light blue vinyl and laughed.

"Gog and Magog," she said, laughing again.

"Well," The Admiral chuckled. "Glad I could give you a good laugh. What is it?"

"It's a coming war that may have just come and ended. It is supposed to be quick, like three days, and very fatal, at least for the followers of Gog. Gog is a predicted ruler of some lands north of Israel, around and beyond the Caspian Sea, referred to as Magog. Magog becomes a confederacy. The war is to be portrayed as Israel's biggest nightmare in the last days; but prophecy says it will end suddenly when enemy soldiers are miraculously slain on the plains, valleys and mountains of Northern Israel. That just happened."

"Is that why you have that grim look?"

Sheryl took a small compact out of her purse and looked in the mirror.

"I don't have a grim look!"

The Admiral sat silently, rubbing his finger around the rim of his glass. He loved Sheryl deeply and completely, so why did he keep finding a way to avoid... marriage? Fear, maybe? But why would he fear marriage at his age.

"I am always happy at IHOP, because I get senior discounts."

"When you get my age, you get double-discounts," The Admiral laughed.

He watched Sally and Katie drive out of the parking lot, and wondered what their story was. A news alert streamed along the bottom of the lone TV. He could not read it from his booth but noted this was a real alert because of the color-code, flashing red.

"Why so interested?" Sheryl asked.

"In what?"

"The two ladies? You were staring."

The Admiral glanced again out the window. The blue BMW sat diagonally in Pleasant Hill Road and was now surrounded by several black Suburbans, unmarked.

"Are we jealous?" The Admiral asked, amused.

"No, no. Too old to be jealous. Staring is just not like you."

He glanced again out the window. The two ladies were laying on the pavement being handcuffed. He looked at Sheryl, and reached across the table to hold her frigid hand. Her hands were always cold, even when it was 110° outside; and he worried. Maybe that was it, he thought. Maybe he feared he would marry Sheryl, and then she would die. He wiped the thought out of his mind.

"They were talking about the War and this Gog character," The Admiral said. "I know nothing about it, except what you've told me. Something magnificent has happened there, in Israel; and I cannot find anything about it on the news."

"That is because we are now censoring the news. The government calls it 'filtering'."

The waitress brought more coffee, and The Admiral recognized her from somewhere. Her ebony skin was flawless. Where had he seen her before? He looked closely at her nametag, trying to focus. The eyes were not what they used to be.

"Mr. Admiral! How are you?" Agatha said, handing them menus. "Where is your friend, the wind-watcher?"

The memory came back as he remembered her from the IHOP at Goddard Space Flight Center in Maryland. She had waited on him and Chadbo.

"Now I remember," said The Admiral. "It was really hot that day."

"And windy. Your friend warned us, because he could see wind comin'. How he do that? It saved our lives, you know?"

The arrests came quick, as Katie and Sally were loaded into the back of one of the Suburbans. Agatha introduced herself to Sheryl.

"Agatha," Sheryl asked. "Do you know what's going on with the two ladies that were here a few minutes ago, the ones that were just arrested?"

Agatha leaned over the booth, glancing around nervously; and she began to whisper.

"The mo-rality police. It is worse than Iran. They have recordin' devices, audio and video, in most restaurants, fitness centers, bowlin' alleys… anywhere that people crowd. They listen for anything terrorist. We had a meetin' here with Homeland Security before they installed their devices. There was an article in the *Gwinnett Gazette*."

"But why would they have arrested them? What did they do?"

The entourage of three black Suburbans left in single file, and a towing company loaded the blue BMW onto a flatbed truck. On the side of the flatbed truck was a sign:

You Blow; We Tow
DUI Task Force

"Were they drunk?" The Admiral asked.

"No," Agatha whispered. "They were talkin' 'bout the Bible and the word of God. That is a no-no with the new laws. Did you know we no longer sell sausage and bacon?"

"Why is that?" Sheryl asked, faking surprise.

"Because it is offensive to the… the Muslims. Our whole, dang world is goin' slap crazy," Agatha sighed. "Those ladies were talkin' 'bout the war in Israel that ended three days after it started. I have a friend who works in Qiryat Shemona, close to the Golan Heights. His name is Benjamin Taylor, and he is a Bible archaeologist, real smart like me. He says it was Magog, too. Like a lot of people are sayin' who still believe."

"How does he know that?" Sheryl asked. "Why does he *think* that?"

"You got me," Agatha said, rubbing her wrist, the one with the implant. "He said that drones over the area where a bunch of troops died sent back video of thousands of buzzards and other vultures on the ground, eating the bodies. Hundreds were flyin' overhead."

Sheryl felt nauseated.

"He just send the video. You want to see?" Agatha asked and left to get her laptop. She returned in less than a minute and took a seat by The Admiral.

"Did you see the news alert?" she asked.

The Admiral and Sheryl both turned to the TV but could not read the stream.

"What news?" Sheryl asked.

"There was another big earthquake in Israel last night, bigger than even the Jerusalem quake. Went straight across the Golan and into Syria. Heavy damage in Damascus, and much of the city has been totally destroyed."

"Damascus has been destroyed?" The Admiral asked.

"Yes," Agatha said, feeling faint. "Just like Ezekiel said would happen twenty-six hundred years ago."

Sheryl sat in wonder. Damascus had been predicted to be destroyed but had never happened, one of the unfulfilled prophecies. Now it had, if Agatha was correct.

Agatha went to a Bible website as though it was her hobby and pulled up Ezekiel.

"Right here it is, chapter 38; and they all read the prediction simultaneously:

" 'This is what the Sovereign Lord says: You are the one I spoke of in former days by my servants the prophets of Israel. At that time they prophesied for years that I would bring you against them. This is what will happen in that day: When Gog attacks the land of Israel, my hot anger will be aroused, declares the Sovereign Lord. In my zeal and fiery wrath, I declare that at that time there shall be a great earthquake in the land of Israel. The fish in the sea, the birds in the sky, the beasts of the field, every creature that moves along the ground, and all the people on the face of the earth will tremble at my presence. The

mountains will be overturned, the cliffs will crumble and every wall will fall to the ground. I will summon a sword against Gog on all my mountains, declares the Sovereign Lord. Every man's sword will be against his brother. I will execute judgment on him with plague and bloodshed; I will pour down torrents of rain, hailstones and burning sulfur on him and on his troops and on the many nations with him. And so I will show my greatness and my holiness, and I will make myself known in the sight of many nations. Then they will know that I am the Lord.'

"Wow," The Admiral said. "Double-wow. Where is the prediction that Damascus would be destroyed?"

A few keystrokes later, Agatha pulled it up from the book of the prophet Isaiah.

"How do you know all this, Agatha?" Sheryl asked.

"I study. I was born and raised in Liberia. Africa a tough life, but Liberia was mostly Christian. We went to the church all the time, sometimes every day. And I love these prophets," Agatha answered "They are a lot more accurate than Nostradamus. It is amazin'. Read this."

The special word about Damascus: "See, Damascus will no longer be a city. It will be destroyed and laid waste. The cities of Aroer are left empty. They will be for the flocks to lie down in, and no one will make them afraid. The strong city will be gone from Ephraim. Damascus will no longer rule. And those of Syria who are left alive will be like the shining-greatness of the sons of Israel," says the Lord of All.

Agatha looked up, startled at the noise. A group of Morality Police crashed through the front entry of IHOP and rushed toward Agatha. Within thirty seconds, Agatha, The Admiral and Sheryl were laying supine on the blue, carpeted floor, handcuffed.

There would be no wedding today.

Chapter Ten

Qiryat Shemona
Israel

Ben Taylor, one of America's prodigy archaeologists, at least in biblical research, sat alone outside the entrance to a Bedouin cave, not far from the Golan Heights and the border of Syria. The removal of a large rock at the back of the cave led to one of the most significant discoveries in modern history, better than the Rosetta Stone, better than the Cyrus Cylinder.

The night air was cool, but not as cool as it once was five years earlier on his first trip to Israel. Then the air had been crisp. But compared to the daily heatwave, a heatwave that took a heavy toll on the diggers and sifters, the night was pleasant. He had no complaints.

The sky was dark and there were no city lights, but few stars appeared, which was odd. Maybe he was losing his sight since that night. The explosions, lightning and falling rocks had been so bright. A group of five shooting stars crossed the horizon in a downward plunge, on their journey of devastation. What was the world coming to…

His mind was elsewhere though, not on the relic of Jesus that he discovered. The small scroll and tunic with a splotch of blood belonged to a man named Y'shua, son of Yousef the carpenter from Nazareth, and would set the archaeology world afire. DNA from the son of God.

While Ben was a biblical archaeologist, the field of study was relatively new for him, about seven years. His interest had drifted toward the biblical specialty, mainly because he thought the Bible and the God of Abraham were mythology.

His plan was to prove the God story untrue and write a book, *The Myth of Jehovah*. But the truth of his discoveries proved otherwise. The more he discovered how Israel got there 3,400 years earlier, the more he began to believe the story. Not only was there really a God, Israel seemed to be his preference throughout most of known history. Sometimes he thought it must be tough being God's Chosen, because his discipline was patient and harsh. Sometimes really harsh, he thought, considering the holocaust.

Still, he knew little about the Gog-Magog War or any of the future wars that were to befall Israel in the last days. Of course, that all changed two days ago when the Golan Heights, a war booty of Israel's, thanks to a previous war in 1967, lit up the night sky like fireworks he had never seen in his thirty-eight years.

The Golan Heights had been a part of Syria, not ancient Israel; and Syria used the strategic location to bombard the newly restored Israel in 1948. The bombardment continued until the 1967 War when Syria attacked, and Israel soundly defeated her archenemy from times past and annexed the Golan Heights. Eventually Israel built forty settlements in the Heights, but they had all been abandoned the last few months. No one wanted to be there when war came. Gog of Magog.

"Can I join you, Mr. Benjamin?"

Ben was jumpy since the scenes of war broke out right in front of his eyes, and he had not heard the Jewish guide approach.

"Did I surprise you, my friend?"

"Sorry," Ben said. "I am a little tense."

"I would imagine," the guide said. "My name is Jon."

The two men sat silently at first, but after a couple of uncomfortably long minutes, Jon commented on the night sky.

"Sure are missing some stars, it seems. The whole sky used to light up on a clear night. They have been disappearing for a couple of years. City people do not know, you know what I mean? Cities have so much light, you cannot even see a single star."

Jon was a guide and knew little about astronomy, but he knew one thing for certain. Stars did not just disappear. Something very odd was going on with the Man upstairs, he reckoned.

"Jon, do you know anything about this 3-Day War Israel just had with Syria?"

Jon sat silently for a moment and stared at the bright lights along the Western horizon. Whether missiles or asteroids had flown overhead, they had missed the Mediterranean and hit the land inside Israel.

"Wasn't really much of a war," Jon said. "The Christians claim it may be the War of Gog of Magog, but that is not as much a Jewish belief. The Jews have pretty much written that prediction off, like the destruction of Damascus."

"From what I hear, Damascus may have met its destruction."

"You know what's interesting about this invasion?"

"What?" Ben answered.

"Israel did not have to do anything, other than launch a few fighter jets. Once the invasion began, all hell broke loose in the Golan; and it was not Israel wreaking havoc. You saw it as plainly as I."

Ben had seen the start clearly, and then the end soon after. Syrians had smart phones, and where there were smart phones, there were lots of video clips. What he saw was truly beyond his expectation, and the video clips did not give the event due justice.

"I saw it plainly," Ben agreed. "I will never forget the sound of the two... what were those things?"

"Not sure," Jon said. "They were noisy, and at first I thought they were missiles..."

"Except they kept climbing," Ben interrupted. "And they did not sound like missiles. It sounded like a horn or dysfunctional marching band. Kind of musical."

Ben remembered running inside the large cave that night, sure a nuke would wipe out the men below; but it never happened. Later reports from the few eyewitnesses who had not been blinded, claimed the two lights climbed straight up in altitude; and as they climbed, all eyes watched. Suddenly, like the atomic warhead that ignited two-thousand feet above Hiroshima, the two lights turned "brighter than seven suns" according to one witness; but there was no explosion, only an unbelievably bright light. The Bedouin cave lit up like a Roman Candle in his hometown on the 4th of July. Ben missed Duluth, and a tinge of homesickness set in. He could not wait to get back to his wife. God had blessed him with Hillary, and he was not sure why. She was way more than he deserved, he was sure of that.

"And then the earthquake," Jon said. "Been having many earthquakes since the Jerusalem quake, too many."

"It would be hard to forget that earthquake," Ben said.

When the earth opened, drone videos showed a giant crevice craftily rearranging the landscape; and giant chasms many feet deep began to appear. From the land of Golan, many who had been blinded but not killed, fell screaming into the bottomless pits. White glowing rocks crashed to earth; and were it not for the extreme heat of the burning rocks, one would have thought they were huge chunks of ice falling from Heaven.

"Whatever happened," Jon said, staring toward Golan, still aglow from God's reward, "all the attacking soldiers got out of their vehicles and were soon killing each other. I have never seen anything like that. They had all been blinded by the two lights."

"I've thought about that," Ben said, "why they would depart the safety of their vehicles. Just prior to the attack, my phone and laptop started going haywire. I rebooted several times. What if the two lights were EMP weapons and fried all the electronics in the battlefield? Not only would the machines be inoperable, they would also be a hellhole with no air circulation. The soldiers would have to get out of their vehicles or cook."

"But there was no explosion with the lights," Jon interjected.

"Yeah," Ben pondered. "There would surely have been explosions with electromagnetic pulse bombs."

After a pause, Jon repeated a part of Ezekiel from memory, the part about the soldiers killing each other with the sword during the Gog of Magog War; and Ben listened, wishing he had studied the Bible a little more. Maybe a lot more. His grandma read her Bible every night before she went to bed, rest her soul; and she disappeared last year while washing dishes.

"I was an atheist at one time," Jon said. "But now I am a good Jew, except…"

Jon's conversation drifted into silence.

"Except what?" Ben asked.

"My family would disagree that I am a good Jew. I have started reading the New Testament, and they find it difficult to believe that I would do such a thing. They are so pro-Morsi and his fancy New World Order or New Age Order, they believe he is the promised Messiah. The more I read the New Testament, the more I believe that Jesus was who he said he was."

"Who did he say he was?" Ben asked.

"He said he was the Messiah," Jon said and paused. "He came to save the Jews from themselves, and the Pharisees just missed it."

The ground shook and bright lights lit the horizon in the distance, toward Mount Hermon.

"Did you feel that??" Jon asked, frightened.

The ground rolled underneath them like a small wave. More lights flashed toward Mount Hermon, and the flash was now more crimson than white. They covered their ears, trying to shut out the loud, scraping sounds; and a flock of vultures flew overhead. What did the vultures know that they did not know?

"Is Mount Hermon volcanic?" Ben shouted to his new friend.

"Yes! Why?" Jon shouted back. "How did you know that?"

There was evidence in Mount Hermon's ancient past, large basaltic deposits from some thirteen million years earlier.

"I'm an archaeologist!" Ben shouted. "I studied the mountain ranges and was sure I read that this entire area, and southward past the Dead Sea, had a violent geological history. When was the last time it erupted?"

"About thirteen-million years ago," Jon said.

The falling rocks came as a surprise and the two men were startled as one slammed into a small growth of wild date palms, turning them into twenty-five-foot torches. The ground continued to roll, not violently, more of a gentle rocking motion; and they were thankful for the cave. The falling rocks glowed a deep reddish-orange, and more crashed outside the entrance and in the valleys below.

Soon the smell of smoke infiltrated the cave as the brush and orchards in the valleys caught fire, and Ben knew that was not good. The drought had taken a toll in Israel, this drought in particular. What little rain Israel received the past year, most of it was red as blood.

"We need to get out of here," Jon shouted, but both men were hesitant to leave the protection of the cave. "What do you think is going on?"

Cautiously, Ben moved toward the entrance. Distant lightening appeared at the top of the now-glowing Mount Hermon, and a river of molten lava edged down the southwest flank of the mountain.

"I think she's gonna blow!" Ben shouted. "We have to go for it."

Chapter Eleven

Wild Willy ran like he had never run before, or at least during the last twenty years. The night sky above Jerusalem had an eerie tint, not exactly a glow but different than he had ever seen in his numerous journeys to the Promised Land; and he laughed at the name. Promised for what? Promised for continuous desolation and war was what he saw. He had to find Aludra. Something was happening to the north, and he was certain it wasn't anything good.

Will had been chatting with Chadbo a few minutes earlier, as Chad explained the coronal mass ejection headed toward Earth.

"This one hit near you, Wild Willy. You guys in Israel never lost power? It should have knocked-out every cell phone in Israel."

"Nothing yet," Will said, glancing around. "Heard there were a few problems north of here. Maybe Israel had another miracle. That seems to happen all the time."

The lights in Jerusalem seemed fine, and people were talking on phones, still celebrating the Golan Miracle and President Morsi. Cafés were crowded because President Morsi was visiting The City of David again.

Israelis rejoiced in the renaming of Jerusalem at the hands of Morsi though Jordan, Saudi Arabia and Egypt threatened war from the South; and more Muslim countries were joining the quickly forming confederation. The City of David was more inclusive.

"Maybe you got lucky," Chad said but wondering how. Power was out in all of Syria and Lebanon to the north, and much of Russia. It did seem miraculous.

The Muslim countries to the south were Sunni, and Morsi was Shi'a. The two sects of Islam had always hated one another. Iran had become the new and improved Persia of old and eagerly endorsed President Morsi. They knew he had a plan in the formation of the

J.L. Robb

Global Government Initiative in which, ultimately, Allah would rule.

On the other hand, the Sunnis also knew that Morsi, the Shi'a pig, had a plan, a diabolical conspiracy with Israel that would end, much to Israel's dismay, in the retaking of Jerusalem by the Southern Confederacy of Islam and the complete elimination of Israel. The Sunni hatred for Morsi was paramount.

Will's heart raced as he ran, and then he heard Aludra.

"Will! Will!"

He looked to the left. She and her brother, the one who once hated and wanted to kill her, sat on a small park bench, also studying the strange sky. Thunder, or something, rumbled constantly from the north toward Golan; though they had heard the 3-Day war ended in a resounding defeat of the Northern Alliance. There should be no bombing.

Muslim warriors from the northern countries of the old Soviet Union made up a large part of the Alliance and had frothed like rabid wolves for war since the rebirth of Israel in 1948. They came from Chechnya, Tajikistan, Kyrgyzstan, Uzbekistan and Turkey, thirty thousand in all; and all had died. Aludra ran toward him, and Will was relieved. He had never had anxieties, but something did not feel right.

Rushing toward Will, Aludra threw her arms around him and smothered his face with kisses.

"Stop. I'm all sweaty."

"I love you, Will; and I love your sweat too."

A tear dropped slowly down Aludra's cheek, and Will was again overwhelmed by his feelings for her.

"What's the matter?"

Aludra sobbed, something Will had never seen. She was always composed, though she had been through living hell; and worry spread across his face.

"What's wrong, Aludra?"

74

"Muhammed is afraid, because … because of what is coming on the world. He wants to kill himself. He said he was the reason, something about a drone war or something; and millions will die."

Jeff had mentioned a drone war to Will during their last conversation and indicated that he was in touch, sort of, with the notorious Vinny, the killer of millions.

Will was not happy about that turn of events but withheld judgment until he could get the scoop. He would kill Vinny at first chance, so why would Vinny be in touch with Jeff? Did Samarra have something to do with it? It was Samarra, after all, who stole the Spanish Flu virus. His mind raced, and he wondered what Vinny knew about a drone war.

"What does your brother know, Aludra? Where is he?"

The low rumble of a motorcycle came from the north, and Will glanced but saw nothing. Ash began to fall from the sky. Aludra turned and looked back at the bench, but Muhammed was nowhere to be seen.

"I do not know where he is. He was right there," she pointed. "He is so depressed that he would ever have been involved in such a murderous rampage. He is going to kill himself, I am sure."

Will embraced Aludra tightly as she sobbed against his chest, and he again glanced up the street toward the sound of the invisible motorcycle. He was certain he heard shouting.

"Tell me what he knows," Will asked softly. "Maybe we can stop it."

The motorcycle came to a halt, and the two riders were shouting.

"Mount Hermon is erupting! Mount Hermon is blowing up!!"

Aludra watched the two men curiously as tears continued down her cheeks; and she wiped them away with the pink sleeve of her shirt. She hoped they were not terrorists, because terror filled the streets of Jerusalem.

"Slow down, slow down!" Will said, instantly on the defensive. "Mount Hermon is a volcano?"

"Yes," said Jon the guide, and Ben Taylor parked the motorcycle at the shoulder of City of David Highway.

"It is definitely a volcano," Ben shouted and walked toward Will and Aludra.

"Been doing some digs up at Golan," he continued. "Jon and I were overlooking the mountains a while ago when it erupted. I thought at first the war had flared up again, but it was Mount Hermon. We came here to let people know, in case they need to evacuate."

Aludra heard the word but was unsure of the exact meaning. *Evacuate.* She did not think it was good news.

Will did a quick calculation and did not feel Mount Hermon would cause problems for Jerusalem. It was about three hours north of the capital, too far away. *Wow*, he thought. *Mount Hermon was a volcano.*

"It's about a hundred and twenty miles north of here, so I think we will be fine," Will said, subconsciously fanning an ash. "Might get some ash, maybe some small earthquakes."

The ground shook softly as Will spoke the words, and the reddish glow of the northern sky continued to expand. A sound like faraway thunder filled the air, as a larger eruption of the ancient mountain continued. Small specs of ash fell to the streets, resembling very fine snowflakes.

✡ ✡ ✡

Dawn Galloway was the President of *Dawn Mallard Galloway Missionary Outreach.* Her mission was often dangerous, but Syria had been her greatest challenge. While most Christians left Syria when the civil war started, seeking refuge in friendly countries, many Syrian Muslims were seeking Christianity. It was a phenomenon, but a dangerous phenomenon. It was also her calling.

Dawn started her mission after retiring as a Cumberland County crossing guard and getting a message from Jesus. Unlike those who sometimes hear God *in their head*, that had not been Dawn's case.

She heard an actual voice and would never forget: *Dawn, let's go save some Syrians*. And she did.

A grandmother of thirteen, she and Pearl, her poodle, had traveled to some dangerous places. Dawn's husband, Kelly, also retired, stayed home and took care of their North Carolina dairy farm. Kelly was a good, strong man, always jolly; and he was proud of Dawn. Whenever someone would ask him what his wife did, he always answered the same: "She works for the Lord." And she did.

"What do you think?" Dawn asked her associate, Charlotte Harris.

Dawn and Charlotte had been friends since sixth grade and had always gone to the same church. As adults, they both had an affinity for genealogy; and Charlotte was an ancestry expert.

"I think we need to get the heck out of Dodge, as John Wayne would say," Charlotte laughed nervously.

The red glow in the night sky over Mount Hermon was surreal; and ash fell heavily from above, like a light gray snow. Their black, 1962 Chevy station wagon was now a fluffy, light gray; and Charlotte was sure there would be no letup anytime soon. She wrapped a scarf across her mouth and nose.

"I think the whole city was destroyed," Dawn said, looking down on Damascus from their hilltop base of operations.

With the power out, light was scarce; and even with each lightning strike, the city's destruction remained invisible, hidden behind a fog of dust and debris.

"It was a prediction," Dawn said.

"Help me, help me. Please."

The cry came from the east, and the two ladies spotted the Muslim woman lying under a fallen tree as lightning lit up the sky. They rushed to her; but no matter what the effort, they could not move the tree. Dawn said a silent prayer, that Jesus might help the poor woman. Three men ran to assist, and miraculously, one had a chain saw. *Thank you, Jesus*, Dawn said quietly. *That was a quick miracle.*

The men removed the tree within minutes; and the woman was freed, a broken arm the most serious injury. They carried her to the missionary outpost and into the small infirmary. Dawn and Charlotte went into action, stabilized the woman's arm and administered pain medication, the last dose they had. They would need to wait for the doctor to set the arm properly, though Dawn had some medical experience from owning a dairy farm for so many years. An explosion rocked the night sky and a large fireball appeared from somewhere inside Damascus.

The Muslim woman moaned, oblivious to the sounds of war, exploding mountains and the turmoil in Damascus, her hometown; but she somehow knew her beloved city was no more. She had escaped most of the civil war in Syria, only Syria was now Persia-Minor. Thanks to the generosity of Israel's new leadership and President Morsi, she and her family had been allowed to move to Israel. She wished now she had never returned to Damascus.

"Did you hear that?" Charlotte asked Dawn.

"What?"

Charlotte leaned over the small-framed, Muslim woman and listened closely to her comments. In the darkness of the room, neither Charlotte nor Dawn could see the small bumps on the woman's upper neck, partly covered by her gray hijab. She shivered violently, somehow freezing in the 102° air. Dawn draped her wrap around the delirious lady, trying to keep warmth in her body.

The woman spoke with a raspy whisper, in ancient Aramaic, a language that Charlotte spoke fluently. It was the language of Jesus. She listened closely, and the woman again repeated her statement:

"See, Damascus will no longer be a city but will become a heap of ruins."

"What is she saying?" Dawn asked, praying again that the poor woman would survive. She did not appear to be severely injured, other than the broken arm.

"She is talking about Isaiah," Charlotte said, "Or maybe it was Jeremiah. Sometimes I get the prophets mixed-up. The prophecy that Damascus would forever cease to be a city, left in ruins forever."

The injured woman moaned once, and her eyes sprung open. Then the young Muslim woman died.

Dawn and Charlotte had seen plenty of death the past two years. Dawn had been threatened twice with beheading for helping others find Christ and the great benefits he offered. The room grew darker as one of the candles blew out, and now there were three.

Proselytizing was forbidden in the violent, my-way-or-the-highway world of Islam; and the discipline was usually death. Dawn had been spared, she was sure, by guardian angels. Her escape had been a miracle, most certainly.

They placed their hands on the still body and prayed silently for the woman, prayed that God would forgive her for her sins and for never recognizing Christ. Dawn knew for sure that God was forgiving, but sometimes, not. That's why there was Hell, for the unforgiven.

Suddenly the still air was ruptured by the wailing and weeping of a man, tall and skinny. His left arm hung limp, as though paralyzed; but in his right, he carried a small, silver sword. Then he collapsed and fell on the still warm body; and he sobbed and clinged to his sister.

"Mary. Mary," he wailed. "Please do not leave me. Please do not leave me."

Thick ash slowly seeped into the room, and Charlotte closed the door. Dawn and Charlotte exchanged glances, her-name-is-Mary?? glances. A Muslim woman named Mary? Then, for the first time Dawn recognized her, one of her first converts. That conversion resulted in the *first* beheading threat, from the young girl's... brother. Her left-handed brother, Abdul.

Abdul slowly stood, maintaining his balance with the aid of the sword; and the sword sparkled briefly as a meteor flew overhead, low in the atmosphere. Dawn's heart raced in fear, and she grabbed Charlotte forcefully.

Abdul saw the fear and then recognized the woman who changed his sister's life forever, the woman who stole her soul from Allah. His left arm was paralyzed because of this woman, of this he was certain.

"Get behind me, Charlotte. Now!"

Charlotte did as told but was confused about the sudden turn of events. She had never seen Dawn so frightened, or commanding.

She had never seen the man who tried to behead Dawn but had heard the story. A tall, unusually thin man held his arm in the air, a silver sword in his hand… His left hand; and according to witnesses that day, God got him in the downswing. A bolt of lightning came out of nowhere, there were no clouds in the sky, and struck the sword. The man was not killed but knocked unconscious. When he awoke, Dawn was nowhere to be found; and the man lost the use of his arm.

Charlotte looked at Abdul, her face filled with fear as recognition set in; and she began to cry. Was she going to be one of the saints in Revelation? One of the Christians beheaded during the tribulation? Goosebumps appeared all over her body, and she began to tremble.

"She has the plague," Abdul said softly and threw his sword to the earthen floor. "She *had* the plague. I know who you are," he said, looking directly at the lady called Dawn. "I was going to kill you that day, but God saved your life. That saved my life."

"How so?" Dawn asked, and a warm comfort came over her body. She walked over to the tall man and held his now swordless, right hand and hugged him like a mother would hug a lost son.

Dawn, Charlotte and Abdul sat on a blanket by a window and talked while Mary now existed in a different world. The room was becoming ash-ridden, but outside was worse. Charlotte worried little about the plague comment. If that did not get her, something else surely would; and in a strange way, she was disappointed. She had been looking forward to being one of the saints, even if it meant losing her head. She would certainly not have rejected Christ for Muhammad.

"She converted the whole family except for my uncle," Abdul said. "He is still consumed with violence and jihad. The more I listened to A'isha... that was Mary's given name, the more I longed for a life of peace and love. Jesus changed my life. And getting the sword knocked out of my hand helped too. I lost my arm, but I found the true God. It was worth it."

Bright light, the brightest light any of the three had ever seen, filled the room. They closed their eyes, hoping to avoid blindness and waited for the sound. They were certain an atomic bomb had been dropped.

After a full minute had passed with no sound, Abdul squinted slightly; but now the room had returned to darkness. He opened his eyes but still could not focus. He would have to let his eyes adjust.

"Are you alright?" Abdul asked the two missionaries, but there was no answer from either woman. Outside the sound of running filled the air, and Abdul wondered what caused the bright light.

"Was it Blip?" he heard someone ask outside the mission room but had no idea what they were talking about.

His focus slowly returned, and he made his way across the small room to say a final goodbye to his sister. She was gone.

Abdul jerked his head, trying to focus in the dim light.

"Where is Mary?" he shouted, but there was no answer. The room was completely empty, except for him. The three women had simply disappeared.

Chapter Twelve

Jeff drove to the Gwinnett County Aircraft Museum in Lawrenceville to check on Wild Willy's airplane, if you could call it that. The behemoth B36J was the largest airplane, part propeller and part jet, at the museum and one of the largest ever built.

He pulled into Morsi's to grab a coffee. *The best part of waking up is Folgers in your cup.* He was getting so old, the best part of waking up was just waking up.

"Hey Dan," Jeff said. "Got any fresh coffee."

"You bet, made a pot just for you, my man."

Daniel Sutton, a part-time preacher and owner of the convenience store, was a friendly sort; and Jeff had long foregone Starbucks since the CEO made his comments about marriage, reaffirming previous comments from the previous CEO. The world had become a sick place in a relatively short time.

Jeff poured coffee into the largest Styrofoam cup on the counter and thought about the great changes that had occurred in his life so quickly.

"Do you miss Little Falls yet?" Jeff asked. The store was completely empty, except for him and Dan.

"You know," Dan said, "I do sometimes. The fishing was great, and there were fishing holes everywhere. I moved here just before the Buford Dam blew up, but I hear the fishing there was pretty good. You know, my grandpa grew up in Little Falls, close friend of Charles Lindbergh. It is one of the oldest towns in Minnesota."

Jeff loved the way Dan said *Minnnesotaaa*. Reminded him of the My Pillow guy who reminded him of Jesse Ventura.

"But rabies got so bad," Dan continued, "and I was worried about my wife and kids. Don't know if you have ever seen rabies in action, but it is something else. Not a good way to go."

"I saw it in action during the Vietnam Conflict, it wasn't a war you know," Jeff said, realizing he still felt a little bitterness at how the conflict was run by Washingtonian egomaniacs. "I was stationed at Bethesda Naval Hospital, and one night they brought a little girl into the emergency room, bitten by a fox."

Jeff recalled the story with sadness, because the same thing that happened then, was happening now.

"There was no way to tell if the fox was rabid, because it escaped. The bite was small, and the parents were against vaccinations of *any* kind, so they refused my advice and did not vaccinate her."

All the details of the young girl's death a month later, the pain and agony the six-year old went through, flooded his mind.

"What happened?"

"She died within a month," Jeff said, suddenly solemn from the memories. "A torturous death."

"That's awful," Dan said.

"It was awful for the little girl, but her suffering ended in a month. Her parents are suffering to this day, I am sure. They brought her back to the hospital within a week, heavily salivating and difficulty breathing. They wanted to get her vaccinated immediately, even though I had explained to them that the vaccine was not effective if they waited until symptoms appeared."

Jeff removed his leather driving gloves.

"So what did you do?" Dan asked, interested. His brother's son had been bitten the day before by a squirrel, and he was very anti-vaccine.

"We gave her the vaccine."

"Ouch," Dan said. "I hear it's painful, twenty-seven shots in the tummy."

"Yeah, at that time it was twenty-seven; but today it is only seven shots, one in the butt and six in the arm. Once a week for six weeks."

"Are there many side effects?" Dan asked.

"Yeah," Jeff said, pausing. "It makes you want to chase cars."

"What?" Dan asked.

Then he got it, and the two men broke out in laughter.

"Hide the fire hydrants," Dan said.

Jeff slid his hand under the scanner and looked into the face recognition device, but he did not hear the usual approval tone.

"It's not working, my friend," Dan said, looking at the red mark on his wrist. "So you did get the chip."

"I know, I know," Jeff said, feeling guilty. "The Mark of the Beast, supposedly. Maybe so, but what do you do?"

Jeff's mood was now dour. How did he get on rabies and now, the mark of the antichrist?

"You can't buy anything without the RFID implant. Thankfully there is an app. I tried to sell my house, and the closing attorney refused because I did not have the implant."

"Are you moving?"

"Yes, we're thinking about going to Israel. I feel like Samarra and the kids would be safer there."

"Yes," Dan said, "Israel is a really safe place to go. Bombings, earthquakes, Mount Hermon erupting, War of Gog-Magog. Good choice."

"I said I am only thinking about it. Wild Willy lives there most of the year, and he seems to think it is safer there than here. Speaking of Wild Willy, I need to get a move on."

"You do not need the implant, Jeff. I do not have an implant either, but my store is stocked."

"It looks like you have an implant," Jeff said, surprised. He could see it plainly.

"Fake implant," my friend. "It is a decoy. There is a whole underground network here in Georgia for the few remaining people who know the 666 story."

"A knockoff implant? Like a knockoff Rolex?" Jeff laughed.

"Exactly."

"Hmmm," Jeff pondered. "How would I sell the house if I decide to move?"

Two men, wearing hoodies, entered the store, picked up three packages of Twinkies and walked to the hand scanner.

"Scanner doesn't work with sunglasses on," Dan said. "Jeff, stand over there if you don't mind, by the ice cream cooler."

"I gotta run. Going to the Air Museum," Jeff said and turned toward the door. "See you tomorrow."

Jeff walked out the door, and the heat was already unbearable. He hit the start button, and his new Tesla Electrocycle came to life silently, like electric bikes do. The two blasts caused him to duck, and he hit the brake. The sound had come from behind, possibly from the convenience store; and his heart nearly stopped. Had the two men been robbers? He ran to the door, approaching from the side and ducking below the store windows, Glock in hand.

"You can come in, it is safe. These clowns aren't going anywhere."

The two hooded men lay on the floor.

"What happened," Jeff asked, wondering if they were dead. There was little blood.

"They're not moving, because I said I would kill them if they moved a millimeter. Shot them in the butt with bird shot. They will have a hard time sitting in the jail."

A distant siren, an approaching ambulance, made its way down Duluth-Lawrenceville Highway as a Gwinnett County police car pulled in the driveway. Thirty minutes later, Jeff left after giving his report to Sergeant McAdoo.

He again noticed the Morsi's sign, wondering when the store changed from Majik Mart… wondering if it had anything to do with the man many were calling the Beast. A knockoff implant did make sense to an entrepreneurial soul. Everything else had a copy, so why not the RFID? He turned on Vinny's private message and again listened.

"Good morning, Mr. Ross. Included in this message is a link to the KFC code words and meanings. Ed Poe at Homeland has also received a copy. You are the only two, so share as you see fit.

"I do apologize about Europe, but what happens there is out of my control."

Thirty-Six Red Mercury Bombs had gone off in Germany, France and England; and many had been killed, burned to ash before hitting the ground. The byproduct had been fire. It seemed most of Europe was in flames, and their resources were thin. Europe was on the verge of total financial collapse. Starvation and plague had become rampant; and the new plague was especially brutal, an easily transmittable HIV/AIDS.

"Your government is infiltrated with sleepers; so when you share, be very selective. The so-named Drone War was to start around Labor Day but did not. This is only because Jumpin' Johnny was killed by the bears, and the sleepers did not know what to do. However, they have since contacted me with coded messages. These messages can be accessed via the Finger_Lickin link below.

"Mr. Ross, most of the RM bombs are relatively small in nature, less than a kiloton; but they can easily destroy four or five city blocks. The heat generated by the bombs is very intense. As small as the RM bombs are, anything within a quarter-mile will melt instantly, including people. You know the Bible verse that describes this, I am sure. The Preacher showed it to me.

'This is the plague with which the Lord will strike all the nations that fought against Jerusalem: Their flesh will rot while they are still standing on their feet, their eyes will rot in their sockets, and their tongues will rot in their mouths.'

"Unfortunately, this happens in nuclear explosions. The body melts before it hits the ground, Mr. Ross.

"The decoded messages only identify the area where the RMBs are located, not the specific coordinates. The drone strikes may not be bomb attacks, because many are equipped with aerosol sprayers. These can dispense most anything from chlorine to anthrax to the SARS 3-virus. A few will carry mustard gas. I would recommend that these areas be evacuated immediately, if you can get this message to the right people.

"The first wave of attacks will be in the Connecticut-Vermont area, the second wave will be the Bible Belt. The plan is to bring the United States to her knees financially, destroy morale and achieve a peace treaty through submission to Shariah Law. The warriors will not stop until they succeed or are dead. My suggestion is to make them dead as soon as possible.

"I will be in touch."

Chapter Thirteen

"She's a beauty, I'll tell you that."

Jeff had never met Sarge, but Wild Willy spoke highly of him. Sarge, retired Air Force Sergeant, had maintained and modified Will's B-36J Peacemaker since Will made the purchase. There was nothing about a B-36 that Sarge didn't know, and Wild Willy had the only privately-owned B-36J in the world.

"She is," Jeff said, admiring the gleam of the shiny, silver fuselage. It looked like a mirror. "And she's really big."

"Careful," Sarge said. "Women don't like someone tellin' them they're big, know what I mean?"

Sarge laughed all over himself, like he always laughed at his own jokes.

"Will asked about the electronics. He wants to know if there has been any damage from the solar storms."

"No sir," Sarge said. "This baby has very few microcircuits and still uses mostly vacuum tubes. Not much to fry, so EMP is not a problem. All electronics are state-of-the-art, except microcircuitry is minimal; and what microcircuitry there is, it is well shielded."

"That was Will's thoughts too but wanted me to check. The Atlanta airport is still closed from all the planes that can't take off. The GPS and other electronics in almost every plane were fried by the last solar storm."

"Yep, I know that's right," Sarge said. "That's why all them planes crashed. Helicopters were falling out of the sky like rain."

The solar electromagnetic storm had caused havoc in parts of the United States; but Jeff knew it would be getting worse, at least if Chadbo was correct and seemed to always be. Much of the Mideast and parts of South America were totally without electricity as the grid system transformers were blown.

"When are you planning on moving it back to Warner Robins?" Jeff asked, noticing for the first time a gun chute of sorts below the belly of the shiny, silver plane.

"Watch it," Sarge laughed. "She don't like to be called *it*." He laughed again. "Pro'bly next month. We got the Mother's Day Air Show at Warner Robbins coming up. Then we might fly it over to Israel."

"What's this?" Jeff asked, pointing to the apparatus, one of three.

"That, my friend, is an anti-missile defense system manufactured in Israel. The system detects incoming heat-seeking missiles and disperses flares and shrapnel. Works every time according to the Israelis. How Will got this from Israel, I have no idea."

"Wild Willy has a lot of connections." Jeff laughed. "How fast will this thing go?"

"Watch it."

"I know. I know," Jeff laughed. "Don't call her a *thing*."

"You're learnin' fast, young fella. Don't want to make her mad. About 500 with a tail wind, maybe 525. Fast for mostly props. We have high-speed propellers on her, plus four jet engines."

Jeff took a tour of the plane, amazed at the great shape *she* was in. He and Sarge became instant friends, and he was more secure about Wild Willy's planned flight to Israel. Having Sarge as part of the crew would be a big plus.

"What's this?" Jeff asked, nodding toward what looked like a small missile launcher.

"Can't tell ya that," Sarge smiled. "I'd have ta kill ya."

Jeff walked under the plane and took a look.

"Looks like a little missile launcher."

The tubes were small for a missile launcher, about the size of a cardboard tube in a roll of paper towels and not very long, maybe four feet. The rotary swivel-mount offered 360-degree coverage, but Jeff wasn't excited.

"Must not have much explosive," Jeff said, smiling at Sarge.

"Don't have no explosive," Sarge answered. "Not even a warhead."

Jeff looked confused.

"Come with me," Sarge said, walking to the rear entrance to the behemoth of a plane.

They walked up the rear stairs and into the fuselage which looked little like a superfortress and more like The Ritz. There were four private sleeping quarters with private baths and a movie parlor with popcorn machine. The smell of popcorn permeated the air, and Jeff's salivary glands did what salivary glands do.

"Getting' ready for the tour groups," Sarge explained. "They love the popcorn. Mr. Will gets all his popcorn from Garrett's in Chicago. Says it's the best. It sure smells the best."

Sarge led them to the midway-point through the large, cigar-shaped aircraft and stopped where the pathway narrowed noticeably. Where walls extended from the outer wall of the plane, a narrow utility door allowed entrance to the enclosures, one on each side of the plane.

"In here," Sarge said, opening the door, "is the coolin' system for the electromagnetic tube-launcher. There's a coolin' system and magnet on each side of the plane. This thing launches a dang skinny, little tube made out of some light-weight metal. That's the warhead, so to speak but don't have no dang explosive. Will said it works ever time. Those little missiles leave the tubes at about six-thousand feet a second."

Jeff did a quick calculation.

"Four-thousand miles per hour?"

"Yep," Sarge said. "A little faster. And these boogers are smart. Got those little AI brains inside. Goes so fast, anything it hits is destroyed by the kinetic energy. Mr. Will and his toys."

The drive back to Duluth seemed longer than normal, and dead deer lined the highway. Jeff passed the American Legion Post, the one that burned; and buzzards were having a feast. Where did all the deer come from... and what killed them? Wild dogs or coyotes fought amongst themselves, great slathers of saliva, flailing through the air. Jeff could almost smell the rabies.

The summer air was extraordinarily cool for a change, only about ninety. He smiled. Ninety was the new seventy and how quickly it had happened, just like his momma used to say would happen in the end times.

"Gonna get a lot hotter, son. You just wait."

He missed his mom.

"Alexa, WOLN-Radio please," Jeff said. A second later he listened to the latest news of the world.

"...rash of disappearing people in Russia. An underground church was raided by the revived KGB Intelligence Network. According to eyewitness accounts, when the soldiers broke the doors down, no one was there.

"What is so interesting," the commentator continued, *"is that the church was surrounded after cameras recorded more than two-hundred people going in. Several Russian soldiers claimed to see people vanish right before their eyes; but in later interviews, those claims were denied. President Morsi has warned of grave consequences to those who modify video footage."*

"So," interrupted the guest, *"Morsi is spinning this as Photoshopped video. We have analyzed the video footage, including actual footage of disappearing people and discovered no modifications."*

Jeff breathed in the air but wished there was an alternative. The smell of dead carcasses oozed through his nostrils and a taste of copper appeared in his mouth.

"Thank you, Mr. Poe," the host said. *"Ed Poe, from Homeland Security, is our guest today; and we are honored. Is it true that you are actually Edgar Allan Poe?"*

Ed laughed. He was used to people commenting on his birth-name.

"Yep, that's true. My parents had a great sense of humor. May I continue?"

"Please do, but first we have to pay some bills."

The jingle played, a Folger's coffee commercial; and Jeff laughed. *The best part of waking up is Folgers in your cup.* That is when the five-pound turkey vulture flew directly into him, knocking him to the road. Jeff lost consciousness but did not realize he was unconscious. His world had suddenly become bright and sunny, the smell of the air as pure as lilacs on a summer day.

He walked through a field of yellow daffodils; and in the distance he spotted a small building, a little white church with a white, picket fence.

Chapter Fourteen

"**G**ot yourself into a real pickle, Jeffrey."

Jeff heard the voice as he walked out of a field of daffodils, but it seemed to come from all directions. By now he did know one thing. He was dreaming.

He walked toward the front steps of the small white church, and organ music flowed out the open doors.

"You are always getting yourself into a real pickle, it seems."

Jeff wasn't surprised when Missy T suddenly appeared on the steps beside him. He always saw strange occurrences when Missy T and Kipper T were around; and he knew Kipper T, his other guardian angel, would be appearing soon.

"Am I dead?"

"No, silly. Why would you think such a thing?"

Jeff's relationship with the guardian angels went back a long time, at least it seemed like a long time. They only appeared in his dreams, no matter how real things seemed. Things are not always what they seem.

"Did I have an accident?" he asked.

"You did," answered Missy T. "You have a lot of accidents."

"Yep, a great big bird knocked you right off your motorcycle," Kipper T laughed.

Jeff had not seen him, but now Kipper T was standing right there beside him. He had a way of just appearing and then disappearing.

"You're going to get killed one day, riding around on one of your toys," Kipper scolded.

"Am I hurt?" Jeff asked, doing a quick examination of his body.

The leather outfit did its job, and he had no abrasions or broken bones. The organist inside the small church completed her melody of old Christian hymns of long ago; and it became eerily quiet. Not even a breeze to make the daffodils dance.

"Not hurt as bad as your fancy-dancy motorcycle," Missy T said. "You only bought it to catch Vinny. Fast and quiet. You do not need to worry about Vinny. BJ has shown him the light of the world. BJ has no idea what an accomplishment that was for the Kingdom. Vinny may make it."

From the front doors of the whitest church Jeff had ever seen, even the ones outside Lukeville, came the voice of Enoch the stutterer, except when he preached. Then he spoke plainly.

"… don'tcha know."

Jeff smiled. Enoch's trademark.

"Is Vinny really going to make the Kingdom of God?" Jeff asked, stunned at the possibility. "He has killed thousands, millions of people. More than a million were killed in Manhattan and millions more from the Spanish flu. How could he possibly make it?"

Jeff's face was red, and Missy T was concerned he might have a heart attack or stroke. God was not through with Jeff.

"The same way you will *possibly* make it, Jeffrey. Forgiveness. You should know by now that Jesus said there is only one sin that cannot be forgiven and that you will be judged by what is in your heart."

Jeff thought about that and wanted to raise his hand, like in high school. He was sure of the answer.

"To not believe in Christ," Jeff said. "The way to make it to the next life. The next good life, I mean."

"Nope," Kipper T said, "and you know better. So many Christians have that impression. No, even *not* believing in Jesus is forgivable, according to Jesus himself; but it would be the rare exception, not the rule. In a lot of ways, Jesus was very much about the exception to the rule, not changing the rule. Jesus will make that determination on Judgment Day, who makes it and who does not. You, Mr. Ross, better hope he is in a very forgiving mood… Vinny better hope the same. Jesus is not a free-ride, you have to totally believe."

"God is not happy with us, don'tcha know," Enoch preached. "No. He is not. None of us. Look at what we let happen! We got porno shops on every corner nowadays, we got abortions galore, we cain't pray in schools or the doggone football games, don'tcha know. We got men marrying animals! Now, that ain't right. We got reality-TV shows about dirty, old men who like little boys. And there ain't many parades of repentance in Washington, DC, don'tcha know.

"School teachers teachin' our kids that there wasn't never no flood, and Adam and Eve came from go-rillas. Now that must have been one heck of a surprise, when that momma ape done dropped a hairless baby.

"Churches teachin' their flocks that God is all-inclusive. No, God is not all-inclusive; and it's well laid out in the Good Book, don'tcha know. Why do you think Jesus talked about that narrow path and the wide super highway? Those on the wide road might say they believe, but they don't; and they won't make the most important cut of their life, I tell ya. Ya cain't pledge your life to God and then continue to live like hell, don'tcha know. And you surely cain't be havin' no parades to celebrate how proud you are about sinnin'!"

Jeff admired Enoch's unflappable way with words, and the common sense he made.

"So what is the unforgivable sin?" Jeff asked Kipper T. He was certain his answer was correct, but how could you argue with angels?

"Do not blaspheme the Holy Spirit," Missy T said, looking Jeff straight in the eyes. She had the bluest eyes and blackest hair he had ever seen. "You have been told that before, Jeffrey Ross. You better pay attention."

"Here you go, read it for yourself," and a Bible mystically appeared in Kipper T's hand, black leather, opened to a verse in the Book of Mark. "Jesus is speaking."

Jeff read out loud.

"Truly I tell you, people can be forgiven all their sins and every slander they utter, but whoever blasphemes against the Holy Spirit will never be forgiven; they are guilty of an eternal sin."

Jeff had never read that verse before, or he must have missed it, nor had he heard of an eternal sin. So any sin was forgivable, except... *that* one. Then he was afraid to find out what it meant. Had he ever blasphemed the Holy Spirit? He hoped not but was sure he probably had, and that was depressing.

The sound of applause filled the air in the small sanctuary as a large crowd, maybe a hundred, applauded the words of Enoch. He was sort of a bottom-line kind of preacher, and people seemed to like his style, at least in Jeff's dreams.

"Now you say, 'I want the CliffsNotes version of the Bible.' Well I guess you do," Enoch continued. "You got so little time, and you are so busy with your *devices*. God ain't gonna call you on your cell phone and invite you to Judgment Day. You want the CliffsNotes version of the Bible? Take a seat."

Jeff interrupted Missy T, asking if they could go inside and listen. He had wished many times for a simple version of the Bible.

"No," Missy T said. "We have heard this one many times. Before you go, you must know this."

Jeff listened carefully, suddenly curious.

"Some bad things are getting ready to happen in the world, worse than what has already happened. The final trumpet of Revelation has sounded. That is the sound that everyone is hearing, wondering what it is."

"Yeah," Kipper said. "Really bad."

Missy T gave Kipper T *the look*.

"You are still so unaware of what is about to take place; but Jeff, you will see Melissa again," Missy T continued. "Then you will understand. Be careful, Jeffrey."

How was *that* possible, Jeff wondered. Melissa was dead, maybe not dead but in Heaven. He had seen it with his own eyes, that night she vanished.

"Do you mean Samarra?" Jeff asked.

"No, I mean Melissa. And Jeffrey," Missy T continued. "Be careful, don't give up, don't give in… and get rid of the RFID. Remember, almost every sin can be forgiven; but that does not mean it will be forgiven. Only that it *could* be. You need to get rid of the Mark of the Beast. Do not tempt the Lord thy God. Seriously."

"How do we eat?" Jeff asked. "How do we buy stuff?"

"If God provides the necessities for the birds of the sky, God will also provide for you. You will be asked to reject your belief in Christ and accept other ideology. There is only one true God, and it is not Allah. It is Yahweh. Ditch the mark and pray for forgiveness."

Jeff heard a loud thump and turned, scanning the field of daffodils, but saw nothing. Probably another chunk of ice. When he turned back to face Missy T, she and Kipper had both disappeared.

"Now let me tell you somethin'" Enoch started. "God didn't make the Bible simple for a reason."

Jeff walked into the small, white church and took a seat at the back pew. It wasn't unusual for his guardian angels to appear and disappear. A Bible and hymnal sat in the rack.

"He wanted you to ponder, to think about, to investigate, don'tcha know? If you really want to know the Bible, you gotta be a Bible detective, don'tcha know."

Jeff felt something in the palm of his right hand and opened it slowly. A small, white post-it appeared, and some writing. He took out his reading glasses. The message was from Kipper T.

We will one day meet again, Jeff. When the electric grids fail, you need to get to Israel. The United States will become a killing field.

Chapter Fifteen

"**A**re you okay, buddy?"

Jeff opened his eyes, squinting in the daylight. He spit something out of his mouth, felt like a feather.

"I guess," Jeff answered, trying to focus his eyes. "What happened?"

"I saw it all," another man said, a short guy with a small clump of strawberry blond hair on the top of his head. Jeff tried not to laugh but couldn't help it. The guy looked like a rooster.

"I think he must be in shock," rooster guy said. "He's laughing hysterically. Did you call 911?"

"No, no. Don't call 911. I feel fine, just a little dizzy. What happened?"

Jeff did not recall his dream, the meeting with Missy T and Kipper T, nor the CliffsNotes sermon. With the assistance of the two rescuers, Jeff stood.

"A doggone turkey vulture got ya. I ain't never seen nothin' like it."

A siren sounded in the distance.

"I already called 'em," rooster guy said. "Sorry."

Jeff saw the dead vulture on the edge of the highway and rubbed the side of his head. A lump the size of an egg had appeared, and he dreaded the coming headache. The paramedics walked hurriedly toward him, scanning the nearby woods for wild dogs, wondering why he was covered in feathers.

"A dang turkey vulture," rooster guy started again, "Done knocked him right off that motorcycle. They out heah feedin' on the dead carcasses, ya know."

After assuring the paramedics that he was fine and thanking his two rescuers, Jeff checked his bike. The motorcycle had continued down the road about fifty feet and into a clump of pampas grass guarding a telephone pole. There was hardly a scratch.

Jeff pulled the cycle from the plant, wiped a few more feathers off, mounted and pushed START. About a mile before reaching downtown Duluth, traffic stopped. A group of three women and four men, dressed in camouflage fatigues, blocked Duluth Highway with pickup trucks; and they all carried rifles and sidearms.

The two cars in front of Jeff gradually made U-turns, turned away by the guards and some colorful language came from the second car, some words Jeff had not heard in years.

"Come ahead, Mr. Ross," one of the ladies shouted, motioning him to come on through. When he reached the guard, he asked her what was going on.

"We aren't lettin' anyone in who don't live here, that's all. Crime is way out of hand, the riff-raff burned the American Legion Post, we're just tired of it. The police are doin' all they can, but they are out-armed. We're just helpin' out. We don't want to get like New Orleans."

Jeff listened but had no idea what New Orleans had to do with blockading Duluth.

"What's up with New Orleans?"

"Now Mr. Ross, I know you watch the news. I see you goin' inside that disco place with all those news stations. And you tellin' me you don't know what's goin' on in New Orleans and Baton Rouge?"

Jeff didn't respond fast enough, and the female guard started again.

"The Voodoo folk are killin' the Wiccans there. The Wiccans are the witches. They into witchcraft, sorcery, other stuff that God don't like. Last night a whole coven was wiped out, thirteen people. They burned them at the stake, like the Salem witch trials all over again.

"And now some Christian gang is killin' the Voodoo folk *and* blowing up mosques. The Mosque folk are retaliatin' and blew up three or four churches last Sunday. So we don't plan to let it happen here. You can pass, Mr. Ross."

She waved him through.

"Thanks," Jeff said, moving slowly forward.

"And one more thing, Mr. Ross."

Jeff paused.

"You lookin' pretty bad. Got a big knot right there on your head."

"Ran into a turkey," Jeff said, laughing.

"Hope it was my ex-husband," she replied. "And please pray that we are successful, and pray you don't lose no electricity. The world's a dangerous place in the dark, Mr. Ross. That dadblame red moon is hardly visible and looks to me like half the stars done burned out. We lost electricity for a week at my house; and let me tell ya, there are some strange animals comin' out at night. Scary."

Jeff made the final, five-minute drive, pulled into his gated driveway in Sugarloaf and into the Faraday-shielded shelter for his motorcycles and automobile collection. Missy T had once suggested he sell the boytoys and help the hungry and sick. Maybe he would. He wondered if he would ever see Missy and Kipper again. It seemed it had been a long time.

Jeff walked through the back gate, planning to put on his bathing suit and sit in the pool awhile. The day had been hot and stressful. Samarra and the girls were volunteering at a home for refugees in Buford, and Jeff let that sink in. A home for refugees in Buford, refugees from California. They were some of the Californians who survived the Ross Wave. Last week several busloads of refugees arrived from Wyoming as the evacuation of everything around Yellowstone began.

Dressed in his blue seersucker bathing suit and a US Navy T-shirt, Jeff grabbed a float and hit the pool.

"Alexa," he said, adjusting the blue, foam float beneath him, "Turn on some soothing music."

"Okay," the Amazon device answered. "Here is a selection of schoolroom music. 'A-B-C-D-E-F-G...H-I-J-K...'"

Jeff liked the ABC song about the alphabet as a kid, but this was not what he had in mind and was annoying.

"Alexa," he shouted, "Play SOOTHING music."

"Okay, here are a few selections from a light jazz station."

Jeff relaxed, supine on his back with hands behind his head, staring at the high cirrus clouds, sitting almost stationary in the sky like cirrus clouds do, fifteen miles high or so. Lullabied by Rosemary Clooney's *Thanks for the Memories*, he was soon dozing. While Jeff slept, he did not hear the soft-jazz station go to a newsbreak.

"... could be the bust-of-the-year. Two nondescript warehouses have been raided, after an anonymous tip, by Homeland Security. Both are located south of Burlington, Vermont. So far, all the drones discovered seem to be non-functional, possibly due to the solar storm that hit the Northeast last week. That storm destroyed, as you recall, many electronic systems and resulted in numerous crashes of small aircraft. More than one-thousand small drones were found.

"Now to Israel where Mount Hermon continues to erupt and..."

The sound stopped as the station went to dead silence, but Jeff continued to doze. The pool pump and the waterfall fell silent, and traffic lights in the area went to emergency backup, flashing red.

Samarra and the kids left the black Mercedes SUV in the driveway, outside the electric gate and tried the manual bypass, to no avail. They used the small gate that had a keyed entry and walked up the long driveway, sweating in the extreme heat of the day.

"It must be a hundred and fifty out here," Audry whined.

The few cars and trucks that continued down the roads throughout Gwinnett County and beyond were mostly pre-1970 models. While luxury automobiles and SUVs failed, old pickup trucks and cars rumbled down the roads. Most of those drivers had no idea why so many cars stopped in the middle of the highways, and traffic backups quickly became traffic nightmares.

As the electric grid system serving the greater Atlanta area failed, elevators in the few buildings that remained occupied, failed. Pumps at the water treatment facilities failed as did the pumps at all gas stations. Backup generators at hospitals and medical clinics failed; because the microcircuits melted instantly, fusing with other circuits and shorting out the electronics. The latest farming equipment, combines, tractors and harvesters, failed in rural fields as farmers quickly moved into the twenty-first century, a century jam-packed with microcircuitry.

From the kitchen of Jeff's house, there was sound as the vintage ham radio came to life, powered up by Jeff's Generac, diesel-fueled generator. The Eddystone EC10 shortwave receiver from 1967 suddenly became busy as ham operators took to the airwaves.

"Chad to Jeff. Chad to Jeff. Are you there?"

Jeff slowly awoke, vaguely recognizing Chad's voice and the sound of Samarra and Audry entering the pool gate.

"My phone isn't working," Audry whined, tired from the day's volunteer work and the exhausting heat.

Jeff lay on the float as his eyes came into focus.

"Wow, Samarra," Audry exclaimed, "Look at that."

Audry pointed to the sky and Jeff focused. He had never seen anything like it. The high, static cirrus clouds were no longer static and moved wildly about the sky, looping suddenly one way and then another.

"Jeff, come in," Chad's voice boomed from the ham radio speaker. "The jet stream is going absolutely crazy. Are you there?"

Jeff swam to the edge of the pool, climbed out and quickly dried with the yellow and blue beach towel. He greeted Samarra and the kids and walked into the kitchen where he took a seat at the ham radio setup and answered Chad, dripping chlorinated water on the tiled kitchen floor.

"Go ahead, Chadbo. What's up?"

Finally, the sound of the generator registered; and Jeff for the first time realized the power was out. The slowly setting sun would soon bring darkness, and the heat of the night would be difficult for those without air conditioning. His Generac was powerful and would continue to operate the air conditioner for the safe-room below the house. He was glad he purchased a generator that was shielded against EMP.

"Jeff, the upper atmosphere winds are absolutely bonkers, nearly black! I have never seen wind this dark!"

Chadbo's concern was notable. Chad's amazing ability to actually see the wind, one of the few who had ever been born with the ability, remained puzzling to Jeff. Apparently, the colors Chad saw were transparent, the darker the color, the stronger the wind. Black was not good.

"The upper atmospheric winds are creating havoc in Canada and the Arctic and are headed our way. Canada has never had an F5 tornado except the one that hit Elie, Manitoba in 2007, *until today*, that is. A tornado swarm is active right now in Toronto, and at least six F5 tornados are on the ground. Large areas of Toronto are said to be destroyed, but reports are sketchy because of the electric grid system failures. Thank goodness we have old ham radios with tubes at Goddard. The handheld hams are crispy-fried."

"Wait, hold on," Jeff interrupted. "You are talking way too fast for me to keep up."

Jeff's head was spinning, and aching. The collision with the turkey vulture had taken a toll.

"Jeff," Samarra whispered. "You have a feather in your hair. You look awful. What happened?"

She gently touched the bruised knot on the side of his head.

"I got hit with a turkey."

Samarra dug lemonade out of the refrigerator, hoping to calm Audry. Audry had become much whinier since Chuck Hutz disappeared. They all missed the odd man, but Audry had been especially attached. He was her mentor, as strange as he was.

"Really?" Samarra laughed.

"I'll tell you later," Jeff said and turned back to the ham radio.

"By the way, how did the wedding go?" Chad asked when Jeff returned. "Did they finally do it?"

Fate seemed to be against a wedding between the Admiral and Sheryl. Every time it was planned, a disaster would happen.

"Well," Jeff said, "They finally got out of jail."

"What?"

"Yep, they got arrested by the Shariah Police at IHOP for talking about Jesus or something."

Jeff referred to the new Morality Police as the Shariah Police, because that was really what they were. The officers didn't act Islamic, they didn't spread prayer blankets out and pray five times a day; but everyone knew.

Outside, another crash and explosion shook the late afternoon air; and the windows of the home vibrated, emanating an eerie tone. Probably another helicopter without proper shielding, Jeff thought. Jenni, Jami and Audry ran out the door to see what happened, and a cloud of very dark smoke rose above the tree line.

"Chadbo, I have to go. Something just exploded."

"Okay, radio me back as soon as you can; and Jeff... watch the weather. It is going to be very windy."

Jeff joined the girls on the patio, alarmed at the smoke. Too much to be a helicopter.

"May Day! May Day!" erupted from the ham radio.

Jeff ran back to the kitchen, nearly slipping on the tile floor.

"Go ahead," he responded.

"My name is Raji. Several of us are trapped in the new Hindu Temple on Highway 120, close to Sugarloaf."

Jeff subconsciously reached for his phone to call 911 before realizing the phones were dead.

"What happened, Raji?"

"We were bombed."

Raji told the story as they waited for help. The smoke was getting thicker, and he was not sure how long they would be able to breathe. Large roof trusses from India, hand carved, heavy and ornate with colorful jewels, had fallen and blocked all the exits. Two members had been crushed to death, and six survivors were now trapped in the burning building. Strong winds fed the firestorm, and Raji knew they were on the verge of burning to death.

Jeff listened.

"If we do not make it," Raji continued, "A group of five Muslim women came here for a visit. They were very polite and made an appointment to meet with us. They said they would like a tour of our new Temple and wished to learn more about our beliefs. I was wary at first, but the lady who called seemed so sincere, and fluent."

Jeff heard the lone remaining fire truck in Duluth making its way toward the billowing smoke, and the smell of plastic and vinyl wafted through the air. He guessed the fire truck must be shielded against EMP.

"The women were dressed in these extreme burqas, I mean head-to-toe with little, tiny eye-slits. Dark blue. But they were very nice and amicable. Jamal, my assistant, took them on the tour and all of a sudden… BOOM! That is all I know. Can you get us help? The fire is raging, some are crushed, we are desperate. If you pray, please pray for us."

Jeff missed the last part of the conversation as he ran across the front lawn, across Sugarloaf Parkway and into the parking lot of the Hindu temple. He ran the half-mile in record time for an old man, which he now realized he should not have done. He was perspiring heavily, and his heart was surely going to pound right out of his chest. Beside him, a woman dressed in scarlet wept as she kneeled on the hot pavement.

"Are you okay?" Jeff panted, fighting the dizziness.

The heat from the fire was unbearable, and he pulled the lady in scarlet away, leading her to a large but mostly dead Maple tree that would provide some shade. The fire truck pulled into the parking lot and the crew of two prepared to do the best they could, but it would not be enough.

"I pray, Lord. I pray Lord that Raji was raptured. Please Lord. He was a good man, he had a good heart. Jesus looks at our hearts in judgment, is not that right, Lord?"

The suicide bombers may not have known of the propane tanks, five of them stored in the kitchen. Had they not been dead, they would have been pleased at their good luck. The first tank to blow shot through the temple roof, across the parking lot, across Sugarloaf Parkway and landed in the center of Jeff's swimming pool, barely missing the patio where Audry sat, still fiddling with the non-working phone. She was not well-versed on EMP.

The second tank exploded, setting off the other three in rapid succession; and Jeff fell over the lady, trying to offer what protection he could. He waited for the debris fall.

The Hindu Temple now lay in splinters and melted plastic, as though an F5 tornado had leveled it. Jeff had been around plenty of large explosions and knew that if Raji was ever found, he would be in small pieces.

The woman screamed in anguish, and Jeff's heart broke. She was truly in agony.

"Is Raji a relative?" he asked, trying to help anyway he could.

"He *was*," she cried. "He was my husband. He found Christ yesterday… and today he is dead. Why?"

"Walk with me. I live right over there," Jeff said, pointing. "Come with me. My wife will clean your tears, and we will talk."

"Was he raptured?" she asked hopefully. "Could death also be like the rapture? He was taken, and I was not."

They walked slowly, and Jeff put his arm around her shoulders. The small-statured woman shook with anguish, and tears flowed like the mighty Mississippi as they made their way to Jeff's home.

"What was that?" Samarra shouted to Audry from the kitchen, making her way to the patio. "Something must have hit the house."

The propane tank that landed in the pool startled Audry; and she rushed into the parlor, almost knocking Samarra to the floor.

"What *was* that?" Samarra asked again, as calmly as she could. Her ears were still ringing.

"I don't know!" Audry cried. "Something fell in the pool. It almost hit me!"

Outside the home, splintered wood fell to the ground, along with several Hindu idols. Pieces of Hindu temple debris littered the neighborhood, and ornate jewels fell from the sky like rain.

The day remained sunny as late afternoon edged toward dusk, and the winds gusted. The smell of fire and burning plastic lingered in the air between gusts; and wild dogs scoured the Hindu site, searching frantically for food. Jeff wondered if these were the winds from Canada that Chad warned of, but how could they be here this fast?

Soon the temple fire spread with the aid of the dusty-gusty wind, and two complete neighborhoods burned nearby. With no electricity, even fire hydrants refused to share their water. The event would become known in Gwinnett County as *The Night of the Fire*; and before the night would be over, the fire would spread northward to Suwanee and on toward historic Buford before turning westward toward Alpharetta and Roswell. Four-hundred seventeen died as a result of the fires, started by five Muslim women in a Hindu Temple.

Jeff walked the still-sobbing woman across the patio and introduced her to Samarra and Audry. Samarra washed the woman's face with bottled water, and the face finally had a name. Mary.

She offered Mary a robe and immediately carried her smoke-ridden clothing to the laundry room. Mary lay in one of the guest rooms, but Samarra could hear her sobs. She said a quick prayer, asking for emotional support for the distraught lady.

"Where is Jeffrey," Samarra asked the twins after turning on the washer. "I need to wash his clothes."

"He went to check his toys," Jami and Jenni said in unison as twins often do. "Something about that EMP thingy. How are you going to wash the clothes if there's no power?"

"Great," Samarra said, flipping the light switch that did nothing.

Jeff made the walk across his two-acre property, to his Faraday enclosure to check the electric motorcycle and other vehicles. Hindu Temple debris lay on the dry ground, and he stumbled over some kind of statue or deity. He was deeply concerned that the electricity wasn't back on and began to wonder if it would come back on. If it was solar related, like Chadbo was always warning, the grid could be out. Hopefully it wasn't out nationwide. Or worldwide.

The all-electric Tesla Roadster started without problem, coming to life with the near-silent electric hum; and he was glad he invested in the protective cage. He then checked his shiny silver, electric motorcycle and was pleased to hear, again, a near-silent hum. Spotting a small piece of white paper taped to the GPS console of the motorcycle, he picked it up and read the note. It was signed: Kipper T.

We will one day meet again, Jeff. When the electric grids fail, you need to get to Israel. The United States and Europe will become killing fields.

Chapter Sixteen

B en Taylor, Jon the Guide, Aludra and the guy named Wild Willy ran for shelter as a sudden rain washed ash out of the air and to the streets of The City of David and people below. The wind blew ferociously.

The wet ash formed a brownish, gray slime on the streets of Jerusalem; and two cars crashed into the wall outside the newly-constructed United States Embassy. Ben thought he may have met Wild Willy somewhere but couldn't place him. He worked his brain.

Running into the lobby of the refurbished King David Hotel, large rocks and small boulders fell to the ground outside; and the sound of breaking windshields and crunching metal filled the night air. The rocks fell from the sky like giant hailstones, and bodies lay in the streets. The hotel shook from the onslaught.

"Hard to believe these rocks came from Mount Hermon. Must have been one heck of an explosion," Will mused.

"It was," Ben answered. "It destroyed much of Damascus, at least that's the rumor. You know, that was a prediction from the ancient Jewish prophets, that Damascus would one day be destroyed."

"Really?" Aludra said, surprised.

"Yep. A clay tablet was discovered a couple of months ago with the passage from Isaiah inscribed.

'*See, Damascus will no longer be a city but will become a heap of ruins.*'

"Some biblical scholars claim that happened already, in 732 BC," Ben continued. "That was when the ruler of Assyria razed Damascus before invading Northern Israel, leaving Damascus a heap of ruins; but it became a city again, once the center of early Christianity. The prophecy said it would never be a city again when it is destroyed in the last days."

"And it has happened?" Aludra asked. "It has been destroyed, yes?"

"Yes," Ben answered. "It appears so."

"So," Aludra mumbled. "It really is happening. It really is the end times."

"Does that surprise you?" Jon the Guide asked. "Did you not see or hear the Two Witnesses when they preached in Jerusalem? Those two guys were a direct fulfillment of what was foretold by the ancients."

Ben had seen the Two Witnesses, after they were killed. Scuttlebutt had it that President Morsi killed them, but many tried without success.

"I saw them rise from the dead," Ben said. "I was visiting the Land Bureau that day, trying to get a permit for an archaeological site-survey and heard all the ruckus in the streets where the two preachers had been laying for three or four days. The smell was hideous, so it was obvious the men were in a state of decay. When I walked outside, there they went. Poof. They disappeared into a cloud. Never saw anything like it."

The group sat silently, except for the sound of rain, wind and falling rocks.

"Did you make any discoveries?" Aludra finally asked.

"Maybe," Ben said after a brief, contemplative pause.

Ben Taylor was quickly becoming a legend in an elite group of international biblical archaeologists. He believed in the God of the Jews, though he had never read the complete Bible, nor did he go to church. He had never been fanatical about his religion and was a private, humble person; but events the last few years had made him more of a fan of God. The events were playing out just as described, especially Damascus.

"Maybe what?" Will goaded. "I know you're dying to tell us. I can see it in your face."

Will had seen Ben Taylor before but could not recall exactly where. He was sure though, because he never forgot a face. The hotel shook but the group hardly seemed to notice. Everything seemed to be shaking these days in Israel.

"Well," Ben started, "There might not be anything to my find. The scrolls I discovered are being dated, but the language has been confirmed. A hybrid of Hebrew, maybe Aramaic, that was common when Jesus himself walked the earth."

The audience of three listened, enthralled with the mystery of Ben's find.

"What is it?" Aludra asked. "What is your Ben-scroll?"

"Ben-scroll?" Ben laughed. "I like that."

Ben rubbed his scruffy chin, wondering why he was sharing this story. He swore to himself he would not spill the beans this time; and here he was, spilling the archaeological beans. For whatever reason, he trusted the small group.

"It may be the earliest manuscript of the New Testament," Ben said. "And it's not all written in Greek. It's not the entire New Testament, only the first four books. The gospels. That's all I discovered. Of the four, three are in a Hebraic language."

What a coup this would be, Ben knew; but he was a humble man and shunned notoriety. He hated speaking in front of a crowd and knew that was part of the find. He would be making appearances all over Israel and the world. He would be despised by some believers, the few that were still around in their hidden churches; because for years they were taught that the Jewish apostles wrote in Greek rather than Hebrew, their primary language. Then again, the dating would be key.

"There was something else that was especially interesting," Ben said, scratching the mosquito bite on his arm, "but it had nothing to do with the find. It was a small section of leather inscribed in Greek. Hold on. I got the text of the translation yesterday."

Ben examined the text history of the previous day and found it quickly.

"Here it is," he said and began to read. "Beware the 9th of Av."

"The 9th of Av?" Jon the Guide interrupted.

"Yeah," Ben said. "What is that? I haven't had time to research."

Wild Willy and Aludra exchanged glances, loving but worried glances. Neither had heard of the 9th of Av, but Will was sure it wasn't anything good. Seemed there were ten bad things for every good thing these days.

Jon pondered the moment. As a Jewish kid, his parents were always saying, "Beware of the 9th of Av," like it was a doomsday of sorts. As a result, he studied the phenom and the history of why parents would tell their children such a thing. He stood, walked to the ornate entrance of the King David Hotel; and a muddy, ashy glue-like mess flowed down the streets.

"Tisha B'Av," Jon said quietly. "The Day of Mourning."

The group waited, but Jon did not offer explanation. The worried expression on his face was not reassuring, Aludra thought.

"And?" Wild Willy finally asked. "What is Tisha B'Av?"

Jon looked out the front entrance of the hotel. The rain had stopped for the most part, but slimy ash covered the streets.

"Av is the fifth month of our calendar," Jon began, still studying the streets outside. The amber street lights gave the ash a kind of eerie glow. "The Jewish calendar."

"Jewish calendar?" Will asked.

"Yeah," Ben said. "The Jewish calendar dates the present year as 5780, based on the biblical ages of folk in the Old Testament. Goes all the way back to Adam and Eve, if you believe that story."

"Ben is correct," Jon continued. "Nissan is the first month of the year and always includes Passover."

"When is this day of mourning," Ben asked. "I mean, this year."

"July 30," Jon said.

An explosion far away rocked the hotel, a low-frequency rock, the kind you could feel in your bones; and Ben guessed Mount Hermon was at it again.

"As in two weeks?" Ben asked.

"Yessir," Jon answered. "Two weeks from this Thursday."

The sound of thunder and a flash of lightning introduced another round of ash-laden rain.

"The dedication of the new Temple," Aludra said to no one in particular.

"Pardon me?" Ben asked. "The new Temple?

"Yes," Aludra answered.

"I did not know it was finished," Ben said.

"It's not," Jon said. "President Morsi is dedicating it because it is two-thirds complete."

"Six sixty-six," Aludra murmured to herself.

Jon spoke to the group, providing a little history.

"According to the Torah, the Hebrew slaves were freed from Egypt and headed to the Promised Land where they waited to conquer the land that God was giving them, land occupied by the ancestors of modern-day Arabs, the Canaanites.

"Moses sent in some spies to gather reconnaissance, but the spies returned with words of woe. The land was guarded by giants and great walls. The Israelites decided against invading the land; and because of their disobedience to God, they would spend an additional 38 years in the desert. Moses never made it to the Promised Land because of this disobedience. The date of the refusal to conquer the land was the 9th of Av.

"The First Jewish Temple was built by Solomon about 800 BC and is believed to have been built according to instructions from God. The dimensions were specified, the colors of the décor and the fabrics were specified. About 410 years later, the Temple was destroyed by King Nebuchadnezzar, destroyed and bulldozed. That happened on the 9th of Av.

"The Second Temple was built after King Cyrus of Persia freed the Jews from the wrath of Nebuchadnezzar. Cyrus allowed all the Jews to move back to their land, and they promptly constructed another Temple. The Romans destroyed and bulldozed the Second

Temple about 650 years later, in 70 AD. That destruction also occurred on the 9th of Av.

"In the year 132 AD, the Jews were certain that their Messiah was the warrior Bar Kochba who revolted against Rome. Big mistake. More than a hundred thousand Jews were killed. The 9th of Av.

"Wow," Aludra interrupted. "I have never heard any of this."

"Wait," Jon said. "There is more."

The King David Hotel shook once again from the low-frequency rumble; and the group considered leaving, but where would they go. The streets were ankle-deep in ashy slime, and the winds had picked up considerably. Another car slid down the road and over the curb.

"The 9th of Av, 133 AD, the Romans ploughed the temple grounds and built the pagan-worship city of Aelia Capitolina. In 1095 AD, Pope Urban II declared the First Crusade on the 9th of Av. Thousands of Jews were slaughtered in the first few months.

"In 1290, 9th of Av, England expelled the Jews and confiscated their property.

"Spanish Inquisition, 9th of Av, 1492. Spain and Portugal expel all Jews from the Iberian Peninsula."

Ben made mental notes of these remarkable events and would do his own research to verify the details. Seemed too much to be only coincidental.

"The First World War began the 9th of Av, 1914.

"1942, the deportation of Jews from Warsaw to Treblinka for slaughter. 1944, 9th of Av, the Jewish Community Center in Buenos Aires is bombed, killing scores of people."

Jon paused at the noise outside the hotel and wondered if the building would withstand the wind.

"There is more," he said, "But you get the point."

"Do you think something bad will happen at the Third Temple dedication?" Aludra asked.

Jon had not considered a connection between 9th of Av and the Temple ceremony, but maybe.

"Maybe," Jon answered. "Maybe."

"It's going to be one heck of a celebration," Wild Willy chimed in. "All the Israelis think Morsi is the Messiah."

"It is odd," Jon said. "Morsi came out of nowhere; I mean, who ever heard of him five years ago? Then he miraculously escaped the Paris nuclear explosion…"

Jon trailed off in thought. How *had* Morsi survived the explosion when he was so close to ground-zero? Not only survived, survived unscathed.

"What's odd?" Ben asked.

"It's odd that so many Israelis, definitely most Israelis except for the Messianic Jews, believe Morsi is the prophesied Savior; and he is not even Jewish."

"No," Will said, "But he has sure done a lot for Israel. Brought some sort of peace, comparatively speaking and helped raise funding for the Third Temple, much to the dismay of the Islamic world."

"That is all true," Jon said. "And there are all the miracles he has performed."

"What if he declares himself to be God?" Ben asked. "Hillary… that's my beautiful and wonderful wife… told me a story years ago about the last days. The Temple would be rebuilt, but the one they call the antichrist would then declare himself to be God Almighty."

"That will not go over well," Jon said, considering the brief two weeks until the 9th of Av. "Even the Israelis, as much as they seem to be blinded by the light, will know he is not Yahweh, the God of Israel."

"That is when the war will start," Aludra said. "At a place called Armageddon."

"Could be," Ben said. "Troops and military vehicles have been gathering in the plains of ancient Megiddo for months. Surprised the apocalypse has not already happened."

"Aludra, you mumbled something a while ago," Jon said, noticing for the first time how beautiful she was, like an angel. "Something about six sixty-six. What did you mean?"

Chapter Seventeen

"Who are all these people?" Abe asked, trying to see through the translucent gates.

Abe assumed the man was Saint Peter. He looked like the Saint Peter he had seen in movies, dressed in a glowing, white gown and white-as-snow hair. He also assumed he was having another wild dream or had been raptured.

"They are the innocents," Saint Peter answered. "The sinless."

"The sinless?" Abe asked.

There were no sinless, with the exception of Jesus; and there never had been. Everyone born had sinned against God. It was one of the first lessons taught in the New Testament.

"The unborn," Saint Peter said. "The children throughout time who have been sacrificed, whether killed in the fire for Molech or for modern-day convenience."

Abe stared into the pearly gates, and Heaven really was beautiful. He did not know the natural elements well; but the walls of many buildings, even the road itself, shined like gold while others appeared built of exotic stone. The reds of Ruby adorned the buildings and turquoise was the color of the sky.

"Yes, Abe. I know what you are thinking. Heaven truly is a beautiful place. All will want it, but not all will get it. In most ways, sacrificed babies and aborted babies are the same. They were not given the free will to sin before being killed, all for some kind of prosperity. Followers of Molech sacrificed their children by fire, thinking that would please Molech. They, the parents, would receive a great life in return. The same with most every abortion. A termination for benefit. Jesus is disappointed in man's weakness, especially of the flesh."

Abe looked inwardly as he had done many times, remembering his jaunt through the days of the sexual revolution of the seventies, eighties and nineties. He had done his part for sexual liberation, including paying for an abortion that summer in 1988. The thought that he had paid someone to kill his unborn child, out of convenience, received little guilt at the time. Human fetuses were not really human. He bought into the skewed logic because he was young and stupid; but the guilt came later in life, when he actually started believing the statements made by Jesus. He had followed the wide road much more than the narrow road.

"So you are telling me that aborted children go straight to Heaven, without judgment?"

"But they have been judged, my friend. They have been judged sinless. They got the last laugh while their parents will be under judgment. That is why people should spend a lot more time in prayer instead of casinos and shady hotel rooms."

Abe was mesmerized by what he saw behind the gates. There were hundreds of thousands, maybe millions of people, men and women of all nationalities, dressed in white and singing songs he had never heard, the most beautiful music. The only road he could see was like no road he had ever seen, paved with stones of emeralds, garnet and exquisite marble, laid on a bed of gold.

"Yes, Abe," Saint Peter continued, "Do you see the young lady standing by the gate?"

Abe looked past Saint Peter, and there stood the most innocent and glowing child he had seen. Demure and beautiful, the young girl looked familiar. Auburn hair shined in the bright light of... wait a minute. There was no sun. Where was the source of the light?

"Yes," Abe answered.

"She is your child, Abe. She had an unusual future planned."

That was why the young girl was familiar, Abe reckoned; and tears formed quickly, streaming down his cheeks.

"Your daughter was to lead a revival, Abe, a revival like the world has not seen since the days of Jonah and the salvation of Nineveh. Only her message of salvation would have been permanent. She was destined to save the world from what is happening at this moment."

"I am sorry I ever did that," Abe said; and sincerity dripped from every word, like the tears now dripped from his face. "I have prayed for forgiveness many times."

"Yes, you have," Saint Peter said. "Too many times. God hears you, Abe. You do not have to ask over-and-over. Praying is not supposed to be ritual. You are forgiven, don't you understand?"

"She is so young," Abe said. "She should be forty-two."

"Yes," Saint Peter said, "We age very slowly here."

As suddenly as Abe's meeting with Saint Peter started, it ended. He wandered back from his daydream or vision, to the present; and Condi held his hand as he told her the story of his latest weird dream, or whatever was happening to him. He was troubled over his vision of the young girl in blue.

Condi had been unaware of the abortion that Abe referenced; but unfortunately, it was a story way too common. Fifty-million abortions a year, worldwide. She forgave him, knowing secrets about her own ghosts in her own closet, the ones only she and God knew about.

"What happened next?" she asked, squeezing his hand.

Abe said nothing, reminiscing his past sins of which there seemed to be more than he thought. He tried to do the math but needed a calculator. How many people were already in Heaven, he considered, if aborted children got a free pass?

"Saint Peter said we should get married," Abe finally said with a grin. "He said you were a good woman and that you deserved a great catch like me."

"Oh really?" Condi laughed. "Aren't I the lucky one?"

Abe's therapy had proven a great help. He remained with a certain insecurity about women, but his feelings for Condi were sometimes overwhelming. He felt for certain he had been blessed, undeservedly blessed; but then, who really deserved God's blessing.

It was only by grace and mercy. Whatever the reason, he was a happy camper.

"I have a question."

"Ask away," Condi said.

"Is your name really Condi? I mean your birth name."

Condi looked at him, a questioning sort of look.

"The reason I ask, I do not recall ever meeting a 'Condi,'" Abe continued, "I don't know… I feel like I have met you before."

"Connie," Condi said. "My younger brother could not pronounce Connie when he began to talk. He called me Condi. The name stuck."

Abe's heart skipped a beat.

"You don't like it?" she asked, arching her eyebrows.

"Was your mother's name, Barbara?"

Now Condi was surprised. How could Abe possibly know her mother's name?

"Are you a psychic? How did you know that?"

"Did you ever go to Jefferson Junior High?" he continued.

Condi said nothing, but her mouth was agape. Abe could see recognition on her beautiful face. His heart was surely going to thump out of his chest; and he glanced downward, certain that his shirt was pounding right along with it.

"Were you in the choir?"

Condi was startled at the ringing sound; it had been so long in coming. When the grid is down, there is little noise. The Duluth Bell Tower at City Hall began to ring, and the railroad crossing came to life.

"The power's back on!" someone screamed from across the Town Green; and from the north, the sound of the Amtrak Express.

The few remaining businesses around the Town Green had resorted to ringing up sales the old-fashioned way, using hand-crank calculators rustled up from the Army Salvage store on Buford

Highway. Employs and patrons made their way outside to the Town Green, as though it was Fall Festival.

The air was electric with joy. Traffic lights were on, and Condi heard the TVs in *The Divide* spring to life. She could not wait to hear some news.

"Let's go," she said, pulling Abe from the steps. "We have news!"

They walked quickly toward *The Divide*, and many others had the same idea. The sound of electricity being restored had invigorated the remaining population, but current news was on everyone's mind.

What was going on with the Asian nuclear war? What about the rumored hailstorms with fifty-pound hailstones? Was there really a worldwide rabies epidemic? Weren't there ham radio rumors about Mount Hermon erupting along the Syrian-Lebanese border? What was this miracle on the Golan that ham operators were talking about night and day? Had Damascus really fallen? What in the world was red mercury?

"Yes," Condi said.

Abe looked at her quizzically as they walked up the front steps of the news bar and restaurant.

"Yes what?"

"Yes, I was in the choir. Seventh grade. How did you know?"

Abe was off for the day, actually off for most days since the power outage; but he would now have to help prepare for the coming crowd. People yearned for news of the outside world. The charging stations were full, thirty-five phones, micro-laptops and other devices plugged in, slurping up a charge like camels at an oasis.

"You were my first girlfriend," Abe said and walked behind the bar. "I lived with my uncle. You were prettier than a tiger lily. I was too embarrassed to tell you."

Abe blushed, and Connie remembered. He always talked about tiger lilies, and she was absolutely certain this was arranged by God's grace. Too weird to be a coincidence.

Chapter Eighteen

Fourty-three days passed before the power grids in much of the South and Midwest were repaired and the first electricity, restored. Most generators had long run out of fuel, and panicked sections of the nation received a taste of anarchy.

The grocery stores and pharmacies had been ransacked the first week without power; and ham radio stories cluttered the airwaves, dispersing tragic news of fire, riots, rapes and pillaging.

There was no insulin to be found, and diabetics died by the thousands. Neighbors shared with neighbors, at least most; but soon water and food ran out. Very few had been prepared for the loss of electricity, and two children in South Carolina were found eating bark from a pine tree. No TV, no phones, no air conditioning, no dogfood. Thanks to a few remaining street preachers, many wondered if they were in Hell.

Within a week of the power outage, gangs loaded for bear set up roadblocks for those foolish enough to wander out of their own safety net. Food, water and medicines were confiscated.

The mayors and town councils in areas affected by the complete loss of electricity were surprised at how quickly society defaulted to decadence and depravity; and two were executed for supporting the new president, unpopular by those with unbiblical beliefs because of his push to overturn Roe-Wade and put the Bible back in the school system.

News was scarce, especially current news; but rumors were numerous from solar-powered ham radios; and the news was not good: Rapes at roadblocks, kidnappings for food, beheadings of Christians and Jews. It was beginning to look a lot like Egypt and Syria.

"I am soooo glad the electricity is back on, Uncle Gray," Audry said to Gray and Andi. The power had been on for nearly three days, and now there was no more darkness.

"I used to think it was dark at night, but it really wasn't," Audry continued. "Compared to the darkness with no electricity or moon, normal darkness is nearly daylight."

Gray and Andi Dorey, passing through Duluth in their not-so-new '57 red Chevy Bel Air, decided to drop in. They had known Jeffrey for several years, friends with him and first wife, Melissa. The friendship went back a long way, through many life-changing events, even the Cayman Island tsunami.

Melissa had been killed in the tsunami, or so they all thought; but she was miraculously saved by Jamaican fishermen and taken to Jamaica.

"It was scary," Andi said. "Were you frightened?"

Audry had been frightened, *very* frightened. The darkness at night was as thick as chocolate pudding, you could not see anything.

"Not really," Audry answered. "Well, a little. The wild animals were scary. Daddy has night-vision glasses, so we could see the animals at night and scare them away. Then the batteries went out."

"Oh no," Andi said. "What did you do?"

"We stayed in the safe room at first; but when the generator ran out of gas, the air conditioner stopped working. It was too hot down there."

The Admiral and Sheryl came through the swimming pool entrance and walked toward Gray, Andi and Audry. They both had on purple tee-shirts with JAILBIRD emblazoned in gold across the front.

"They've been in jail," Audry squealed and laughed.

"We heard," Andi said. "Talking about the Lord at IHOP is not okay with the morality police."

The Admiral and Sheryl quickly told the story, laughing; but it had been far from funny at the time. They had been separated and interrogated for three days, before the President himself placed a call requesting their release.

"Yeah," The Admiral laughed, "They didn't know we had friends in high places."

"Where are Jeff and Samarra?" Sheryl asked.

"Daddy's fixin' the TVs. Everything has to be reset," Audry said, twisting her long, red hair between her fingers. "It takes a long time."

"You mean Jeff has been without news?" Sheryl asked.

"He has the ham radio back now that we have power. And he listened to the news this morning in the car. Did you know the Temple is being dedicated next week? I hope we have the TVs fixed by then."

"Yes, we heard," Gray said, troubled. He had read an article recently about the Ninth of Av, the date of the Third Temple dedication and all the bad events that had occurred that day in Jewish history.

"How did you know that, Audry?" Andi asked.

"Know what?" Audry answered.

The sound of an aircraft came from high overhead; and the wind picked up slightly, now blowing from the northwest. The stench of the burned Great Smoky Mountains, still on fire, assaulted the air.

"About the Temple dedication. Most little girls do not know this kind of stuff, know what I mean?" Aunt Andi winked.

"Mr. Hutz told me," Audry replied.

"I thought Mr. Hutz died?" Sheryl said. She had seen him disappear that night on TV during an interview.

"Raptured, actually," Audry said with no sadness. "But he still talks to me in my sleep."

"Tell Gray and Andi what he said, honey," Samarra whispered, carrying a tray of coffee and a box of Krispy Kreme donuts. "Sorry. I lost my voice."

Audry paused, grabbing a vanilla covered, glazed donut with colorful sprinkles on top. She licked the sprinkles, then attacked the donut.

"He said lots of stuff, Sam," Audry started. "He said they should not dedicate the new Temple on July 30, because it is the ninth of Av on the Jewish calendar. He said bad things happen on that day."

Gray and Andi exchanged glances.

"He said that the crackdown on the Jews in Israel and around the world will begin that day. He said it would be like Hitler all over again but on a worldwide scale."

"Do you know what Hitler did to the Jews, Audry?"

"Uh huh," she said. "Not just to the Jews! He killed Jehovah's Witnesses and gay people too. Did you know Elton John said Jesus was gay?"

"No," Sheryl said. "Go on."

"He said a humongous war was coming; but I should not be scared, because I am special."

Audry *was* special. Everyone sitting around the table knew she was unique, and a little odd. She sometimes knew things before they happened.

"He said the wind was going to blow like crazy, more than four-hundred miles an hour and light would be blinding."

The Admiral listened carefully, because Audry's prediction track record was phenomenal. He could think of few man-made structures that could stand up to four-hundred mile-per-hour winds, especially for a sustained period. The winds in Jupiter's red spot were this speed.

Audry told of more predictions from the infamous Chuck Hutz as Jeff made the final corrections to the large, outdoor TV. The news was coming soon.

The Admiral and Sheryl stood to leave as Abe and Condi made their way in. Everyone was meeting at Jeff's house, it seemed. Sheryl explained that the new President, the most Christian president in years, was landing at Warner Robins Air Force Base in four hours, and she had to be there. They would leave Button Gwinnett Airport on a private military jet at three o'clock.

"Everyone, hold your breath," Jeff said as he hit the remote POWER button. The set was tuned to FOX News, and of course there was an alert.

Sheryl and The Admiral said their goodbyes and wandered toward the gate.

"This just in from Reuters, some tragic news."

The Admiral and Sheryl stopped and turned toward the news. The news host, ReAnn Ring from Holland, could not continue and left the news set in tears. The TV went to an advertisement for the latest reality show, *People Who Think They Are Dogs.*

Jeff grabbed the remote and changed to Omega Letter Network News.

"... in the Atlantic about twenty miles east of Savannah, Georgia. The President's plane was expected to arrive at Warner Robins later today. Some fishermen were eyewitnesses to the explosion, though they have conflicting accounts. Some say the plane simply exploded in the air; others say a missile was fired from a speedboat as the plane's altitude lowered.

"We repeat, the President of the United States is dead, killed when Air Force One exploded high above the Atlantic Ocean."

Chapter Nineteen

The Palestinian miners worked tirelessly but slowly, taking caution to deceive any snooping eyes of the Israel Defense Forces. Their efforts in Gaza, the Sinai and West Bank had taken years.

The latest jihad group to appear on the borders of Israel was ruthless, more ruthless than Jihad's Warriors.

The Warriors had a fervent and restrictive belief in the teachings of Islam and were on the verge of collapsing the economies of the West. Things had gone smoother before Vinny defected or was killed. There was still no answer to that question.

"Mohammed," Sai'imi said. "What do you believe happened to Aboud?"

"I was only now thinking about this," Mohammed answered.

Aboud, Mohammed's twin, became known as Vinny, once in America and played the part well. Mohammed was respectful of Aboud's abilities and his genius. It was impossible to believe he had defected. Certainly he was dead. Almost all lethal activity had ceased in the United States over the past year, as had any communications from brother Vinny.

Sai'imi had become Mohammed's right-hand-man over the past couple of years, and life would be tough without him. He was a mastermind at almost everything, from astronomy to drone technology to mining.

"How are the mines?" Mohammed asked.

"The mines are complete, Mohammed. We are in testing phase. Allah has been good to us. Not even one has been discovered by the Israeli scum. It is a sign for success."

The mines were not really mines. They were tunnels lined with the foam insulation boards delivered to Palestinian territory by the Israelis. The IDF would blow up their buildings, the Palestinians would build them back and the Israeli jackals would blow them up again. It was a never-ending battle, and foam insulation boards were a hot commodity. Only these foam boards were used to line the walls of underground tunnels, helping to silence the digging.

"It has been much work, Mohammed. We have tunnels along the West Bank close to Jerusalem. Next week when the Jews gather to celebrate the opening of the supposed temple, Morsi and the other scum will succumb to their wickedness."

"Who knows about this, Sai'imi?"

"No one, Mohammed. We are all sworn to secrecy."

"What of the Arabs who will be in the area? How will they be warned?"

Sai'imi paused, certain they had discussed these details.

"No warning, Mohammed. If we give warning, someone will surely spill the corn. They will be sacrificed to Allah, and they will be the fortunate. They will be in paradise by the end of this Jewish ninth of Av."

"Have you any news about Air Force One?" Sai'imi asked.

"Not yet. But soon. It has either happened now or it has been a failure. We are scanning news outlets."

The pause was uncomfortable. Sai'imi knew that Mohammed suffered greatly, worried about his twin brother. Aboud had done well, no matter the end-result. No one could match his accomplishments and glory.

With the help of Jumpin' Johnny Hussein, Vinny had wiped out the tunnels of New York City and nuked Manhattan. Three dams had been blown up, including the Buford Dam, the largest. There were rumors that Vinny had a part in the Panama Canal disaster that cost the world trillions of dollars. Vinny carried out the Mother's Day massacre with precision and finesse, destroyed Surprise, Arizona and spread death by Spanish Flu all over the world. Sai'imi even wondered if Vinny played a part in the spread of Gay Plague through mosquitos that was killing Europeans by the tens of thousands.

Mohammed's phone vibrated, and he quickly read the text.

Check Al Jazeera.

"Turn on Al Jazeera," Mohammed barked; and Sai'imi did as told. The old tube-type television was virtually invincible to EMP, and Sai'imi clicked Channel 226. The high-definition upgrade worked, but only barely; and the video was fuzzy.

"*Again,*" the somber newsman started, "*I hate to be the bearer of tragic news; but if you are just tuning in, President Ronald Travis is presumed dead, the victim of the crash of Air Force One. At this time there are no witnesses to the crash, other than the fighter escorts; and the military has them under wraps. At this time, no authorities have mentioned terror.*"

"Those people are so stupid," Mohammed mocked. "They do not even know when terror strikes."

Mohammed and Sai'imi did not celebrate their success, knowing that war would surely follow, a war like the world had never seen. According to the Persians, the Twelfth Imam was alive and well on planet Earth; and soon President Morsi would have the world in his hands.

"How did you do it, Mohammed? How did you manage to take the President down?"

Mohammed divulged the details to his friend. Japanese investors, still angry over the Hiroshima bombing in World War Two, donated a boat to the cause, a luxury submarine-yacht, two-hundred feet long and more silent than most military submarines.

Under the pretense of shooting a cover for *Sports Illustrated*, the submarine surfaced about thirty miles southeast of Savannah, Georgia. The intelligence was more forthcoming with the newest president of the Satanic United States. The chances Air Force One's flight path would pass just south of Savannah were about ninety percent.

The plane would approach from the east; and fifty miles out, a small, inaudible explosion would take out two of the plane's windows. Rapid decompression would probably kill President Travis; but if not, the FIM-94VIR Stinger missile would.

The Air Force One pilot would descend rapidly, trying to reach ten-thousand feet where the pressure and breathing were manageable. At a height of, hmmmmm, maybe fifteen-thousand feet, the plane would pass within a few miles of the *Sports Illustrated* photoshoot.

The missile, purchased on the black market, was shoulder-fired with a range of fifty-three miles. It was also the world's most advanced shoulder-fired antiaircraft missile. The VIR technology homed in on its target by sensing the heat of the planes exhaust via infrared sensing. It also maintained a visual image of the plane and sensed the difference in temperature of the plane's exhaust and the phosphorous antimissile system employed by the plane.

The plan went pretty much as Mohammed described to Sai'imi.

Faraj, Abdul and Darius, one of the few Shi'a Muslims in *Jihad's Warriors*, all thoroughly trained in firing the FIM-94VIR shoulder-fired missile, began their near-silent journey to the surface of the Atlantic. The site was accurately pin-pointed by the yacht's GPS system.

"Is this the spot?" Esther, the model from Britain asked.

"It is," Abdul answered as he maneuvered the joystick.

The three models giggled with delight. Bridgett and Celine, from Paris, were twins. The women, all younger than twenty-five, squirmed into their tiny bathing suits, excited about the cover opportunity. This would be their route to fame and fantasy, they were certain.

The *Sports Illustrated* theme this year, concocted by Jihad's Warriors, was *SCUBA Meets the Luxury Submarine*. There would be many digital photos of the ladies that would make their way through internet heaven; and they would be rich.

"At such a young age," Celine, twenty-four, said.

"At *such* a young age," the other two repeated; and all broke out in laughter, "And we will be rich!"

The luxury submarine broke the surface, suddenly evolving into an ocean-going yacht, and leveled off. From a large storage closet in the bow, the crew of three gathered and uncased the three missiles and carried them to the enclosed helicopter deck.

There would be a ten-minute wait for the President's plane to appear, assuming the small explosive below the two passenger windows detonated properly. A lot of ifs, but if Allah was willing, it would happen. The world would be surprised by how simple it had been to take down the President's plane; but a steward, a computer-hacker and a drone would soon be heroes in the Muslim world.

The three squealing models made their way to the deck but were surprised when there were no islands. For three-hundred sixty degrees, nothing but water could be seen. The contract called for an island-shoot.

"Hey," Esther said, "Where is the island?"

The rope seemed to come out of nowhere and wrapped tightly around Esther's young and tiny throat. At the other end, a thirty-pound weight was secured. In less than five seconds, Esther went from squealing, soon-to-be-rich European model to a mermaid, on her way to death at the bottom of the ocean.

As each of the young women stood in complete shock at what they had seen, they suffered a similar fate; and Celine watched her twin sister sink below her to the depths of the ocean. In desperation mode, her only desire at the time was life; and she tugged with all her might at the heavy rope wrapped around her throat. Her tiny fingers pried and clawed.

The three *Warriors* waited, listening carefully. Each had a pair of electronic, high-magnification binoculars; and Darius scanned the horizon. It was 2:15, and the afternoon sun journeyed westward toward Warner Robins Air Force Base and the new White House, high above the fluffy, cumulus clouds. A bright shaft of sunlight broke through the confines of the clouds, like a giant laser from Allah; and the beam seemed to penetrate the surface of the ocean.

"Allah is with us, my friend," Darius said. "Look. His sign."

The men waited, but the drone of aircraft engines was nowhere to be heard, no sounds except the lapping of small waves against the side of the yacht. After fifteen minutes, Abdul was sure the plan had failed; and he wished they had not thrown the three women overboard. He especially liked the one named Celine.

"We should have waited to kill the girls!" Abdul shouted to no one.

"Listen!" Darius shouted.

The sound of screaming jet engines became barely audible in the distance. The three *Warriors* grabbed the missiles, hoping they would not misfire. When Air Force One appeared between two large, fluffy-white clouds, the fighter-jet escort slowly leveled off. To the escort pilots, it seemed the President of the United States had a miraculous escape. In their rescue mode, none of the pilots spotted the yacht, now only a mile away.

Air Force One did not pass directly over the terrorist group of jihadists. Now at eighty-five hundred feet, the plane passed more than a half-mile away and flew directly into the sun, temporarily blinding the pilots. Radar was picking something up from the sea, but it appeared stationary. In the heat of the moment, it was assumed to be a fishing boat. One of the fighter escorts veered left and started a circle-search to verify.

The F22 Raptor's missile detection alarm sounded, but the fighter was not the target. The reconnaissance jet, now four miles away, saw the exhaust trails from two missiles and sent a warning to Air Force One.

The Air Force One pilots were the best in the world, as were their responses. As the antimissile system activated, surrounding the President's large jet with exploding phosphorous deterrent, the deck crew waited in anticipation. Would the missiles filter the phosphorous from the jet exhaust, as advertised?

"See any other escorts?" Darius asked.

The fighter escorts were not unanticipated. Under normal circumstances, the President's plane had no fighter escorts; but these days, nothing was normal. In today's world, the President's plane was always escorted.

The explosive force of the two missiles as they detonated simultaneously a millisecond after penetrating the plane's outer skin was complete. The cockpit crew of three were weightless for a few seconds as they began to fall through the warm air, strapped inside the front section of the plane, tumbling end-over-end, toward the deep, blue Atlantic below. The impact would be less than a minute into their future, and the senior pilot texted an *I love you* to his new bride, knowing he misspelled the words.

The rear portion of the plane with the wings and four engines still attached, lurched upward as the weight of the cockpit broke away. Resembling a large hollow log, now near-vertical, the once-presidential jet slowly did a backflip, then slammed into the sea.

Abdul still held missile number three but knew it would not be needed. The three men high-fived and prepared to dive. They would simply disappear.

Celine, miraculously freed from the rope around her neck, made her way upward toward the surface of the water. Every cell in her body screamed for oxygen. The young Parisian model, a Catholic, thought a silent prayer, and it looked like it would be answered in the affirmative.

Breaking the surface as quietly as she could, she could not tame her gasp for air. A hundred feet away, she spotted the gray silhouette submarine-yacht and the three men who tried to kill her. To the right of the silhouette, a ball of fire fell from the clouds. The three men high-fived in celebration over something?

She lay still in the water, floating on her back, praying the men would not spot her.

Faraj scanned the horizon, searching for other fighter escorts. He spotted a streak of yellow in the calm waters, about five-hundred meters to the west.

"What is that?" Faraj asked, pointing toward the horizon.

Abdul picked up the electronic binoculars and searched the water. Nothing.

"What did you see?"

"Maybe nothing," Faraj said. "I thought I saw a yellow rescue vest. Let's dive."

Celine was vulnerable, supine in the water; and a small wave elevated her tanned body as she bobbed up and down.

Abdul spotted the flash of yellow and picked up the binoculars one more time.

"It's the girl," Abdul said. "Allahu Akbar."

"Yes, He is," Faraj said, grinning; and the three men laughed in their future pleasure.

The crew checked the airspace; but it seemed that one fighter escort had disappeared, and the other was circling the site. They knew they should dive and be gone, but the hormonal call only gained strength.

Mohammed paused his story. That was the last word he heard from the crew. The President's plane was shot down, and one of the models somehow survived.

"The crew was chasing the whore?" Sai'imi asked, surprised and angry. He hated all women; they were the work of the devil. Mohammed had strict rulings about interaction with women.

"Yes, apparently. There has been no word since the President's plane was shot out of the sky."

"Mohammed," Sai'imi said. "Do you understand what you have done for Allah? You have rid the whole world of the American devil himself. You are a hero, Mohammed. Maybe *TIME* will put you on the cover."

"Yes," Mohammed laughed. "Maybe. I would like to know how the story ended."

"Turn on OLN News. They always break the story."

Chapter Twenty

He opened the shaft of the bottomless pit, and from the shaft rose smoke like the smoke of a great furnace, and the sun and the air were darkened with the smoke from the shaft.

Then from the smoke came locusts on the earth, and they were given power like the power of scorpions of the earth.

Revelation 9:2-3 ESV

Ben, Jon, Aludra and Wild Willy awoke in the lobby of the King David Hotel two days after Mount Hermon erupted in the north. Streets remained ash-ridden and slippery in the deluge Israel was suffering after several years of drought.

"It has stopped raining," Jon said, rubbing both eyes in disbelief.

The four had become good friends during their night's confinement inside the hotel lobby, but all were tired and needed a hot bath.

"Maybe we should chip in and get a room," Ben suggested. "Everyone could clean up a bit."

"Do you know how much a room costs at the King David Hotel?" Jon laughed. "It has a history."

The sound of news interrupted their thoughts, something about the President of the United States. They ambled across the ornately tiled floor and to the Roman-themed coffee shop, Pomegranate Café. They grabbed a small table, ordered four coffees for fifty US dollars and listened to the OLN News commentator, Judi Ainslie Jackson, live from Covington, Georgia.

"I think she used to be on FOX News, one of their beauties," Jon said and listened to the latest news alert. "Not sure where they find all that beauty and intelligence."

"*…terror not involved according to the White House. The crash of Air Force One, reportedly, is the result of a tragic, atmospheric event. Only one of the two fighter escorts returned to Warner Robins. The other apparently went down at sea from the same atmospheric condition, a downburst.*"

Pomegranate Café, packed with the early-morning crowd, became utterly silent as everyone absorbed the tragic news.

"*The United States military is on high alert because of the 'state of the world' according to the White House.*"

"That makes no sense," Ben said.

"What makes no sense?" Jon asked.

"If this is not terror related, why is the military on high alert?"

Out of nowhere, Israeli jets screamed over the city, heading north. The walls of the hotel shook; and the still silent, early-morning crowd, rushed outside to see what was going on.

"Good question," Wild Willy said.

"Don't go outside," the maître d'hôtel yelled as the guests rushed out, paying no heed to the plump, little man.

Because of the Temple Dedication Ceremony, the crowd was festive and many were unaware of the eruption of Mount Hermon during the night.

The first to exit the King David Hotel immediately slid to the ground in the slick ash. Those behind, in their rush to get outside, stampeded over the fallen with no clue they were there. Rocks fell from the sky, most pebble sized; but a few were the size of bowling balls. Ben wondered if the bowling ball-sized rocks could be the hundred-pound hailstones that John envisioned in Revelation. In less than a minute, forty-eight people were killed from the rock storm.

"What a mess," Wild Willy said, watching the activity outside. The sound of sirens grew louder.

The End: The Book: Part Seven

"… three tunnels. The discovery in the Golan Heights was not unexpected, according to Israeli sources. General Ben Avi, working with Mossad, stated that the tunnels might be 'diversions.' Apparently they were easily discovered."

Judi concentrated on the news script as it displayed on her small screen, but her mind drifted. Fortunately, she had the ability to do both, and she recalled the dream the previous night, a dream about tunnels and drones. The ending was not good.

"This just in," she continued. *"The crew of an oil transport witnessed the crash of Air Force One. Though nearly two miles from the crash scene, every man claimed to have seen missiles or rockets leaving the sea and shooting down the President's plane. Stay tuned."*

✡ ✡ ✡

Thirty miles off the coast of Georgia, the submarine-yacht edged closer to the French model in the yellow bikini. The men laughed and mocked, thanking Allah for their good fortune.

"So you thought you escaped death, but you lived. A miracle!" Faraj shouted to the frightened girl, laughing. "Do not fear. Death will soon find you."

"Yes, but not until we have a little fun," Abdul said. "Maybe you can be one of my wives."

The small dinghy, large enough for three or four moderately-sized men, was cautiously lowered to the ocean surface, with Abdul as the only crewman. None of the men could swim, and the bright-orange life vest lay on the floor of the boat. Abdul started the small, gas engine and aimed the dinghy toward the young girl. The other two jihadists waited patiently in anticipation. They would get the girl, submerge and that would be that.

The F-22 Raptor pilot completed the circle-search and had spotted only two vessels. The oil tanker appeared harmless and was too far away to have fired the missiles. He rapidly guided the fighter jet downward until only a few feet above the water, cutting a deep crease in the calm, ocean surface. The F-22 *Heads-Up* display spotted the girl floating in the water and the small boat headed toward her. The pilot quickly went to Plan B.

Plan A was a quick hit by an air-to-surface missile, but the girl in the water changed everything. The pilot pushed the plane almost to the speed of sound and flew no more thirty feet above the dinghy.

Abdul kept his foot tightly on the orange life preserver. He was almost there. He never saw or heard the plane until it screamed overhead, and the force that was creasing the ocean surface knocked Abdul up and over the side. He never resurfaced, and his orange life vest floated in the sea.

Celine seized the opportunity, swam thirty feet to the dinghy and climbed in. The men on the yacht scrambled, trying to dive before the F-22 returned. The dinghy motor, remarkably, was still running.

Celine had been in plenty of boats. Most of her modeling sessions were on boats, from the most luxurious yachts to sixteen-foot runabouts at boat shows. She thrust the throttle, and the small boat moved away from the yacht as fast as the engine could take her. She did not want to be near the yacht, because she was certain its demise was near.

"Dive! Dive!" Faraj screamed, and the men could hardly function. They shook in fear.

They loved Allah but suicide had not been part of the plan. The yacht slowly began to submerge, too slowly; and the evolution from surface yacht to submarine began.

Kristi Tanner Walker had been enthralled with fighter aircraft since she was a little girl watching the A-10 Thunderbolt blow the snickers out of anything and everything around it. It was the first time she decided her future career.

A homecoming queen, valedictorian and magna cum laude honors graduate from the Air Force Academy, she never made it to the A-10. She preferred the F-22 Raptor and was the first female U.S. Air Force Raptor pilot for the magnificent work of art.

The yacht appeared to be submerging, and that was a first for her, a yacht that could dive.

The missile dropped from the plane and sped toward victory. The hundred-million-dollar ship blew up just like a thirty-foot cabin cruiser, only the explosion was larger.

Kristi, from a distance, circled the girl in the dinghy and waited for the rescue helicopter. Her life would never be the same after this day; and with the realization that the new President, the one so many loved, was at the bottom of the ocean, she cried.

An orange and white Coast Guard chopper appeared as a small dot on the western horizon.

✡ ✡ ✡

The winds in the West Bank blew hard and constant. Mohammed and Sai'imi met in a small church coffee shop, about a mile from the Wall. Occasionally stones fell from the sky. Many Palestinians and Jews had resorted to the hottest product on the market, The Kevlumbrella. Made of Kevlar, some limited protection was offered. Plus, it was protection against the glaring sun.

"Tunnels are prepared, Mohammed."

Sai'imi explained, in detail, the sequence of operations.

"There are six tunnels behind the West Bank wall, just east of Jerusalem. The tunnels open into the small shanties that line the border boundary, seventy-five meters from the wall.

"The evening of the ninth of Av, this so-called holiday, the shanties will be pushed over and the tunnels will open to the night sky. Other shanties, away from the drones, will be set on fire. The stupid Jews will think it is just another night in Palestine but will focus attention on the burning shanties."

Mohammed smiled. The thought of interrupting the opening of the Third Temple and killing a lot of Jews in the process would be most pleasing to Allah.

"Each drone is black and will be difficult to spot, at least visually. Yet they are so small, they look like hawks on radar. Some will make it through, Mohammed. Even if they spot the swarm, they cannot get them all. The drones are individually programmed via coordinates by Google Satellite, thank you. No joysticks or monitoring. Each knows exactly where to go. Then we blow this wall up, insha'Allah; and we will drive the inhabitants of Satan into the sea."

The Israeli-Palestinian wall was painful for Mohammed, but not the same way it was a burden to the Palestinians. They had to live with it, and he was only a visitor. Soon he would be handling affairs in Europe again.

"Why did you not go under the wall?"

Sai'imi explained. The Israelis had ground sensors on both sides of the wall. With the drone plan, it would not matter.

"The wall is virtually impenetrable, Mohammed. It goes ten meters into the ground."

"What will the drone swarm do, Sai'imi? What is the plan?"

The plan was simple as long as the wind remained calm. The volcano had not helped, Sai'imi was sure of that. It had been windy since the eruption.

Each drone or set of drones, Sai'imi explained, were programmed for their individual duties. During early morning darkness while most slept, the tunnels closest in proximity to the Temple site will open. A fleet of near-microscopic drones will fly over the Temple grounds and dump their loads.

"What is the load?" Mohammed asked.

The red-mercury bombs were reserved for Europe, Russia and the United States. Sai'imi wanted to blow up one of the enhanced bombs and would handle Tel Aviv, what was left, and the Dimona nuclear facility.

"Wherever people stand, walk or touch, the nearly invisible powder will be. This is military-grade anthrax with a ten-day incubation period. Most will show symptoms after that. Until then, they will not have the knowledge of their exposure. They may spread it to others who might touch their clothing. Each mini-drone will carry three grams."

"And how many are there?"

"There will be two hundred. They are almost silent and invisible. Once the mission is complete…"

The ground jolted; and a loud noise, not a boom, more like a very large fingernail scraping a very large blackboard, frightened the men.

"Never heard anything like that!" Sai'imi said worriedly, looking around. "Over there," he shouted, pointing toward the wall. A large crack had appeared.

"The plan will work if earthquakes do not collapse the tunnels, my friend," Mohammed said, maintaining his balance; and ash stirred in areas that had not suffered the rainfall.

"That is not all, Mohammed," Sai'imi said, still looking around nervously for some other disturbance.

"I did not think so, my friend," Mohammed said, slapping the small man on the back.

"The mini-drones cannot be reused and are programmed to crash into the Dead Sea. Security during the dedication will be difficult to penetrate; but if God is willing, our drones will get through.

"Do you remember the small drones that change color?" Sai'imi asked.

"Do you mean the one claimed to have been developed by the Jews, the stealth drone that cannot be seen in the daytime?"

"That is the one. It is called Chameleon."

"What of it?" Mohammed asked.

"We have five."

Mohammed was astonished at the good news.

"How in the world did you manage that, Sai'imi?"

"Russian black market. They were very expensive."

Mohammed had researched the drone when the rumors started but thought they were only rumors. A drone that could lift three times it's weight and could change color to blend in with its environment would be a great weapon.

"They even have the Star of David insignia," Sai'imi added. "The Israelis have seen the drones, often monitoring crowds. They were used extensively when those two crazy preachers were preaching."

Sai'imi paused, focusing on the crack in the border wall. It appeared to be getting larger.

"And?"

"And," Sai'imi said, "When the crowds see the drones, if they do, they will think they are crowd monitors, watching for signs of trouble. What looks like an extra camera is a Teflon container full of acid. Actually, it is a superacid and the strongest acid known to man."

"Fluoroantimonic acid?" Mohammed questioned. That would explain the Teflon container. Fluoroantimonic acid dissolved glass and most anything else it touched. A drop on the arm would burn all the way through.

"That is it, Mohammed. How do you know that?"

"Chemistry degree from Oxford," Mohammed answered.

"Do you know what will happen to the Jews when this acid hits their skin?"

A disturbance at the Israeli-Palestine wall from a landing military helicopter interrupted the conversation, and Palestinian children ran outside to watch. Six armed IDF soldiers exited the chopper; and in fifteen minutes, they set up a small outpost to guard the crack in the concrete base of the wall.

"Let's go," Mohammed said. "We do not need to be seen by those jackals."

Chapter Twenty-One

<u>July 22, the First of Av</u>

"*A*n unprecedented phenomenon has occurred in downtown Athens Thursday morning: a tornado!*"* The news commentator paused, out of breath.

Ben, talking to his wife Hillary on the phone, listened to the news subconsciously. Solar interference with all things satellite made getting through to Duluth, a challenge.

"Hillary, I have a bad feeling about this, about what is going on over here. The Israelis are jubilant over this Morsi guy. They think he is the messiah. I swear."

"Really?"

"… *significant, historical landmarks have been destroyed, totally, including the Parthenon.*"

"Really. Have you ever heard of the ninth of Av?"

"Nope."

"It is a date in the Jewish calendar…"

"I didn't know they had their own calendar," Hillary interrupted.

Ben paused, listening. Did the reporter say the Parthenon was destroyed? Nah… That could not happen.

"Yeah, it is in mid-summer; and a lot of bad stuff seems to happen to the Jews on that date. Has been going on for thousands of years."

"… *unprecedented wind-speed of 650 kilometers per hour. That is more than 400 miles per hour for our friends to the West. The historic Acropolis is no more, just rubble.*"

"*The buildings, constructed twenty-five hundred years ago, were built using the most exquisite Pentelic marble and withstood the climate and wars, until yesterday.*"

Ben talked with Hillary but was now watching the report. The news commentator was crying.

"Ben, are you there?"

"Yeah, I'm sorry. I think I just heard the Parthenon got blown down."

"That happened yesterday. It is unbelievable, the damage. Did you know the tornado is still on the ground after twenty-four hours?"

"*… on the ground for nearly a full twenty-four hours,*" the TV droned. "*Can you imagine? Another unprecedented event. The tornado is now in Istanbul where the Turkish Ambassador has reported the city's history has been destroyed, including the famous Blue Mosque. The last five columns of the monument at Side have fallen, standing since the sixth century B.C.*"

"Un-dang-believable," Ben mumbled.

Ben told Hillary about his new friends in Jerusalem, the eruption of Mount Hermon and the hailstorms. Turned out he really did recognize Wild Willy. Will traveled to Duluth, regularly.

"Small world," Hillary said, and she longed for her husband, especially if something bad was about to happen in Israel. "When are you coming home?"

"In a week or so. I have some work to finish up if Mount Hermon stops doing its thing. I would also like to stay for the Third Temple Dedication."

"I wish you wouldn't," Hillary blurted. "You know the story about the Temple and the last days. It is not a joke, Benjamin. Listen to me."

Ben was well-aware that Hillary had been raised going to church; and her grandpa was a holy-roller preacher, spoke in tongues and other strange stuff. She was somewhat aware of the end-times prophecies, and now he wished he had not mentioned the Temple dedication.

"*The Weather Channel acknowledged that the tornado was off the Fujita scale, faster and wider than any recorded throughout history.*

"The weather is weird, ladies and gents. Alaska hit 92° in March and did it three times. Ninety-five percent of the remaining vineyards in France and Italy have been wiped out by hail, some stones as large as basketballs. Thousands of livestock are dead from the storms. Now to the nuclear war in Asia…"

"Why don't you fly here, Hillary?" Ben asked. "The dedication is going to be a really big deal. The Israelites are going whacko."

"Yeah," Hillary whined. "I bet so if they think the Persian guy is the messiah; but I think he is the antichrist."

Ben supposed Morsi might be the antichrist. He and his new friends had to submit to temporary tattoos on their wrist or side of the neck before they could check out of King David Hotel, but there was no mention of converting to Allah or anyone else.

"He may be," Ben said, knowing little about the character mentioned four times in the Bible. "He has done some amazing stuff. Did you know he survived the nuclear attack in Paris?"

There was no sound, only static; and he knew he lost contact with his wife. He would try later. The sun was no one's friend on Earth anymore. It was noticeably brighter, obviously hotter and was throwing out solar storms like beads at Mardi Gras.

He went to the counter in his small hotel room and made a cup of coffee, picked up his notes on the Ben Scrolls and smiled. He liked the name, suggested by Will's wife. The Ben Scrolls.

Twenty minutes later, Ben poured his second cup of coffee, sat in the lone chair and continued his analysis of the little that had been translated; but his attention wandered back to the news at the mention of drone swarms. There had been warnings.

"… in Europe. Thirteen capitals were hit during the night. Brussels, Madrid and Lisbon suffered extensive damage; and an Israeli analyst claims the bombs were in the 100-kiloton range, six times more powerful than the bombs that destroyed Hiroshima and Nagasaki in 1945.

"Though no one seems to have witnessed any activity prior to the explosions in the capital cities, amateur astronomer Heather Decker

Cook says she witnessed a fleet of objects fly over about midnight and had this to say:

'I am visiting from America and was planning to sing *Amazing Grace* at a funeral tomorrow for a good friend who retired in Old Town. Guess I won't be doing that. Anyway, I was across the river about midnight, maybe a mile from Almada and set up my telescope to watch the newly-discovered comet that everyone is talking about. In the process, I scanned the sky with my binoculars and saw about twenty drones fly over. I think they were pretty small. Five minutes later the whole sky lit up. When my husband saw the shape of the fireball, he was certain it was nuclear. It was scary. But you know what was weird? We found all these small notes on the ground and rooftops, like the Israelis sometime drop from aircraft as a warning; and they all said the same: Remember the Inquisition.'

"Heather went on to state that her husband, a military journalist, said there was no way a few small drones could have caused the explosion in Lisbon and said it must be the Red Mercury threat.

"This is Alana Jammison with BBC World News Today. We will be right... Wait! This coming in from Reuters. There have been two earthquakes in America at Yellowstone National Park, a 7.6 followed by a 7.8. This can't be good. Back in three minutes."

Alana enjoyed her career as a journalist and investigative reporter. It was educational, her mother would always tell her; and that was an understatement. She quickly did a Yahoo search for red mercury, something that had alluded her. At least until a week earlier when she interviewed President Morsi, *off the record.*

Morsi was discussing the coming Ninth of Av dedication of the Third Temple in Jerusalem when he mentioned red mercury, claiming it was a myth. Completing her Yahoo search, she pulled a tissue from the Kleenex box and wiped her brow. Suddenly, it was warm. She hoped to God it was a myth but did not think so. How could so many capital cities be destroyed in a single night?

The phone rang but Ben could not find it. Frustrated, he searched frantically. He was certain it was Hillary. Finally, on the fifth ringtone, he found it in his shoe.

"Ben," Hillary said and sounded breathless. "I have been trying to call. Yellowstone is going to blow. Two earthquakes in the last hour, big earthquakes."

"Yeah, I just heard."

"I am coming there. If I can get out of here, that is. Who knows? Everything is a mess, airports are closing down and several planes have reportedly crashed from the ash. US Geological Survey says the eruption is small at this point but could blow at any moment."

Ben interrupted.

"Stop talking and get to Hartsfield-Jackson Airport."

He looked at his watch. If Yellowstone erupted, hundreds of square miles would be destroyed in the west; and the entire country would be ash-ridden and covered in darkness.

"There is a direct flight to Tel Aviv in four hours. Call this guy if you have any trouble. He may be able to help."

Ben gave The Admiral's phone number to Hillary.

"If you need to call him, let him know that I met his good friend Will in Jerusalem. He told me if I ever needed anything, The Admiral's wife is a very important lady. Maybe it is his girlfriend. Can't remember if Will said he was married, but I'm rambling. Go and call me from the plane."

"I love you, Benjamin."

The line went dead, and Ben found himself glued to the news and depressed. The news was like a never-ending, Shakespearean tragedy; only this was not a play. Maybe God's play. He said a silent prayer for Hillary's safety.

Chapter Twenty-Two

"*Don't Mess With Mama* just caught another one," The Admiral said, laughing. "We ought to go to Huntersville and visit them."

The Admiral and Shirley met Kenneth and Sonya Richardson one day on a research trip to Boone, North Carolina. The year was 2006, a cold winter morning; and breakfast was calling. They pulled into the small parking lot of Huntersville Family Café a few miles north of Charlotte at the invitation of a sign in the large, plate-glass window: two eggs, two bacon, two sausage, grits, toast and coffee for $4.99.

"Who did they catch?" Sheryl asked. "Wasn't their specialty tracking down sex traffickers?"

"Yeah, that used to be their niche but looks like they have expanded. This time they apprehended a terrorist group that was posing as Muslims, can you believe that? Now let me ask you, why would you disguise yourself as an Islamist if you are a terror organization?"

"Well, that is certainly different. Same militant group Jeff talks about all the time?" Sheryl asked.

"Nope. A new one. These Christian terror groups are blowing up mosques and synagogues, and they are popping up everywhere in Appalachia."

Sheryl nervously twisted the engagement ring, subconsciously wondering if today would be her wedding day. In some ways, with all that was happening in the world, the wedding seemed less important.

"Now this is interesting," The Admiral said as he continued to read. "In tracking down this militant group in mountainous North Carolina, they discovered a warehouse full of large, commercial drones and barrels of chemicals."

The Admiral picked up his phone.

"I am giving Kenneth and Sonya a call. Drones and drone swarms are coming up way too often."

Before he could key in the number for *Don't Mess With Mama Agency*, his phone sounded.

"Good morning, Jeff. What's up so early in the morning?"

"A lot," Jeff said. "Have you heard about Europe?"

"Nope. Haven't even cranked on the TV yet. Why?"

"Well, crank it up," Jeff said. "Europe is ablaze."

The Admiral grabbed the remote off the table and hit the on-button.

"I heard an interview with an amateur astronomer who was visiting Portugal. She claimed that right after midnight, Portugal-time, a fleet of fifteen to twenty drones flew over. A few minutes later, a large part of Lisbon was nuked."

Sheryl, eyes glued to the breaking news and mouth agape, watched in horror. Why hadn't she been called? Since the President's death, the government was in more disarray than normal disarray.

"… *amateur astronomer and American Idol winner, Heather Decker Cook. She was the only eyewitness so far who claims a swarm of small drones caused the terrific blast in Lisbon. Interestingly, thousands of dollar-sized leaflets have been found around Lisbon, and also Madrid, that state 'Remember the Inquisition.'*"

"So far," Jeff continued, "The death toll is estimated at nine million. They also found flyers all over the ground about the Inquisition."

"Hmmm. Wonder what that is about?"

"Well," Jeff said. "It would point the finger directly at Islam."

"Why is that?" The Admiral asked.

"About six-hundred years ago, the Iberian Peninsula, especially Spain, was religiously diverse. While the rest of Europe was purely

Christian, Spain was open to Jews and Muslims as well. Under the reign of Henry III, many Jews were forced to convert to Christianity or face persecution. By 1500, the Christian wrath turned to the Muslim population. Muslims received the same offer, convert or die; and by the time the Inquisition ended, more than 160,000 Jews and 300,000 Muslims had been expelled. Did you know all that?"

The Admiral listened to Jeff's history lesson and read the news scrolling beneath the photo of Heather, the amateur astronomer; and she was clearly stressed out.

"No," The Admiral said. "Sounds like Christianity in the 1500s was a lot like Islamism today. Thanks for the history lesson. Jeff, I don't mean to be rude; but I have to call a guy about just that, a drone swarm. I'll call you back. And don't forget the wedding. Berkeley Lake Chapel."

The line went dead, and two minutes later The Admiral was greeted by the receptionist at *Don't Mess With Mama.*

"Thank you for calling *Mama.* What's your pleasure?"

"Good morning. Could I speak with Kenneth or Sonya?"

"This is Sonya. What can I do for ya?"

The Admiral reintroduced himself and explained why he was calling.

"I remember you and Sheryl?" Sonya said excitedly. "Did you ever marry that girl?"

"Today's the day. You and Kenny should come and be our guests."

"Kenny's at Yellowstone. I was flying out today, we were taking a week off; but I have not heard from him since the two earthquakes hit yesterday. I'm not worried though," she lied. "Kenny is one tough man."

Sonya explained how she befriended a loner at church one day.

"Henry would always sit in the back pew and never talked with no one, so I befriended him. Over the next year, he began to open-up and kept talking about this Christian community in the Smoky Mountains. I acted friendly and Kenny took him fishin' a couple of times. Next thing ya know, Henry's done told Kenny about a plan to use drones to set off something called red mercury bombs."

Sonya paused and then asked, "Why the interest?"

"Did you hear about the European capitals?"

"Nope," Sonya answered. "Been here since early, early morning; and the power came back on about fifteen minutes ago. Why?"

The Admiral explained what he knew so far but did not mention the conversations between Jeff and Vinny. He was certain that Sonya would not approve, even with the news that Vinny had pointed Homeland Security, via Jeffrey Ross, to three other warehouses filled with drones. How many were there, he wondered?

"We believe the drones are being used as signal devices more than transportation. They may be used to transport small amounts of aerosols or chemicals, but the drones we have found so far can only carry a kilogram, about two pounds. Possibly this astronomer in Portugal is correct that drones initiated the red mercury nukes."

"Well, I got some news for ya, hon," Sonya interrupted. "The drones we discovered were commercial drones, like the drones Amazon and Walmart are using to deliver goods, some even bigger than that. These bad-boys could lift about fifty pounds. That's a lot of bomb."

Fifty pounds. The Admiral considered the damage from fifty pounds of anthrax.

"And there are those barrels of deadly chemicals, from sarin poison to fluoroantimonic acid."

"Wait," The Admiral said. "What kind of acid?"

"Yeah," Sonya laughed. "I hadn't heard of it either. Fluoroantimonic acid. $HSbF_6$. It's a superacid; and if you spilled a drop on your arm, it'd burn right through and not stop until it got to Hong Kong, China."

"Tell me about it," The Admiral said and turned to Sheryl.

"Ever heard of fluoroantimonic acid, Sheryl?"

She shook her head *no* and shushed him, trying to focus on the reports out of London. Buckingham Palace was no more.

"She hasn't heard of it either."

"Wow," he said. "They blew up Buckingham Palace."

"What?" Sonya said in shock.

"Yeah, the news is just coming out." He hit the record button. "Tell me about this acid."

Sonya tried to overcome the news about the Queen of England's house and hoped they weren't home at the time.

"This is the strongest acid in the world. It cannot be stored in glass containers, because it dissolves the glass. The containers we found were coated with a half-inch of Teflon. Not sure why Teflon is resistant. I am not a chemist by a long shot.

"If fluoroantimonic acid ever hits water, it causes a heck of an explosion. Then the reaction with the water causes a toxic gas, hydrogen fluoride. If you get exposed to enough, you can kiss your eyes and lungs goodbye, and maybe your butt too.

"Now get this. Any acid stronger than a hundred percent sulfuric acid is considered a superacid. Fluoroantimonic acid is twenty-quintillion times stronger than sulfuric acid. A quintillion has eighteen zeros."

The Admiral's mind ran at high-speed, considering the damage fifty pounds of the acid could cause, especially if aerosolized. Might be worse than anthrax.

"And here's something else you might find interesting, Admiral. This Christian militant group with no name burned that historic church in Nashville last week and left two Korans. Everyone thought it was Muslims. Hold on. Let me check this text."

The line became silent with a dose of static, now the norm with all the solar activity.

"Sheryl, what are they saying about London?"

Sheryl turned to face him and tears streamed down her red cheeks.

"The entire Royal Family was at the palace, Justin," and she broke down in sobs.

"Admiral, I gotta go. Kenny's in the hospital. A new geyser opened, and Kenny was standing too close. Apparently, many new geysers are appearing at Yellowstone; but Kenny was forty-seven miles from Steamboat Springs. He has been severely scalded."

The line went dead.

Chapter Twenty-Three

But the day of the Lord will come like a thief. The heavens will disappear with a roar; the elements will be destroyed by fire, and the earth and everything done in it will be laid bare.

2 Peter 3:10

Baikonur Cosmodrome
Kazakhstan

L ittle Nikita, short and plump, was named after his great-Grandfather Nikita Khrushchev. Dressed in Coca-Cola red boxer shorts with a hammer and sickle embroidered on the side, he sipped a glass of warm bourbon like he did every morning when he woke up and ran his crippled hand through his shaggy blond hair. Thirty minutes 'til showtime.

Little Nikita was even more ruthless than his namesake. While his great grandpa threatened to overthrow the United States from within, Little Nikita made no threats. In all appearances, one would think that Little Nikita and the United States president were best friends forever. Only it was all for show. No matter now. The U.S. president was dead. He wondered if the Japanese group had anything to do with the crash and figured they surely did.

This would be the third meeting between Little Nikita of the Russian Federation and Chairman Tseng of China. They were in agreement for the most part, though Little Nikita wanted to attack right after the Ross Ice Shelf collapse. The U.S. Navy lost seventy percent of their strategic assets in that natural disaster, and he felt that the time was right. Twenty minutes later, precisely at 7:00AM, the two leaders met again.

The early morning temperature at Baikonur averaged a comfortable 68° until the past five years. Today it was already approaching the century mark. The air conditioning was running wide-open.

The men met at the Cosmodrome because security was tight, and the discussions were beyond top secret. There were no generals or commanders present, and their conversation was camouflaged by white-noise generators. No one would be able to record their voices.

The Cosmodrome was the world's oldest and largest space-launch complex. Leased to Russia by Kazakhstan, the facility was originally built by the Soviet Union in the 1950s. Sputnik 1, the world's first artificial satellite, was launched from the base as was the first manned space flight.

After a few minutes of niceties and a cup of tea, the meeting began.

"The timing could not be more perfect, Chairman Tseng. I am most happy we waited."

"Yes, Nikita; but not today my friend. The western United States will be useless if this Yellowstone Volcano erupts. Right now, we only have earthquake activity."

Little Nikita contemplated before speaking. Tseng made a good point, but how long would this wait be? He was not a patient man. Besides, any place they hit would be useless for many years to come. Even the food sources would be irradiated.

"When?"

"The woman in Arizona, the volcanologist," Tseng continued, "I think her name is Lynn Tomay, told OLNN that there was a fifty-fifty chance of a major eruption within thirty days.

"The Steamboat Geyser is the largest in the world. In the past, it erupted every decade or so and would shoot steam three-hundred feet high. Then it would stop for another decade. Now it is erupting daily.

"Last week an eruption shot steam twenty-five hundred feet into the air. Something big is about to happen. This is the largest super-volcano in the world. We may not even have to attack. Let's wait two months. If it has not erupted, we nuke every major city. Does not matter about the radiation, my friend. We do not need the United States or Canada. Mexico and South America, we will conquer."

Little Nikita wiped his forehead on the sleeve of his camouflage uniform. The A/C could not keep up. Reluctantly, he once again agreed for a delay.

"What will happen if Yellowstone has a major eruption?"

"According to the volcanologist, it is long overdue; and everything within a five-hundred-mile radius will be covered in ash. Death to millions of people and tens of millions of plants and animals," Tseng smirked. "For the world, it will be cooler. That is a good thing."

The pause was conspicuous as each man pondered the significance of the damage to the United States and Canada. Canada had many natural resources, especially oil.

"I want to nuke some cities," Little Nikiti said with a loud laugh, and the two world leaders fist-bumped.

"We will my friend, we will. Most of the remaining U.S. military forces are dispersed around the Middle East. Ninety percent of her remaining ships are in the Mediterranean, including the last aircraft carrier group. St. Mary's Submarine Base is nowhere to be found after the La Palma wave. The timing could not be more perfect."

That would be the first target, Nikita thought. Sinking the last U.S. carrier group would be noteworthy. Soon they might rule the world if they can kill Morsi. He seemed un-killable, like those two preachers in Israel. But then, even they were killed.

"How many ships do our forces have in the Mediterranean?" Chairman Tseng asked. "China has four in the Eastern Mediterranean and one in the western part. Three more should reach the Suez Canal today."

Tseng checked the time.

"Actually, they should be crossing the canal at this moment."

"We had two spy frigates in the Mediterranean, but I have withdrawn them. It would be prudent to keep your ships far away from the U.S. carrier group, if you understand my meaning."

Chairman Tseng understood Little Nikita's meaning and was amused at his hatred for America.

"Then we agree on the targets?"

"We agree on the targets, Chairman Tseng, but not the order of execution. I want to prioritize the carrier fleet. We sink that fleet, and the United States Navy, for the most part, will be at the bottom of the once deep-blue sea. It will also send a message to the remaining ships to get out. Then we can sail in via the Suez Canal and bring troops in from the north, across the Tigris and Euphrates rivers. We will control the world's oil."

Chairman Tseng endorsed the plan thoroughly, though there were some questions still. Russia and old Soviet Union could man a five-million-man invasion force. China could add another twelve-million.

"What about NORAD?" Chairman Tseng asked.

The North American Aerospace Defense Command was a joint venture between Canada and the United States. Conspiracy theorists claimed for years that it was closed, but then last year there had been the semi-space war that most knew nothing about. Thirty-seven communication satellites had been deactivated in a millisecond.

"NORAD is located deep inside Cheyenne Mountain in Colorado," Chairman Tseng continued. "The main entry is a 25-ton set of mega-doors designed to withstand a nuclear detonation. It is a self-contained facility, Nikita. Once those doors shut, they can exist a long time. There are five lakes inside. One is diesel fuel in case of door closure, and the others are water for industry and personal use. Every building is supported with huge springs so they will bounce as necessary."

Little Nikita paused, listening and thinking.

"Have you ever seen what a 150-megaton bomb can do to a person, Chairman Tseng?"

"No, I have not," he admitted.

Nikita paused again, seizing the moment.

"Carpe momento," he laughed like a jolly, old man and bumped fists again with Chairman Tseng. "Neither has anyone else."

Little Nikita began to explain the devastating effects of the 50-megaton Tsar Bomba that was tested over the peninsula.

"It was to be twice as big, but concerns about the military's safety arose. No one knew what could happen in the atmosphere. Some scientists said it would set the entire atmosphere on fire. In retrospect, that may be true," and Little Nikita pondered the possibility if an atmospheric fire could explode above Colorado and spread all the way to Russia.

"There is one thing certain, Chairman Tseng."

"What is certain, my friend?"

"Any person within seventy-five miles and not underground will be melted, if not evaporated. Above the Arctic peninsula where Tsar Bomba was tested, there had been lots of trees and brush. Much growth and large rocks and boulders. After the bomb, across the entire peninsula, there was not a plant or rock. The ground was smooth as a baby's behind, my friend. Every rock had melted.

"There is a verse in the Christian Bible about that, that even the elements of Earth would melt. It was a hot bomb, my friend."

The two men laughed again, and Nikita motioned the security camera. Within thirty seconds, a Japanese waitress dressed in black and white short-shorts, silver silk blouse and silver high-heels, strode to the table.

"Cognac for you, kind sir?"

"Yes, thank you," Chairman Tseng said, moved by the beauty of the young girl.

Chairman Tseng and Little Nikita sniffed the cognac like cognac drinkers do, and Chairman Tseng immediately recognized the pre-hand-warmed and very rare brand.

"Here's to the poor people," Little Nikita said, chuckling; and the two men slowly sipped the $15,800 *Hardy L'Été* cognac from the Four Seasons Collection.

"So this Tsar Bomba III or whatever can melt the mountain, my friend?"

"They will be delivered in triplicate, Chairman Tseng. We have five, and we have twelve capable delivery systems. Two will be used on NORAD and one at Warner Robins' Little White House."

"Every missile is the 10-headed MIRV system. Independently guided warheads will reenter the atmosphere, and several will make it. Our stealth technology has well surpassed the technology of the Islamic States of America," Little Nikita smirked. "We will hit them simultaneously, NORAD and the carrier group."

Chairman Tseng nodded in agreement. Little Nikita seemed to be the man with the plan, but too much hatred skewed a man's perception.

"Do you know who was in power in Russia when the Tsar Bomba exploded?"

"Of course. Your grandfather."

"Great grandfather, Mr. Chairman. In 1961 over the Novaya Zemlya archipelago in the Arctic Ocean, the largest nuclear weapon ever exploded to that day and ever since, blew up two-and-a-half miles above the islands. Windows were blown out in Norway, and the flash of light was seen six-hundred miles away, my friend," Little Nikita laughed.

"Animals sixty miles from the blast, burned to death, incinerated in a flash like this rapture the idiots keep mentioning," he continued. "The bomb was never used because it weighed too much, fifty-thousand pounds; but we continued work. We have one-hundred-fifty megaton weapons; and with the help of an element called red mercury, the bomb only weighs five-thousand pounds, less than the bombs that killed all the Japs in 1945."

Chairman Tseng laughed.

"I do not think the term 'Japs' is politically correct, Mr. President."

"Even to this day, Chairman Tseng, a larger nuclear weapon has never been detonated," Little Nikita said, making a point that he hoped Chairman Tseng would understand. No one had a bigger bomb.

Chairman Tseng smiled and held up his glass of cognac in a toast. Thirty minutes later, the meeting was over. It was time to exchange gifts.

Chairman Minsheng Tseng handed Little Nikita a small box with a standard LED lamp, a piddly gesture compared to the crystal set of Chinese artifacts presented by the Khrushchev regime.

"As you know Little Nikita, China is the largest provider of LED lighting technology in the world. Our goal is to decrease the world's electrical usage through the use of these magnificent lamps. Global warming is out of control," he continued, wiping perspiration from his head, "as you well know; and we can help.

"I present this lamp to you, my good friend; and we will offer a complete lighting conversion for the Kremlin... and of course, your friends. Through a gesture of good will, we are offering our LED technology to the world at ridiculously cheap pricing. We want the whole world to go green."

Little Nikita examined the lamp and focused on the tiny, individual LED diodes.

"Do not look directly in the light when they are on, or you will temporarily lose your sight. These are very bright."

"Do you know how large our Kremlin is; it would be quite a job."

"My friend, you will not believe the difference. We give you the lamps, and you have them installed. Your first shipment will be sent as soon as you can send the specifications on what you are presently using."

The men shook hands and parted ways with big, comradish bear-hugs. Chairman Tseng fully understood the bomb message.

✡ ✡ ✡

"How did it go, Minsheng?"

Chairman Tseng took a seat in the soft leather chair, in the president's office at Ningbo Limited Lighting in Guangdong. Though still early morning, the temperatures along the shores of the South China Sea approached a hundred.

Guangdong, the most populous province of China, had seventy-five million citizens and forty-million migrants. With a Gross Domestic Product that approached the whole of Mexico, Guangdong contributed twelve percent of the total Chinese economy. A lot of it came from the production and sale of highly sophisticated LED lamps and private detection electronics systems.

On the horizon, large, dark thunderheads appeared.

"It is early for thunderstorms, Bingwen."

Bingwen knew more about LED lighting than anyone in China and possibly the world. The only thing he knew more about was stealth detection devices.

"It has become normal, I think," Bingwen replied. "Last week we had a waterspout that took out several miles of Guangzhou Harbor. It was the widest waterspout in history."

"How was your trip to see Little Nikita?"

Bingwen had a great resentment for Little Nikita, and it had stirred in his gut for many years. He was a happy man to be in on the destruction of Russia and the United States; and particularly, Little Butthead.

"It was good," Chairman Tseng said. "He had his agents check the lamp for explosives and install it in a laboratory. They gave it an A-OK, though they will carefully check every lamp and fixture. Are we certain that nothing is detectable? Little Nikita wishes to help the environment," he smirked. "When can you have the first shipment ready?"

"What are we shipping?"

Chairman Tseng and his grandson went over the list of product. Bingwen was the developer of an LED diode that doubled as a camera with recording device, but only a few in China had that knowledge. Of the few, Bingwen doubted that any would be spared in the end; but the murders would appear to be accidental.

This would be too easy, Bingwen assessed silently; and he was overjoyed. All the systems China donated to the new White House at Warner Robins Air Force Base were working perfectly. Not a single office or home on the base was spared as LED lamps whirred away, providing lighting and great subterfuge.

The microscopic LED nanocameras fit in the Light Emitting Diodes with room to spare; and when not in use, they would act as the power-indicator light for the fixtures. The faint red glow would not affect the operation, and all recordings were boosted through the WiFi system of the targeted facility.

"Ten containers of flood lights and interior light fixtures to start. All the fixtures for the Kremlin should have the gas dispersant option like used at Warner Robins."

Bingwen was especially pleased with his gas dispersal option and his ability to hide detection of the dangerous VX agent. Weaponized LED lighting, able to kill in an instant, monitored activity and conversations all over the globe, at least any countries that were deemed a threat. A simple indoor lamp could disperse a half-ounce of VX gas or fentanyl aerosol. Outdoors was a little different because of the wind; but as listening devices, outdoor lighting was everywhere.

"I hate Little Nikita. His grandfather caused great pain for our family. I have a special fixture for him."

Chairman Tseng learned nothing new from Bingwen's comments. His feelings were well known. The Soviet-Sino split in the late fifties and the Chinese war with India resulted in the loss of Bingwen's twin brother and great humiliation. He held out a photo of a statue of Little Nikita and his dog, a Russian Wolfhound. Tiny points of light framed the statue and at the bottom, an LED banner: Death to America.

"This is a bomb?" he asked, looking at the sculpture.

"Yep. Perfected by the North Koreans," Bingwen replied. "It will be activated remotely when it is delivered. On July 30, bomb go boom."

The two men laughed, but Chairman Tseng remained troubled. If Little Nikita was not killed, his anger would be deadly; and the results could be mass destruction. Nonetheless, it would work and within a year, China would be able to monitor the entire globe via LED lights. Who would have ever thought?

"Make sure it works, Bingwen. For your brother."

Chapter Twenty-Four

"**W**e need to get these people evacuated. ASAP!" Lynn screamed over the sound of the newly erupting fissure that appeared out of nowhere. "We're sixty miles from Yellowstone, for Pete's sake."

Jackie knew for sure that Lynn was right. The volcano was going to blow; and if fissures were opening this far away from ground-zero, it could not be good. Her husband, Moose, had been taken by the Good Lord one Saturday when a sinkhole opened beneath their house. The house disappeared in a flash, and Moose's body was never found. The entire bedroom was never found.

"I know that's right," she yelled back. The ground temperature was increasing, and her ankles began to sweat profusely. "Have you noticed all the bugs are gone?"

The previous night was ridden with bugs. Flies, beetles, ants, even frogs had invaded the land. Jackie thought it was a scene right out of Cecil B. DeMille's *The Ten Commandments*.

"They're evacuating," Lynn screamed.

The noise was deafening as steam shot from the fissure. Lava could not be far behind, and the sudden fear of having their skin scalded from their bones became reality.

"Did you see that?"

Yes, Lynn had seen. Two antelopes running across the flat fields collapsed to the ground as the boiling water from the fissures fell back to earth, cooked in an instant.

"Let's knock on some doors," Jackie yelled, and they drove the Jeep Ranger into the trailer park, blowing the horn as they drove.

Jackie Poolton and her deceased husband, Moose, moved to the Yellowstone area two decades earlier, trying to escape complexity and the urbanization monster. Yellowstone had been rockin' and rollin' a lot the past year. Antelope and Elk died in their tracks from carbon dioxide gas emanating from new fissures that seemed to appear daily. And the sinkholes.

Jackie felt guilty thanking God that she wasn't at home the night the house fell into the hole… because Moose disappeared in an instant. He was a good and wholesome man, and Jackie briefly wondered if that might have been Moose's rapture. At least he would not have to endure what seemed to be coming on the planet.

Lynn Tomay and Jackie met by accident a couple of years earlier when Yellowstone experienced multiple earthquakes in a thirty-day period. Lynn was an earthquake and volcano guru, and Jackie's respect for her only grew more with each encounter.

"Try to watch for upswelling," Lynn shouted as she drove, and the road became bumpier as the ground shook.

Lynn had conducted lectures in the area, warning people about Yellowstone; but the more the ground shook, the more tourists came. Lynn was certain that most folk did not understand that volcanos like Yellowstone did not look like volcanos. There was no high, conical-shaped mountain with smoke and lava spouting out the top of a quarter-mile wide crater.

Yellowstone's crater was flat and uninhabited for the most part. Over the years, independent farmers and pot growers camped in the 45-mile-wide caldera where rich, volcanic soil contributed to super growth.

The second pass through Caldera Springs Campground and Park saw some people stirring and walking around in the small, bleak front yards.

Lynn stopped the Jeep by a group of curious bystanders and exited.

"You have to evacuate! Now!" She shouted. "The volcano could blow any moment!"

"Yeah," an old hippie-looking man yelled back, oblivious to the increasing sound. "We been hearing that fer years. I ain't going nowhere."

And so it went. Lynn and Jackie went from campground to campground, many of which had become permanent residences after the National Park Service budget cuts, and warned as many as possible. Some listened and adhered to the advice; but most, like Old Hippie Man, decided to test the Almighty.

"Slow down, Lynn!" Jackie shouted.

Campground Road was always bumpy, but the earthquake activity had caused small ripples in the asphalt. The smell of sulfur was heavy in the air, and their eyes screamed out for more tears to quell the itching. The occasional stench of dead elk permeated the sulfurous smell, and Jackie would gag each time.

"Nothing smells worse than rotting animals," Lynn said. "Just trying to get out of here before the ground gives way. Like that over there." Lynn nodded to the east.

Jackie quickly turned to look and saw a complete forest of tall pines disappear into the ground.

"That can happen anywhere."

"Go. GO!" Jackie shouted, and the Jeep zoomed at thirty miles-per-hour down the bumpy but paved trail.

"I'm burning up!" Jackie yelled, and the sound of crunching ground was deafening. Thirty yards off the trail a large section of land swelled into a small hill, then collapsed.

"It's the ground temperature," Lynn said. "Magma is getting closer to the surface. Help me look for melting asphalt."

Lynn had lectured about global warming and the effect of ground temperature. Some places in the world, like Yellowstone and the Dead Sea, had abnormally high temperatures because of deep geological activity. The past two years, the temperatures had been elevating at a slow-but-steady rate. Undersea geological shenanigans, according to Lynn, were the cause of elevated ocean temperatures. The hotter things became, the more violent the weather. Like the record-setting tornado that hit Greece and Turkey.

"When do you think it will blow, Lynn? I mean, like a week, a month?"

"Probably July 30," Lynn said nonchalantly. Her year had flown by.

The quick answer took Jackie by surprise, because Lynn seemed to be non-committal on possibilities.

"Why do you say that?"

"Because July 30 is the ninth of Av on the Jewish calendar. It is also the day that the Jewish temple will be dedicated in Jerusalem. The Jews have a history of bad experiences on the ninth of Av. I think this year the whole world will have a bad experience. Just a hunch."

"I've heard nothing on the news about this," Jackie said.

"Yes, the 'news.' The news is talking about important stuff, like how cool the new pedophilia laws are."

Jackie guessed that was probably right. Europe decriminalized *youth love laws* a long time ago, and America's desire to be all-things-Europe was an insatiating hunger. Washington fought the Revolutionary War so not to be Europe, but what did the Founders know?

"Or the T-shirt the new First Lady wore to Texas," Jackie added with a laugh. That was the moment their lives changed drastically.

"Whoa," Lynn screamed. "Did you feel that?"

"Yeah. Felt like we were sliding."

Lynn's premonition was evident. The road was melting. Then the tires would blow.

"We have to get to a dirt trail. The road is melting."

Lynn did not expound. Both women knew now that they would likely not make it through this morning alive. Before Lynn could make it off the paved road, the earth opened.

The Jeep bounced violently, avoiding the fissure, and slid into a ravine where the SUV became lodged on the side of the hill between two scrub bushes.

Noting the precariousness of the situation, Lynn and Jackie exited the Jeep cautiously, hoping to avoid a fall to the bottom. Jackie held her cell phone tightly. They would need it, and she silently prayed for a signal. Then came a sound from behind.

"Thank ya Lord Jesus. Ya done sent me two angels."

Chapter Twenty-Five

God moves in a mysterious way
His wonders to perform;
He plants His footsteps in the sea
And rides upon the storm.

Deep in unfathomable mines
Of never failing skill
He treasures up His bright designs
And works His sov'reign will.

William Cowper, 1774

Jeff walked into *The Divide* to catch the latest news, and he was not disappointed. An unusually raucous crowd livened up the upper level, toasting Mexico in the World Cup.

He took a seat at the bar, and Abe the Bartender sat a glass of iced tea with lime on the counter.

"When did you start showing sports?"

"We've had a couple of complaints; but since the World Cup is coming to Atlanta, Pam wanted to make an exception. Some pre-promotion."

Pre-promotion. Jeff thought about that, a little perplexed. It was interesting how life somehow goes on, even when we know the end is right around the corner.

"I suppose it depends on how far away the corner is," Jeff said.

"Say what?"

"Oh, never-mind. I was daydreaming. Abe," Jeff continued. "You know it's the end. I know it's the end. Yet, we keep making plans for the future, as though it's really not going to happen."

A roar and laughter exploded from the soccer level, and a cry for margaritas caught the waitress' ear. Lana headed to the table. She worried a little about the world events, especially the weather; but she was too young to fully understand what was coming. She was sure of one thing: The soccer fans were oblivious to what God was planning. Most were.

"I mean, how hard and how long did it have to rain before the people figured out that Noah really wasn't crazy as a loon."

"Loons are not crazy, Mr. Ross."

Condi Zimmerman pulled out a stool and took a seat.

"Coffee for me, Mr. Handsome," she said, smiling at Abe.

How in the world did I win this woman's affection? Abe considered the fact and hoped his *issues* were in the past and laid to rest. His mom had tried her best, maybe; but she had programmed him to always have doubts about romantic love, and about himself.

"The world does not like the Jew, Abe. Do not ever forget that. And in the end, the whole world will turn against us." She said that often when he was a child, but he had not seen it personally.

He and Condi would be married this day, an unusually cool day for July; but there would be no family planning going on. Who would want to bring children into this mess?

"Have you talked with Sheryl?" Abe asked, and Condi shook her head in the negative.

"What were ya'll talking about?"

"The signs of the times," Jeff said. "My mother used to tell me about them, but I thought she had lost it. One has to ask oneself, 'How many signs do we have to see before figuring out they are signs?' How many hailstorms, how many eruptions, how many earthquakes, how many new diseases…"

"How many new TV shows promoting pedophilia?" Condi chipped in.

Condi learned much from her report on the *Push for Pedophilia*, or the youth-love movement. It was disgusting enough on its own merits, but the surprise was the people pushing the sickness.

The movement grew out of Europe as Islam overtook the once Christian land. Condi read the Quran, had just finished as a matter-of-fact, and did not recall the endorsement of old men and young boys; but it must be there somewhere. There were the *Dancing Boys of Afghanistan*, performers in dance, song and male-on-male sex. American soldiers had been prosecuted or given Dishonorable Discharges for preventing rendezvous between Afghan soldiers and the young boys. It was their *culture*, therefore their *right*.

"Exactly," Jeff said, glancing at the news special on the large screen over the bar, something about the fires in Asia, caused by the small but extraordinarily violent, nuclear skirmishes. There were plenty of internet video footages of folk running, burning incessantly as they tried to escape.

"That will be here soon," Jeff said, nodding at the screen. "These weapons used by Pakistan, India and North Korea are more devastating than the people realized; and the cities nuked will be uninhabitable for many years to come, maybe forever.

The News Special showed satellite photography of Europe and Western Asia at night. Much of the world was in darkness, mainly due to power failures; but parts were aflame. Large parts.

Greece, Spain, Portugal, France, England and Finland seemed to have been hit the hardest, and bright, orange patches glared from the screen.

A sudden crash and laughter erupted from the upper level as a score tied the international soccer match. A wave of vulgarities flowed through *The Divide Disco & Café* like Abe the Bartender had never heard since it opened. Abe through the bar towel on the counter and headed upstairs.

"Leave it alone, Abe," Jeff advised. "It's not worth it."

The crowds had become more-and-more raucous and vulgar since so many believers had disappeared Abe noted many times. Each day seemed to be more vulgar, and debauchery was the word of the day.

"Abe, please," Condi said.

"It is my job," Abe said and walked from the bar to the steps.

Fight-or-flight was an interesting human phenom, and the hair on the back of Jeff's neck stood at attention. He had not worn his fighting shoes but would make do as best he could, considering his senior-citizenship.

"… to Yellowstone where two researchers have been found alive in a deep ravine. Lynn Tomay and Jacqueline Poolton have been hospitalized for observation, as they survived the fall with few injuries. In the process, they discovered a man who had been missing for two days. He was hanging on for dear life," the commentator continued.

Abe walked up the steps, cautious as he went. The soccer fans were not Hispanic for the most part, which was interesting. Soccer had taken over the country, and young millennials had turned into the new hooligans. Another crash, and a large TV screen fell to the floor. The young group broke out in laughter and cheers.

"Tomay is a volcanologist and earthquake specialist. She insisted that they be flown to Atlanta for hospitalization. Said she wants to be far away from Yellowstone; and get this Dr. Schneider, the commentator said to her guest. *Ms. Tomay said it may not be possible to get far enough away, at least in this hemisphere."*

Abe took the remote from his pocket and tried to shout over the rambunctious crowd, as The Admiral walked in the front door. No one noticed him as he made his way toward Jeff and Condi. He was *sans* Sheryl, because the groom-to-be dare not see his bride on the wedding day. He stood silently by Condi as their focus was on something upstairs.

"What did Ms. Tomay mean by that comment, Dr. Schneider?"

Dr. Chrissy Schneider surprised her family when the thirty-something woman decided on a science career. She was majoring in English Lit at an Ivy League school when she tired of the elitist attitude and transferred to Georgia Tech, not knowing that scientists were also elitists, at least, many.

Chrissy enrolled in the School of Nuclear Nanotechnology, the study of nuclear-powered, miniature drones that could fly aloft for days at a time, filming and spying as necessary. However, her hobbies included anything volcanic or connected with sinkholes which were swallowing large parts of the world's landscape.

"I am not sure what Dr. Tomay meant," Chrissy said. *"But I would heed any advice she might give. If Yellowstone should erupt… I mean majorly erupt like it did six-hundred-thousand years ago, there could be complete and utter darkness in the Midwest. It is possible that an ashfall of four meters or more would cover everything within a one-hundred-mile radius. That is about twelve feet deep.*

"Air travel would cease in much of the world as ash is distributed throughout the atmosphere, possibly at altitudes of twenty-plus miles. The volcanic ash contains small particles that grind aircraft engines to a halt."

"What kind of effect would it have on the world's weather?" the host asked.

Abe tried, to no effect, to get the attention of the youthful but destructive crowd; and he fell to the floor, following a punch from nowhere. The Admiral saw the punch, ran toward the set of five steps, and Jeff followed closely behind.

"Most plants will die because the sulfur dioxide ejected from Yellowstone will remain suspended in the atmosphere for years. Sulfur dioxide reflects sunlight, so the heat spell will end and a possible ice age could begin.

"Additionally, there are some volcanologists who theorize that an eruption of Yellowstone's supervolcano may initiate eruptions of the earth's other supervolcanoes. There are several that we know of, and some we do not."

A shot rang out from the soccer crowd, and the crowd scattered. Jeffrey Ross collapsed to the floor, and blood permeated the front of his blue and white seersucker shirt. He would not be attending a double-wedding ceremony this day.

Chapter Twenty-Six

God, give us grace to accept with serenity the things that cannot be changed, courage to change the things which should be changed, and the wisdom to distinguish the one from the other.

The Serenity Prayer
Reinhold Niebuhr
(1892–1971)

Abe the Bartender, mood now one of melancholy and despair, cried over his good friend, sometimes sobbing in the tranquility of his abode in Jeff's basement. It was safe-and-sound, just steps from the safe-room; but he felt anything but safe. He put on his shoes, grabbed his keys and headed to Duluth Medical where he would meet the gang of extremely close friends.

The perp with the 9-millimeter, concealed weapon was quickly arrested by Duluth's Finest as he fled down Buford Highway; and it would have been better for him if he had not jumped from the car to run. Outrunning the K-9 Police was unlikely, and the young man in the black T-shirt screamed in pain and fear as he lay on the hot pavement. Abe answered his phone, and Condi explained that Jeff was in Intensive Care but was alive.

"Did you talk to him?" Abe asked.

"No," Condi said. "But the doctor came out and told me that Jeff wants us to go ahead with the wedding and take lots of pictures."

Jeff lay in ICU, believing fully that it was the coldest hospital room in history. He felt the small wound in his chest with his finger, contemplating the chain of events leading up to the shooting, and the miraculous outcome. No visits to Kipper T and Missy T this time, so he figured he missed the near-death experience. Dr.

Harrison walked into his small room and pulled the privacy curtain fully open.

"Am I going to make it, Doc?" Jeff asked.

"Jeffry Ross. You are the luckiest human being I have ever met. I hope you go to church today and thank Jesus for saving your life. And this," she included, holding up the small pocket-sized New Testament. "There is no possible way this skinny Bible could stop a 9-millimeter round."

"Maybe it was the seersucker shirt," he said laughing.

"I wouldn't make light of the matter, Jeff. You are fortunate to be here. The bullet penetrated your skin enough to pop a few blood vessels. You will have a small depression in your chest, maybe a bruise; but that's it. All your bloodwork is good. Blood pressure is good. Great shape to be such a really old man, know what I mean?"

"Thanks a lot, Nancy. You know how to make a near-critically wounded man feel all sunny inside."

"You are welcome, Jeffrey. I don't see any reason to keep you here. Plus, the air conditioning is having problems. Put this on your 'critical wound' to prevent infection," she repeated.

Jeff looked at the small tube of ointment, admiring the red, white and blue color scheme.

"Very patriotic for the 4th of July," Jeff laughed. "J-Kinsella Vaccine Antibiotic Ointment 5%; never heard of it."

"Something you never heard of," the doctor said sarcastically, "is hard to believe."

"You are correct, Miss Politeness; and now I do remember. Kinsella is that guy in South Carolina who owned the crop duster that flew through the stadium."

"That's the one. He was one of the first people raptured, is that what they call it?"

"Yep, that's what they call it."

"Looks like you didn't make it," Doc Harrison said, winking. "You were a bad boy when you were younger. I remember."

"My work's not done, Doc. That's all," Jeff said, hoping that was the case.

Duluth, Georgia, like many small Southern towns, had renovated the town square, installed antique-looking decorative street lamps and adorned the ornamental trees and crepe myrtles with tiny, twinkly-white LED Christmas lights. The air was cosmopolitan, but the culture was still Bible-Belt all the way. A lot of what he considered true Christians were still here; and a few he considered far from Christian, had disappeared. It was like the *Twilight Zone*.

"You can go to The Admiral's wedding today. I see no reason why not. Don't forget the ointment. It is a wonder-drug. Your first application was this morning, and the wound will be totally healed in twenty-four hours if you follow directions."

"Doc?" Jeff asked. "Why did such a superficial injury knock me out? I remember nothing."

"Probably fear of death. We all have it when push-comes-to-shove. And the injury was not nonexistent. You had about a half-inch deep wound. Very lucky… or something."

Jeff gathered his bloody, seersucker shirt and Bible with a hole in it, walked down the hall on his own, down the elevator and into the lobby. His clique of friends waited anxiously and were shocked to see him walking. They had been under the impression he was almost dead. Jeff put the small Bible in his pants pocket, not mentioning the miracle.

"Dead man walking," were the first words from The Admiral's mouth, and Jeff smiled. He was very happy not to be dead.

"Where'd you get the black eye," Jeff asked.

He seemed to have some memory of The Admiral being punched or hit with something, and Jeff again considered the possibility that his life was running backwards, that his dreams were real and his reality was a dream.

"Sheryl smacked me," The Admiral said, and Sheryl reacted with a jab in the ribs.

"When you were shot, Sheryl said I would do anything to get out of the wedding and socked me right in the eye."

The small group laughed, and many said a silent prayer of thanks. They exited, started toward the steamy-hot parking lot, then turned around and scurried back under the Medical Center's entry awning.

"Wow," Jeff said and began to feel a little woozy. "Seems a lot hotter for some reason."

"Can we pray?" Condi asked quietly, glancing around the facility with unease. "What happened today is a miracle. Jeffrey was shot directly in the heart three hours ago, and he is walking around as if nothing happened."

Praying in public was a prohibited activity; and though the Duluth Police Department did not agree, it was now the law. They were required to enforce the newly-passed law. Congress had acted quickly on this one, and Jeff felt somewhat amused. Six years earlier, he would have been screaming about the separation of church and state clause. He would have applauded the congressional law. But now... what a great turn in his life's direction. He momentarily wished once again that he had come to belief when Melissa was alive. *God, give us grace to accept with serenity the things that cannot be changed*, Jeff mumbled quietly to no one but himself.

"Did you say something?" Samarra asked, squeezing Jeff's hand.

"No, no. Just mumbling."

The small group of friends stood in a circle, held hands and Condi began to pray.

"Our Father who art in Heaven, please continue to protect us from harm in a world gone wild. We know what is happening because of Your blessed prophets, the bearers of future news, both bad and good. Thank you for protecting Jeff and The Admiral today, and we say this prayer in the name of Jesus, your one and only Son. Amen."

Across Howell Ferry Road, a lady in a navy blue dress and a yellow scarf looked out of place. It had to be the north side of one-hundred degrees, and she had on a white sweater.

Samarra noticed the woman, and her heart skipped a couple of beats. That was Miss Bodkin, the Town Busybody.

"I would suggest we split up and meet at our house in an hour," Samarra said. "Miss Bodkin is probably talking to the police right now. She is such a nosy… well, I won't say it, but you know."

Miss Bodkin was new to Duluth; and where there was trouble or conflict, Miss Bodkin always showed up. It was uncanny. Always stirring up trouble. She especially despised *church* people.

"Remember during the last power outage, the one that lasted about forty days?" Sheryl asked. "Miss Nosey turned in Old Lady Bivins for running her generator during the wrong hours."

The policeman showed up, the new cop from Charleston, and told her that Mrs. Bivins had a permit because of her ventilator.

"You got a problem with this lady breathing?" Gus Longo had asked the cranky woman.

Gus was known in the police community as a good guy, poised and calm, not easily excitable; but since the Charleston earthquake and floods, his mood had become more dismal, and curt. He was glad to get the job with the new Duluth-Suwanee Combined Police Services, but Miss Bodkin would get on Jesus' nerves, he was certain.

"Don't you have something to do besides mind everyone's business?" he asked, knowing a reprimand would be coming from the Chief.

"We need to get the heck out of here," Condi emphasized, watching Miss Bodkin's frustration. Apparently she was having phone issues, and perhaps that was a small miracle. They seemed to be happening more often.

"Our house at five," Samarra said and could not hide her excitement. She loved weddings. "And wear your wedding shoes!"

Samarra squeezed Jeff's hand again as they walked toward their SUV. The heat from the parking lot was overwhelming, even though the city had painted all parking lots a light gray. The light gray color did keep it cooler, but the increased glare was overwhelming. Drought-dead azaleas lined the sidewalk, and she guessed the water system didn't work too well in the power outage.

"You seem troubled."

Jeff didn't answer for a few seconds, quickly analyzing his demeanor.

"I guess I am a little troubled," he answered. "Not sure 'troubled' is the correct mood, but something."

He took the tiny Bible out of his pants pocket and handed it to Samarra. She examined it, wondering why he would drill a hole in the Bible. The back was stained with blood.

"I have never seen you with this Bible before," she said, puzzled.

"It wasn't mine until this morning," Jeff replied. "Remember the little kid playing in the Town Green the past few days, looks about twelve years old?"

Samarra pushed the pre-cool fob, and she could hear the Range Rover start a hundred feet away. Hopefully the steering wheel cooling system would have done its job by the time they got there.

"The black kid?" she asked. "The one who wears the Superman costume?"

"Yeah. That's the one."

Jeff slapped a bug of some kind. Bugs were everywhere, despite the on-and-off drought, mainly off.

"What about him?"

Jeff recounted his morning encounter and conversation with the young boy named Noah.

"Mistuh! Mistuh!!" he recalled the kid yelling as Jeff crossed The Green toward *The Divide* for a coffee and some news. He turned to look at the kid. His skin was ebony, and Jeff thought the accent was Nigerian. The child had unusually cobalt-blue eyes, a genetic abnormality for such a dark-skinned person.

"Yessir," Jeff said, stopping to face the kid.

His small, red Superman cape blew in the warm wind; and the kid ran over with several small objects in his hand.

"I hate to say it, Sam; but I was a little paranoid as he ran over. I guess it's the times, but I remember wondering what those dark objects he was carrying might be. In Vietnam, there had been lots of kids running toward United States soldiers with small, dark objects in their hands that turned out to be hand grenades. Then he hands me that," Jeff said, nodding at the small Bible.

"Mistuh, you want a Bible? The Lord's comin' soon, don't you know?"

Before Jeff could answer one way or another, the kid put the tiny Bible in Jeff's hand and folded his fingers around it.

"Well, thank you kind sir. That print is so tiny, I don't think I can read it even with my glasses."

"Suh, this Bible is not for reading. This here Bible is for protection. It is a life-saving Bible. Keep it in that pocket close to your heart."

Samarra ran her left finger around the small hole in the Bible.

"What?" she asked, astonished. Was she hearing this story correctly? Was Jeff hallucinating? "What kind of drugs did the doctor give you?"

"None," Jeff said, "Except for the miracle antibiotic ointment."

They opened the doors and climbed into a world of coolness, and Samarra gently touched the steering wheel. Cool as a cucumber.

She drove toward the Medical Center exit, turned right on Howell Mill and headed to their Sugarloaf home. Traffic was daunting because the traffic lights were all flashing, and she hoped for normalcy soon. She knew, subconsciously, that normalcy was far, far away.

"So I put the Bible in my left shirt pocket and forgot about it. You know the rest of the story. Doc told me it was a miracle, that the Bible could not physically stop a 9-millimeter."

The two drove in silence. Duluth's lone firetruck zoomed down Buford Highway past closed and deserted buildings, and a pall of smoke rose a few blocks away.

"They set the new restaurant on fire when they left," Samarra said. "When you were shot, the crowd scattered, yelling obscenities I never heard before. They set some trash bins on fire and torched the new restaurant. Thankfully it was closed."

Jeff heard the near-silent jingle of a Breaking News Alert and turned the volume up. The Range Rover sound system was the best, but they listened mostly to news. It was a never-ending mystery.

"... *455th Air Expeditionary Wing at Bagram Air Field in Afghanistan. Attacks also occurred at the U.S. bases in Jalalabad and Kandahar. Afghanistan news sources are reporting that all three bases have been destroyed by drone activated bombs. Associated Press is reporting that the bombs were of the red mercury variety, also used on the twelve capitals in Europe. An estimated three-thousand troops may be dead or severely injured. The Afghan military has lost an estimated twelve-thousand.*"

"I will tell you another miracle," Samarra said, listening to the news as she turned onto Sugarloaf Parkway.

"What's that?" Jeff asked.

"It will be a miracle if we pull this wedding ceremony off today."

The white Range Rover shifted left as a gust of wind nearly blew them off the road. Jeff's phone played *Bad Boy, Bad Boy; Whatcha gonna do* and he answered the call from Will.

"What's up?"

"Taxes, rent and temperatures," Will said. "I'm in Lawrenceville."

"What?" Jeff responded, surprised.

"Yep," Will continued. "Sorry I didn't call. A lot is going on, and I came back to rescue you guys."

"How did you get here?" Jeff asked.

Most commercial planes in the Western Hemisphere had been inoperational since the solar-initiated EMP a few weeks earlier. If the planes were not totally inoperable, important safety systems collapsed and made flying very dangerous

"You don't need to know," Will said matter-of-factly. "Get your bags packed."

"We can't leave Wild Willy. You're crazy," Samarra said.

"Oh, the wife's with you," Will said.

"Yes, I'm driving. Jeff got shot in the heart."

Will paid no attention to the comment, assuming it was not serious.

"Get Sheryl and The Admiral, Abe, Chadbo, the gang. I will need help flying the plane."

"What plane?" Samarra asked, whispering to Jeff, "Can Will fly a plane?"

"The one parked in Lawrenceville, Miss Samarra."

"When are we leaving?" Jeff asked in jest.

"Tomorrow if I can get her fueled and prepped, maybe the next day."

"Did you bring your dancin' shoes?" Samarra asked.

"Nope," Will said. "Why, are we going dancing? Won't Jeff be jealous?"

"Don't be silly," Samarra said, laughing. "We're having a wedding."

"Really? The Admiral finally making the big hitch?"

"Yep," Jeff said. "Abe and Condi too."

A small flash to the left caught Samarra's eye and she glanced out of reflex. A tiny but growing light appeared about thirty degrees above the horizon. Her first thoughts were a meteorite or asteroid, though they had been rare lately.

"No way," Will said. "He finally landed the Queen of News. Good for him. What time and where?"

The white light suddenly flashed brightly and the sky lit up.

"Whoa," Will exclaimed, simultaneously. "What the heck was that?"

Will counted the seconds after the sudden flash, and twelve seconds later the audio followed, a low but loud rumble. He estimated the distance quickly, about two miles away.

Chapter Twenty-Seven

The Wedding

Berkeley Lake was beautiful, a small village-like community about two miles south of downtown Duluth. With an eighty-acre lake and lots of hills and winding streets, Berkeley Lake resembled a small retreat. Folk found it hard to believe that the small community was a quarter-mile away from a major industrial thoroughfare.

The small, intimate chapel was non-denominational and right on the shores of the pristine lake. A year earlier, the chapel had been painted white; and in the spring, the landscaping would bloom with thousands of bright yellow daffodils. Jeffrey Ross pushed for the changes, saying it had to do with a church in his dreams; and the community bought in. Actually, Jeff bought in and paid for the complete transition.

The parking lot began to fill, though only a few were invited; and the late-afternoon sun made its way toward dusk. Sheryl wanted small and intimate, and The Admiral always tried to please.

Two white swans floated on the clear, placid water behind the chapel; and three children threw bread, hoping the swans would swim closer. A blue and silver pontoon boat edged closer to the dock and finally unloaded the six passengers, close friends of Abe the Bartender.

"You clean up good, Admiral," Wild Willy volunteered. "I like the tux."

The Admiral shook Will's hand and laughed. There would be no tuxedos at this wedding with a Jimmy Buffet theme, but there would be margaritas.

"Too hot for a tux, Wild Willy. But these are designer shorts and sandals."

Chadbo stood in the front door of the chapel, admiring the landscape and the beauty of the community. Then he decided to pray. Chad believed in Abraham's God, he believed that Jesus was the one proclaimed to be the Messiah; and he believed that the prophets of old were an unexplainable phenom. Unfortunately, he had trouble praying.

It's just a conversation with God. Talk to Him like you talk to a friend. He is your friend.

That was Abe's explanation of prayer, and Chadbo turned and walked into the chapel. The air conditioning was set on sixty-five and a chill filled the air. The chapel was empty but filled with tropical Margaritaville-type flowers. Taking a seat in one of the dark-stained, wooden pews at the front of the chapel, Chadbo lowered his head in prayer.

Oh God, he started, praying silently. *I apologize for feeling so uncomfortable talking to you. Abe has been giving me tips. He really does love you, but I guess you know that. I ask you today, it seems I am always asking you for something, to bless these two marriages and their lives together.*

Is this the end? I ask that for many reasons, but I guess the major one is, there seems to be a lot of Christians being beheaded lately. Lord, I was really expecting to miss all this. I mean, people have surely started disappearing... but I am still here. And things are getting really terrible. I am glad everyone can't see what your winds are doing, high in the atmosphere. It is scary, and I have never seen it like this before. Are you going to take us, me and my friends? We are all believers. Thanks and amen.

Chadbo knew science, but he was not knowledgeable about the supernatural spectrum. He knew it happened, because he was on that Jamaica beach when Melissa vanished in thin air. His concern of having to live through what he was sure was coming made his heart beat like a marathon runner's. The USA seemed as secure as ever, but he knew... that was not the way the story was written.

The wedding was simple, quick and quite romantic.

Darrell Edwards and wife Tacy did not bring their eighty-piece orchestra but did bring Darrell's silver Schilke trumpet and Tacy's 10K Yellow Gold Custom Powell flute. The plan called for an inside wedding because of the heat; but remarkably, there was only a slight breeze and the temperature hovered around seventy-four. The plans changed, and Tacy figured that God must be smiling on the wedding ceremony.

Darrell and Tacy played a selection of duets proposed by the two newly-married couples; and at the moment they played Condi's favorite, *What a Wonderful World*, first performed in 1967 by Louis Armstrong. The crowd of twenty-four sipped margaritas, spellbound by the musical performance.

"Hard to believe that sound comes from only two instruments," Abe whispered in Condi's ear, and his head spun from the aroma of her perfume, fresh gardenias.

Unlike The Admiral and Abe the Bartender, Sheryl and Condi dressed to the nines for the ceremony and were absolutely stunning but quickly changed to shorts after the wedding.

"Never seen The Admiral so happy," Jeff said, squeezing Samarra's hand. He thought her hand felt clammy but considered it might be the heat. Only, it was not hot.

"He has probably never been happier in his life," Samarra said. "He is a lucky man to have Sheryl. She is beautiful and has a strong faith in the Lord."

"And she cooks," Jeff laughed.

The evening began to wind down as the sun gradually set in the west, and the bride and groom toasts came to an end. Darrell and Tacy were the first to notice the light and both pointed skyward.

"What is that?"

"I have no idea, Tacy."

Darrell, though not from Duluth, was very familiar with the area. He conducted the Gwinnett Symphony several times on the Duluth Town Green for New Year's Eve celebrations. During his times in Duluth, he had seen some amazing signs in the sky, including Dark Comet that hit the moon.

The light was not an asteroid because the speed was too slow. The light would hover over the lake and then move a short distance and hover.

"Could it be a helicopter?" Condi asked. She had observed plenty of helicopter searchlights in her news career.

"No noise," Abe said.

Condi listened carefully as Sheryl completed her toast.

"And finally," Sheryl concluded, "I want to thank Jesus Christ. Without his tremendous grace and mercy, I would not be here. I was bombed and then kidnapped; and were it not for God's grace, I would have never been found. Thank you."

Everyone toasted the two couples, holding their champagne high; and that is when they all became aware of the slowly undulating light, high over Lake Berkeley. The silence was deafening.

The end is near. Beware the Ninth of Av.

No one in the crowd said anything, but a low murmur began as everyone asked each other: Did you hear that? Was that a voice?

Sheryl held The Admiral's hand tightly.

"Was that a voice, Justin?"

The Admiral was not certain. He heard something… something like a whisper.

"I think so," he finally answered.

"Was that a voice?" Jeff's doctor asked.

"I don't know, Nancy. I could not decipher it if it was."

The spellbound crowd watched the strange light as it began to brighten. It was a small light, not like the flying saucer Jeff once spotted over the lake; but the intensity grew.

"Was that a voice?" someone else asked.

"BEWARE THE NINTH OF AV!"

Everyone heard the voice this time, and the light zoomed away at a speed many thought impossible.

"The earth is shaking!" someone shouted.

"Duluth does not have earthquakes," came another voice, and the crowd began to fall to the ground. A few seconds later the shaking stopped.

The Admiral held up his remaining glass of champagne in a salute, trying to add an air of humor and calm, and said, "I told you the wedding would be an earth-shaking event."

A few continued looking skyward, pondering what they had witnessed; but Jeff and Abe knew exactly. It was *Blip*.

Abe and Condi were the last to leave Berkeley Lake Chapel, but Condi was certain she could still feel the ground shaking. She was aware that people experiencing an earthquake would think the ground was shaking for weeks afterward.

"Do you feel the ground shaking?" she asked, as Abe turned right on Berkeley Lake Road.

"No," he answered but thought he might have felt another slight jolt. "I'm not sure exactly what that was, but I do not think Duluth, Georgia has ever had an earthquake."

They rode silently along the winding road toward the dam, but the wedding day had not ended the way she had expected. No one was hurt in whatever happened, and the chapel was still standing with no apparent damage; so that was good, but... something did not seem right. The air was cool, the wind was calm and Duluth had an earthquake.

Abe's GTO moved slowly along the road below the dam, and the 1964 automobile engine sounded more like an Indy car with the new exhaust system. He hit the gas slightly and listened. He heard something, he was sure. When you owned a car as long as he owned the GTO, unrecognizable sounds did not go unnoticed. He stopped the car and listened. Nothing. Then a low rumble. A siren sounded and Condi nearly jumped out of her skin.

"What is that?" she screamed.

"The dam warning," Abe shouted, starting the engine. The whole car began to lurch.

He rammed the car into first gear, popped the clutch like he never-ever did and hit the gas. A small crack creeped across Berkeley Lake Road; but the shiny, red GTO peeled away as water rushed down and the car fishtailed.

Condi screamed when a rush of water fought to get in; but the powerful engine accelerated the car to seventy, twice the speed limit. In the rearview mirror, Abe saw a flash of blue lights and was certain a cop would not be pulling him over. Then the blue lights disappeared as the Duluth Police SUV washed over the side and down into the valley below.

Abe was surprised that the water would climb up the hill so fast, and he hit the accelerator again. Topping the hill, now at the highest point in Berkeley Lake, Abe stopped the car. Getting out and facing the dam, or where the dam once existed, the roar was deafening. In the twilight, Condi could see the rapidly draining lake and mouthed a silent *Thank you Jesus* at the timing. A second later, and they would be at the bottom of the valley.

"I guess this is a *Thank you Jesus* moment," Abe shouted, and Condi laughed.

A crowd now gathered at the top of the hill, and the cries of six passengers in a blue and silver pontoon boat could be heard over the roar as the boat disappeared to the valley below. In less than ten minutes, the eighty-acre lake was no more. The crowd, mostly residents, knew what was coming. Lots of mosquitos, lots of mud and alien odors.

Many sobbed.

Abe and Condi rushed to their new home, left the motor running and were back in the car in less than three minutes. Both dressed in jeans and knee-high boots, Abe threw a couple of pair of waders in the back- just in case. They headed back to Berkeley Lake to join the rescue efforts, and Abe worried that the subdivision in the valley was no more, million-dollar homes.

"You know what, Abe?"

"What?" Abe answered.

"Duluth, Georgia does definitely have earthquakes," and she quoted the scripture from Matthew.

"Nation will rise against nation, and kingdom against kingdom. There will be famines and earthquakes in various places."

The quote sounded appropriate to Abe as he sped down Peachtree Industrial Boulevard.

"I guess Duluth is a *various* place."

Chapter Twenty-Eight

<u>July 24, the Third of Av</u>

J eff, Chadbo and The Admiral studied the graphics, courtesy of Goddard Space Center. A picture was worth a thousand words, and the answer was plain. The data indicated the sun was twelve percent brighter than a decade earlier.

"It is interesting," Chad commented, "that the temperature is not increasing at the same rate. While it is getting much warmer, the temperature is not increasing at the rate of the luminosity. Thankfully."

"I think about things."

"What do you mean," Jeff asked, responding to The Admiral's statement. It seemed to come out of the blue.

Another large hailstone slammed into the earth outside and the small tremor it generated was easily felt in the safe-room below Jeff's home.

"Things in the Bible about the last days. Like the hailstones landing outside," The Admiral said; and Sheryl listened intently. She had heard his thoughts many times, his private thoughts. "And the sun."

Audry listened for more impacts and was thankful enough to say a silent prayer, thanking God that only a few of the hailstones were so big. They shook the house, and she wished she hadn't left the new scooter outside.

The safe-room was much more than a room, more like an underground ranch-style home. Three bedrooms and two baths, the underground structure had a unique HVAC and air-filtration system, powered by an underground generator that was vented into the rose garden in the southwest corner of the lot. Communications, should power be lost, was provided by two separate ham radio setups with multiple backup batteries.

"The sun first," Chadbo interjected. He had theories of his own.

"If the sun is twelve percent brighter, what is the percentage of the heat increase on Earth. And twelve percent brighter than what? What are we comparing it to? Is it twelve percent brighter than yesterday?"

"It talks about that in the Bible," Audry said as she rode her old, not-so-shiny scooter through the den where the men were glued to the computer, as usual.

"What did she say?" Chadbo asked. He was amazed that her voice was so… different. She was like a little woman.

"Her voice is changing," Jeff said, smiling.

"I said, 'That is in the Bible,' that the sun would get brighter in the last days. Seven-times brighter."

Audry turned a few figure-eights; and Chadbo figured that took the guesswork out of, is it the tribulation or not. If odd Audry said it was, that was pretty much it.

"Then it goes out."

"What goes out?" Sheryl asked. "The sun?"

"Yes ma'am. But the question is???" Audry continued and paused, taking one foot off the scooter for balance. Her red hair, long and not so curly anymore, seemed to have a glow.

"And?" Jeff asked. "The question is?"

Jeff raised his eyebrows, a *we are waiting* kind of look. Jeff, The Admiral and Chadbo waited in anticipation.

"Well," Audry started, "We do not know the starting point."

"What do you mean, Audry?" Jeff asked, his impatience beginning to show.

"Does the Bible mean the sun will get seven-times brighter than it was a year ago, or will it be seven-times brighter than when the sun was made on the fourth day of God's creation?"

The three men exchanged glances.

"The sun was made on God's fourth day. That may not be mankind's fourth day, but it was God's. So on the fourth day, when God made the sun, the stars and the moon, the sun was brand new."

Audry popped a fresh strawberry in her mouth and was glad Brazil still had strawberries. Dad's garden had not done well in the strawberry department the last few years; and she had become a strawberry addict, especially the Plant City strawberries.

"That is also when we had the first 24-hour day. It is likely that the newly-formed sun would have been dimmer at first, so the earth back then would not have been as bright as now."

Audry scooted out the door, through the kitchen and onto the tiled entryway and wondered if the large, gray door could really stand up to an A-bomb like Dad said.

"How does she know all that?" Chadbo asked no one in particular. "She's a daggone genius."

"Mr. Hutz," Audry said as she strode back into the den.

The Admiral and Jeff exchanged looks again. Chuck Hutz was dead. Or raptured. He disappeared on-camera and live.

"Mr. Hutz is in Heaven, but he still talks to me in my sleep. We have dream-talk. He said it would get hotter, and the weather will be worser."

"Worser?" Jeff corrected.

"Worser," Audry said with a most serious look. "I have started writing a book, and authors can make up their own words."

"Has he told you anything about the hailstorms?" Samarra asked.

"Yes," she said.

Audry picked up another strawberry, dipped it in the chocolate-almond mix and placed it on a ladyfinger. She put the dessert on a paper plate and ran into the kitchen to get a napkin.

"Are you planning to tell us what Mr. Hutz had to say?" Jeff asked upon her return.

"He has not said much about the hail except it will get a lot worser too. He told me the really-really big hailbombs... that is what he called them, have nothing to do with weather."

Chadbo, The Admiral, Sheryl, the twins, Samarra and Jeff waited for further explanation, but none came forth.

"Is that it?" Jeff asked.

"Mr. Hutz said the hugest hailbombs will come from a denigrating comet," Audry continued. "He told me it has always happened throughout history but were only discovered recently. The scientist that discovered them in Spain in the nineteen-seventies named them megacryometeorites. His name was Jesus too. Jesus Frias."

Audry smiled at her new word, the biggest word she had ever spelled so far.

"Disintegrating," Jeff corrected.

"What?"

"Disintegrating, not denigrating."

"For Pete's sake, Dad," Audry said with a frown. "He said the big hailstones we have now, like the ones falling outside, are a result of the jet stream. He said the winds that blow up, you know, back up into the sky..."

"Updraft," Jeff interrupted.

"Whatever, Dad. Mr. Hutz said that is the cause of those watermelon hailstones they had yesterday."

The story was still all over the news. Watermelon-sized hail falling out of the sky over Topeka killed thirty-three people and injured thousands. Twelve of the dead died in a homeless shelter when the building was pounded to the ground, pulverized concrete.

"Anything else?" Samarra asked.

"No," Audry said before scooting. "That was it."

The small group exchanged glances and could not help but be mesmerized by Audry's intelligence.

"Wow," Chad said. "Talk about gifted."

"Oh," Audry said, returning to the room. "One more thing. Mr. Hutz said to start collecting water, because some of the hail is poison."

An hour later, the storm stopped and Jeff gave the all-clear sign. He remotely opened the ten-thousand-pound door, and it swung slowly to the right. The group trekked up the flight of concrete stairs.

The house was a mess but not as bad as Jeff expected. Ceiling debris littered the floor but only one hailstone had penetrated the heavily reinforced slate roof. Audry ran past and out the patio door, in search of her shiny, silver scooter.

"Wow," Samarra said, looking at the back landscaping.

The hard ground, covered with dead or dying grass, looked like the cover of a golf ball; only instead of dimples there were small craters everywhere. The ground was white with hail, and some places had drifts up to six or seven feet.

The large magnolia trees were stripped bare, and only the vertical trunks made it through the storm, standing stoically at attention. Next door, the brand new Land Rover rested in the driveway, four flat tires and a heap of metal rubble. Two horses lay on the ground in the pasture across Sugarloaf Parkway, unmoving.

Audry found her scooter and considered it a miracle. Not a scratch but had been blown into the azalea garden.

"Oh my goodness," Samarra cried. "Look at the poor azalea plants."

The Admiral and Sheryl saw the azaleas, or ex-azaleas, small piles of twigs and leaves all that remained where there had been a hundred. They heard the beginning of mourning as residents cautiously left their homes, or what remained and discovered their pets who were caught outside.

Trees, bushes and flowers lay under the piles of hail, along with deceased pets; and the afternoon air had an uncommon chill as the temperature plunged thirty degrees.

"It's freezing," Audry said, riding her battery-powered scooter into its proper parking spot under the awning.

The clouds cleared and the sun appeared, and Jeff donned his dark sunglasses. As he accumulated years, his eyes became sensitive to bright light; or maybe it was that the light was twelve percent brighter.

By four-o'clock, the afternoon had regained its equatorial temperatures; and Audry was glad the power had not gone out. Life was difficult without air conditioning, even for kids.

Jeff called his private gardener; and within an hour, James was there with a small crew to clean up the debris. James Murphy, proud owner of Murphy's Amazing Lawn Care, shook his head. He had worked for Mr. Ross for several years and had never seen a mess this catastrophic.

"I woulda be heah fasteh, Mr. Jeffrey," James blurted, out of breath at what he had seen. "The trees and limbs layin' all across the roads; and Mr. Jeffrey. Oh Lordy-Lordy, I seen bodies layin' ever'where. You know that new neighborhood up there, the one off Buford Highway?"

"Yeah," Jeff said. "The twins spent the night there. What about it."

"Oh no, Mr. Jeff. Oh nooooo," and James began to cry. "That whole naybahood be gone."

Jeff ran into the house, grabbed the keys to the electric motorcycle and headed toward Norcross, south on Buford Highway. He would be there in less than four minutes, depending on the roads.

"Daddy, Daddy. Wake up!"

Jeff glanced over his shoulder, knowing for a fact that Audry was not sitting behind him. *I must be going crazy*, he thought; but he was absolutely certain that he heard Audry's voice. Or maybe it was old age. Older meant slower, in all departments.

He gunned the silent cycle, crested the hill at Hilltop Street; and in the distance where Plantation Estates had once been, he saw nothing but smoke and fire. There was only one firetruck at the scene, and the fire hydrants were inoperable.

The neighborhood and surrounding parts of the area did not even remotely look like the work of a demon tornado. No, this was the work of God's pulverizing machine; and he found himself wondering why. Jami and Jenni were only thirty-one years old, and tears again rode down Jeff's aging cheeks, and he thought… I am so ready for the next life.

Chapter Twenty-Nine

<u>July 25, the Fourth of Av</u>

"*The hailstorm that hit the small, southern town of Duluth, Georgia traveled south down the town's main thoroughfare, destroying homes and livestock along the way. The freak storm had wind gusts in excess of one-hundred thirty miles per hour, and the Southeastern Railway Museum has suffered major damage. The death toll is expected to rise but now stands at two-hundred thirteen dead and several thousand injured. The devastating wind and hailstorm continued southward through Atlanta and dissipated just north of Peachtree City, a trek of fifty miles. The Weather Channel, based in Atlanta, claimed the storm was unprecedented. We have been hearing that word a lot lately. Now to the war in Kansas.*"

Carolyn Morrison listened to the news and was saddened. Before moving to St. Louis, she spent fifteen years in Duluth; and she still had family there. Her nursing career had been a Godsend, at least until yesterday. It seemed to her like the Lord's green earth would not last much longer. She was well aware of the last days scenario, and it was playing out, big-time. It seemed Christians all over the world were being killed, mostly beheaded; and she knew it was only a matter of time before it happened to the largest Christian country in the world, at least it used to be. She turned the volume up to get a better grasp of the tragedies of the day.

"*… just west of Kansas City. The entire neighborhood of twenty-two homes was rounded up after midnight and reportedly taken to one of the homes where they were given a choice: Denounce Jesus and pledge devotion to Allah. Only one person refused initially, a mother of three. After her two oldest children were beheaded, she relented to save her youngest. What a sad story.*"

"Yes, it is," Abdul, the guest on OLNN, responded. *"I am a Muslim, and this is a disgrace to my religion. This has been going on everywhere. Last week, more than a thousand Christians were beheaded in the Chechen Republic."*

"How do we stop it?"

Carolyn drove west, hoping to escape the frequent earth movements Kansas and Missouri were experiencing. The rebuilt St. Louis Arch collapsed again yesterday after the latest shaking by the New Madrid fault. While the Midwest and the eastern United States continued to shake, rattle and roll; the news from the west was more positive. She would stay far south of Yellowstone. According to news reports, Yellowstone could blow at any moment.

"The Muslim community has to stop it. Like the Christians eventually stopped the KKK, Muslims need to stop their own extremists. The Ku Klux Klan philosophy was very similar to the religious extremists of Islam. That seems to be the way it is in the world of religions. Take the pope for example."

Before her momma disappeared that night at the dinner table, Carolyn questioned her about all the disappearing people. Her momma was a deeply religious woman with a strong faith in Christ, yet she had not experienced this rapture-thing going on. Why not?

"Jesus did not escape his tribulation, child," Momma told her that night at dinner. "Read your Bible. Jesus knew what was 'bout to happen. He prayed to God, that God would take his 'cup of poison' away. That's what Jesus called it, don't you see. He called his trial, tribulation and death a cup of poison."

"I remember, Momma," she had responded.

"That there is an example of Jesus praying and not getting the answer he wanted. Sometimes God answers and the answer is 'no,' even for Jesus. Did you know that Jesus even told his apostles to pray they would not have to endure the times of tribulation? See, Jesus did not know when the tribulation would be. It coulda been then, in their day; except the prophecies about the exile of the Jews throughout the world and their return to Israel had not been fulfilled. People been waiting for a long, long time, child. And now it is here."

Then, after eating her last bite of strawberry shortcake, Momma got up to take her plate to the kitchen and vanished in an instant. All the family at dinner that night knew full well what had happened, and no one wanted to call the police. Carolyn picked up Momma's broken plate and began to weep.

"Last week it was reported," Abdul continued, *"that Pope Pius is planning to announce his support for President Morsi as Ruler of the New World. Privately, according to our sources, Pope Pius told a small group of Cardinals that Morsi was the return of Jesus."*

Carolyn nearly drove off the road upon hearing the words. Momma told her many times that Pope Pius XIII was the False Prophet of Revelation, even when everyone thought he had been crucified. She watched the video of the pope's crucifixion, and it looked real enough. Then he showed up, alive and well.

A glimmer, maybe a flash outside the windshield captured her attention as she merged on the bypass around Springfield; and she focused on the five tiny objects flying over her car, maybe a quarter-mile or so high. The drones were barely visible; and they disappeared from sight, heading north toward the city she was now bypassing. The traffic came to a sudden halt; and armed young men, shirtless and angry, went from car to car, robbing and assaulting the occupants. Not far enough away, three gunshots rang out over the Interstate. There seemed to be no escape from lawlessness.

✡ ✡ ✡

The lead drone was followed closely by four subservient drones. Springfield, Missouri, was the location of three red mercury explosive devices of an unknown capacity. The detonation frequency was fixed, and the four drones in the rear began to veer off in various directions, sending silent signals that would detonate the devices if all went as programmed.

The dominant drone began a broad sweep of the downtown area. Unlike the other four, this drone did not transmit a single frequency. Programmed by the North Koreans, the autonomous drone ran through a group of three-thousand frequencies each second, transmitting continuously. If any frequency input was wrong, the drone's high-powered transmitter should eventually hit the detonation tone.

The temperatures were high and the humidity was low, making for a dry-heat day. The 85th Annual Ozark Empire Fair, one of the largest events in Springfield, was in full operation. The late-July crowd was sparse, compared to previous years, maybe twenty-thousand people a day according to the news, as parents kept their children safely at home. The world had gone crazy, and street crime was rampant.

Hotdogs and sizzling turkey delights were the delectables of the day; and parents with small kids stood in the hot sun, waiting.

"I want a hotdog! I want a hotdog!!" a small boy whined as his mother handed him a funnel cake.

The smell of livestock permeated the air, and the wind-stirred dust called for safety goggles, available for free throughout the fairgrounds. A large Ferris wheel, two-hundred feet in diameter was a permanent structure and the latest addition to the event.

"Let's ride the Ferris wheel, Mom," and the two headed to the ticket line, funnel cakes in hand.

The line was short, and only half of the safety-seats were occupied. As the seats filled, Rhonda and her son slowly advanced toward the top of the wheel. They had a grand view of the fairgrounds and surrounding villages; and as hot as this day was, the fairgrounds began to fill.

Across the vast East Parking Lot, a shuttle-train traversed, picking up families along the way. The temperature display read 112°.

"Do you know why the Ferris wheel was invented, Mom?" Jake asked.

"Nope, can't say that I do," Rhonda answered.

She was certain of one thing though. Jake knew. Autistic since birth with an assortment of learning disabilities, Jake had a phenomenal memory, a gift she thought.

"It was the United States' answer to the Eiffel Tower. There was a huge movement to build something that competed, and a man named George Washington Gale Ferris, Jr. came up with the idea. When it opened, it was two-hundred fifty feet in diameter, even bigger than this one; and it had thirty-six cars. Each car could carry sixty people."

"Wow," Rhonda said, duly impressed.

"That drone almost hit me, Mom," Jake suddenly cried out. "Did you see it?"

Rhonda looked and sure enough, a tiny drone was hovering over the Ferris wheel. The crowd below began to point, and Rhonda thought it was part of a promotion.

"I don't think this is good, Mom."

Across town, the annual Price Cutter Charity Golf Tournament was fortunate, attaining some of the greatest golfers in the country for this year's event, along with the two top-qualifying amateurs. One of Springfield's most successful charity events, millions had been raised for children's causes.

Reggie Boyd, born in Liberia, was an immigrant and a senior at North Carolina State University, majoring in Drought Farming. Drought Farming was a new curriculum in the NCSU School of Agriculture, a result of the world's dry condition.

Reggie did not claim to be African-American, though he clearly qualified. He had received his citizenship after serving the required Five-Year Citizenship Program in the U.S. Military. His choice was Navy all the way. Reggie was the number-one amateur golfer in the country, six-foot five, skinny as a rail and skin like ebony. He considered himself to be American, and that was all he wanted to be his whole life.

"So tell me about Liberia," his cart-mate, the other amateur, asked.

Because of the heat, the tournament officials decided to allow air conditioned golf carts, compliments of the Golf Pro Outlet Mall. In the world of golf, air conditioned carts became the norm with the rise in temperatures around the world. Though the carts were not enclosed, the cold air blasting from the small vents added some relief. Reggie wiped his face again with his golf towel.

"It is a hard life over there, sir."

"I have never heard of Liberia."

"It is in Africa and the country was carved out of the land for the freed slaves," Reggie explained, not going into much detail. "I grew up with dirt streets that turned to rivers of mud when it rained, the people are very poor but the education system is grand."

A transport plane flew low overhead, preparing to land at the new Springfield-Branson International Airport; and Reggie wondered if planes always flew over at such a low altitude. That would be very distracting to his golf game.

"Do you like America better than Liberia?"

"You must be kidding," Reggie laughed. "I only wish my ancestors had chosen to stay in America instead of going to Africa when the slaves were freed. I guess they hated their masters."

He paused, considering once again if all slave masters were demons; but he had studied American history thoroughly and knew that was not the case. After a single generation of slavery, no one really knew anything about what had once been their homeland; and many considered the white family to be their family too.

"I would love to have been raised in America. I do not understand why so many who have so much from this great land, hate it so much. The people are silly."

The buzz from above went unheard until Reggie stopped the golf cart. At first it sounded like the overloaded transformers in Liberia; and the two amateurs scanned upward, guarding their eyes from the bright sun as best they could. Reggie saw the source of the sound first, two small drones on a mission, flying quickly toward the clubhouse and the eighteenth green. Probably a promotion of some kind.

"That's interesting," Reggie said, mostly to himself and withdrew his small opera binoculars from his golf bag. He focused on the drones. Though the magnification was minimal, he could plainly see a small container beneath each of the drones. "Wonder what the containers are for?"

The two young athletes were relieved as they climbed into the cart, glad to have the cool air blasting away. Reggie drove toward the clubhouse.

The electric cart was amazingly quiet, but the hum of the air conditioning was annoying. However, the sound of the air was not enough to drown out music coming from one or both of the drones, *Come Fly With Me* by Frank Sinatra. Reggie had not noticed any speakers. Then they heard the screams, screams of agony as they approached the crowded stands of the eighteenth hole; and Reggie pressed the accelerator to the floorboard.

Springfield's new international airport was equipped with the latest technology; and today the airport was especially crowded as young teenage girls crowded the lobbies waiting to see their American idols, plus a few from Europe. The all-night concert at the fairgrounds had not sold the tickets the promoters hoped to sell, but the crowds at the airport to greet the rock stars was huge. Later estimates would claim a crowd of three-thousand plus.

The large transport plane that flew over the Price Cutter Charity Golf Tournament a minute or so earlier carried six bands from Europe and all their equipment. The inside of the plane, now quiet with all the passengers strapped in their seats, reeked with the pungent smell of marijuana. The pilot, prepared for landing, gently lowered the transport toward the runway on final approach.

"We have two UFOs!" exclaimed an air traffic controller. "Two o'clock, one mile out, five-hundred feet altitude."

✡ ✡ ✡

Mohammed and Sai'imi cursed the Syrian heat. The night had been sleepless; and even at four in the morning, the temperature finally hit a daily low, 109°. Air conditioners could not possibly keep up, and most homes that had air conditioning maintained a temperature in the low nineties.

"Every night is hotter, my friend."

Mohammed did not answer and frustratingly searched the sky for the moon. It would be full tonight if he could only find it. His mood was dour, and the heat did not help. Nor did Sai'imi's constant jabbering. Sweat rolled down his back, beneath his tunic, offering relief but minimal.

"And the days are brighter," Sai'imi added, laughing.

Sai'imi had strong and devoted feelings for Mohammed at first, but his humaneness to his enemies was disgusting and unislamic. Why simply blind the enemy when you could kill him?

"It will be a success," Sai'imi said. "The drones are tested, programmed, locked and loaded."

Sai'imi loved the United States military, especially the toughness of the Marines and SEALS; and he knew he would be a Marine had his family immigrated there. Unfortunately, border security and immigration rules were tightened, not long after Manhattan was nuked; so here he was, in the hot desert night with Mr. Personality.

"We will know soon," Mohammed said, listening to vultures circle above. The air smelled of dead animals… or people. It was a common odor in Syria.

"When?" asked Sai'imi.

Mohammed finally spotted the full, dark red moon, almost invisible. He noted the angle to the horizon and guestimated the time to be a little after four. That would be concert-time in Springfield, Missouri.

"Soon, my friend. Soon," Mohammed said. "This is our practice run, and we must pray it is flawless.

Chapter Thirty

Jeff focused on the U.S. Geological Survey charts, forwarded to him by Chadbo. There were many small earthquakes every day, thousands that are low magnitude and go undetected by humans. Wildlife seemed to be more sensitive, either to the feel of the earth movement or the frequency of sound they may hear; and many who lived in earthquake-prone areas pay careful attention to God's creatures.

"What are you studying?" Samarra asked.

Still dressed in her pink robe, she made her way to the kitchen, not waiting for his answer. She must have coffee.

"What are you studying?" she asked again, upon her return. "Oh. Turn on the news. Something is going on in Missouri."

Jeff turned from his desktop computer, picked up the remote and activated the TV but wondered why he had not already done so. A creature of habit, it was the first thing he did in the morning. His worries about the earthquake activity, though mostly minor swarms, had taken priority this morning. Every known fault line was dotted with activity. The images made the earth look like a cracking, round eggshell.

"A lot of small earthquakes going on," Jeff answered, adjusting the volume. "More than I have ever seen in a twenty-four-hour period. Four thousand, plus a few."

The large screen pixilated and images turned into small, square bits of color; but that was the norm in this day of super solar activity. Even the Northern Lights could be seen in St. Thomas and Puerto Rico.

"More news is breaking. Please stand by."

"Really? Four thousand?" Samarra asked, surprised. Jeff was obsessed with earthquake and weather data. "That is hard to believe you did not know that, Mr. Weather Wizard."

Jeff smiled, winked and refilled his coffee cup.

"It just started overnight. Chadbo sent me the graphics."

The early morning sky was cloudless and a deep blue as the ten o'clock sun continued its drift upward. The morning did not seem as bright as usual, which he found odd. It seemed that every day was brighter. Plus, the sky was unusually blue, a deeper blue than he could recall; and he considered macular degeneration.

"*... as the transport plane attempted to land, air traffic controllers reported two unidentified objects approaching the plane that was carrying several European bands for the concert last night.*

"*An eyewitness cutting grass on the airport grounds stated that she saw a drone fly directly at the plane, exploding on contact about two-hundred feet above the runway. She claims it was a bomb that caused the crash, not a drone flying into the engine.*

"*And John, this could be true,*" the commentator said with a hoarse voice, speaking to a reporter from a secure location in Springfield. The airport was closed indefinitely. "*There was a witness interviewed on another station who corroborates drone activity. Listen to this clip; and I warn the audience, it is difficult to listen.*"

There was a brief pause, some sort of satellite glitch maybe. There were lots of interruptions these days, but soon the sound resumed.

"*Carolyn Morrison, a nurse trying to escape the lawlessness of St. Louis had just entered the Springfield bypass when she saw a cluster of small drones, she estimates there were five, flying toward Springfield. Nurse Morrison, thank you for talking with me. What happened next?*"

"*My goodness! My goodness!*" Carolyn started, and her distress was noteworthy. "*Oh... my... God. I haven't ever seen nuthin' like that before, I'll tell you that right now. Nuthin'.*

"Why, those things flew over then a couple went left, toward the airport over there."

Nurse Morrison pointed toward the smoke and shook her head, still in disbelief as the entire terminal continued to burn, along with four jetliners that had the unfortunate mishap of being at the gates, boarding passengers. Dark and acrid smoke tainted the surrounding air.

"That lady's going to have a stroke," Jeff said.

"That plane exploded or somethin' just before it landed. I mean, it was close to that runway. That runway right there! Why would they have a runway so close to the road? Makes no sense. Then…"

The nurse dabbed at her eyes, trailing off into space somewhere, disheveled and confused.

"You know," Nurse Morrison continued. *"I could hear folk screamin'. They were on fire; and you could see them runnin', like a torch."*

Carolyn Morrison continued to sob and struggled to tell the story.

"You know, we could smell the burning flesh after the plane hit the terminal. There must've been lots of people in there. Some of these people stood right here by the highway, vomitin', includin' me.

"Then the big bomb exploded, at least I guess it was a bomb. I have never seen nuthin' like that. Look at me. LOOK AT ME!"

Jeff and Samarra watched with sadness. It was difficult. The top half of her nurse uniform was riddled with frays from the heat blast, and the right side of her face was blistered. Many cars were burning, while others appeared untouched.

"You see all those young men layin' on the street over there?" Carolyn said, pointing toward a large group. *"They were out here robbin' and beatin' folk before that plane crashed. Now look at 'em, dead and mangled, layin' on the scorched pavement."*

The cameraman scanned left toward the gathering crowd, and several men were trying to lift some cars and a pickup truck off a group of teenagers. There was little crying and moaning, and the screen faded back to the studio. The commentator dabbed her eyes with a tissue.

"*Okay*," the commentator said, embarrassed at showing her emotions, "*I apologize for that. Now we are going to FNN journalist Bud Weiser. Bud, I will not even comment on your name. Your parents must have a great sense of humor.*"

"*No,*" Bud answered. "*Dad just liked Budweiser, Angela. Plus, Mom's ex worked for Miller Lite.*

"*Angela, I am standing about a half-mile from the 85th Annual Ozark Empire Fairgrounds; and I have with me, Rhonda and Jake Fest. They are here today to help in the aftermath of this terrible tragedy; and you know what, Angela? I just received a newsfeed, and apparently this was not the only city to suffer from these mysterious drone attacks.*

"*Angela, can you tell our listeners what you saw or know about the events last night?*"

Angela held Jake's hand tightly. He had been fidgety and anxious since the drone nearly hit him the day before.

"*My son and I were at the top of the Ferris wheel yesterday, late morning. Jake and I were enjoying the view when a drone almost hit him and hovered over the Ferris wheel.*"

Jami and Jenni strolled through the room and out to the pool to check the weather.

"Where you gals headed?" Jeff asked the twins.

Jeff said another silent prayer, thanking God for once again looking out for the twins. They had been two of the few survivors of the hailstorm to hit Plantation Estates.

"Over to the shelter, Dad. We told you last night. You never listen."

"Come and watch this news. This is why I worry when you go out. The world is not what it used to be five years ago. It has gone crazy."

"We have to go, Dad. The hungry and ailing are waiting, and there are more of them than ever."

"Take your pistols, and watch out for wild animals. The Jackson boys were almost killed by three deer last week. Came out of the woods and chased them up a tree."

"Men are the wildest animals out there, Dad. You know that."

The girls kissed Samarra and Jeff, and they would be at the Duluth-Suwanee Hands of Mercy Shelter in ten minutes. The twins debated whether to continue helping when the shelter was renamed from the Hands of Christ Shelter; but in today's world, Christ had been blocked it seemed. The news continued, like a never-ending Shakespearean tragedy; only this was no play.

"*...Jake started screaming to get off, and the Ferris wheel operator obliged. We got home early evening, turned on OLNN news channel and that's when we saw it. The whole darn fairgrounds was on fire. Something exploded...*"

"*It was the Ferris wheel, Mom,*" Jake whined.

"*Yeah, that's what he's been saying since last night.*"

"*Jake,*" Bud said, "*Why do you think the Ferris wheel was the cause?*"

Jake pulled at his chin and said nothing for a few seconds.

"*Be patient,*" Rhonda said.

"*Because I saw it on Discovery Channel last week. They had a demo.*"

Bud and Rhonda waited a few seconds, but Jake did not offer more information.

"*A demo of what?*" Bud asked, recognizing the symptoms of autism, similar to his own son.

"*Well, there are these red mercury bomb accelerator devices that are planted everywhere. The small drones then fly over the site and activate a timer. The bombs look small, but the red mercury makes them really humongous. That is what happened last night.*"

"*Angela, that may be true. I have not heard of red mercury, but some of these kids are very smart,*" Bud said, winking at Jake; and a big grin covered Jake's blushing face. "*What we do know is, the bomb was huge but not nuclear. No radiation. And at least thirteen*" *hundred are dead, along with a whole lot of farm animals. And get this, eyewitnesses claim that some people disappeared before the explosion, vanished into thin air. Of course, those reports have been proven to be nonsense in the past. Nevertheless, this area will not be the same for years to come. Back to you, Angela."*

"Wow," Jeff said. "Thirteen hundred killed at the fair?"

He walked over to glance at the graphs; and the earthquake activity was incredible, especially in fault lines located in the Middle East, Europe and Asia.

"Now to the final incident, at least we hope. Everyone in this area is well-familiar with one of the largest charitable events in the state, the Price Cutter Charity Golf Tournament. Folk, this is an awful story. Let's go to Jane Marsh, one of our investigative journalists, who actually played in the event. Jane, I've heard bits and pieces of this story, so please fill us in."

The screen briefly flashed an extraordinarily gruesome video clip, people walking slowly like zombies on The Walking Dead TV show. Pieces of something, possibly flesh, hung from their faces; and many clawed at their eyes.

"If there is any good news in this report," journalist Jane Marsh started, *"it is the low number of fatalities. This sick, sick terrorist attack, and it is what it is, was designed to blind and torture people, anyone. There was no concern for the innocents, the elderly, the children. I interviewed a gentleman not long after the attack occurred, one of the golfers; and here is the video."*

The clip started with Jane turning and grabbing the sleeve of a dark-skinned man. The man appeared dazed.

"Let me introduce you to Reggie from Liberia. Reggie is the top amateur golfer in the world. I see you have a bandage. Were you injured in this attack?"

Reggie tried to answer but at first, could not find the words. The paramedics had sedated him slightly, to handle the pain; and he felt lightheaded.

Jeff glanced at one of the security camera displays and was surprised to see the twins coming in the gate.

"Are you okay, Reggie?" Jane asked and held his arm, hoping to give some support.

"Yes, I am okay. Thank you. Just a little woozy."

"Why don't you have a seat," Jane suggested, and Reggie sat down in a golf cart.

"Were you wounded?" she asked again.

"Yes. Apparently. I must have been splattered a little. I never saw anything…" he trailed off.

"I never saw anything, and then my hand started burning. Really burning. I looked down and there was a hole in my hand."

"A hole?" Jane queried.

"Yes," Reggie continued. *"I never felt it until it had burned all the way. It was very speedy. My golf hand."*

Jane was astonished at the young man's calmness and attitude. He acted much older and wiser. Growing up in Liberia must be a learning event, she reckoned.

"I was lucky," he said. *"These drones flew over, flew up to the finishing hole where all the crowds were. They were almost silent, and hardly anyone heard them. Everyone was enjoying the golf, and you could barely hear over the large fans. It was hot."*

"How were you lucky?" Jane pushed, as gently as she felt necessary.

"I have my eyes. You see, the drones, they fly slowly over the crowd, and no one knew. Then, suddenly they started blaring out music, some song I never heard in my country. Almost everyone stopped and glared at the drones, not knowing what they were. Then the drones dispensed their cargo, some kind of acid I guess. The big cooling fans blew droplets everywhere. People were screaming."

"Yes, I see some over there clawing at their eyes, waiting for more doctors."

"I do not know what the substance was, but the plotters were devils. I am hoping to never again see people have their eyes burned out… never!"

The clip ended, and Jane Marsh handed the reins back to the station, which promptly went to commercial.

"Wonder what kind of chemical was used?" Samarra asked. "What kind of acid could instantly burn through someone's hand?"

The twins walked in, frustrated and in a hurry.

"They didn't eat much," Jeff said, amused.

"No," Jenni said, pouting. "Jami left her phone. Again."

Less than a minute later, Jami and Jenni were headed back to the shelter, singing a song into the wind.

What a friend we have in Jesus.

Jeff had no idea he would never see them again.

Chapter Thirty-One

Vinny paid for the old, black man's waffle and eggs as he paid for his cup of coffee at Omelet House.

"Twenty-four dollars for two eggs and a waffle, monsieur? Must be some delightful eggs."

"Egg's a whole day's work fer a chicken... mon-sieur," the cook said, grinning. "You know that black feller over there?"

"No."

The cook, Isaiah according to the name tag, was tall and lanky, pale skin and a neatly trimmed beard.

"It's nice, what you doin' fer that-there feller. Since food prices done jumped through the dang sky, he don't come here often."

"Merci," Vinny said with a near-perfect accent. "Keep the change."

Isaiah the cook grinned again, feeling the fifty-dollar bill. He could feel a counterfeit in an instant. This one was real.

"Why, thank you, young feller."

Vinny turned to leave the small restaurant, paused and turned back to the cook.

"Do you know of a place in this area called *In the Woods*, or something similar?"

"Yessir. Go left outta the parkin' lot, and go two miles or so. You'll see an old Exxon sign on the left, an abandoned fillin' station. 'bout a hunnerd feet up on the right you'll see half the sign, just says *Woods*. There'll be a burned out church. Used to be a Methodist campground 'til somebody burned the church down last year. They found a Ko-Ran at the scene, but it turned out to be planted. Maybe they thought it'd grow into a Ko-Ran plant."

Isaiah broke out in laughter at his joke. Vinny thanked the cook again and exited. This would be his last meeting with BJ the preacher, and he guessed a burned out church campground was as secure as any place these days. BJ was waiting when Vinny turned into the ash-gray parking lot.

"Thank you," BJ said as they shook hands at the conclusion of the brief meeting.

"Thank you, my friend, for telling me the truth about Jesus. You saved my life, my eternal life. Even though I was a hardline Muslim, I still had doubts about another life. Maybe I read and studied too much, I do not know. But when you explained the resurrection the way you did, it suddenly became clear. You were a gift to me, BJ, at a time that I deserved only death."

The men parted, and BJ would get the codes to Edgar Poe. Agent Poe indicated that he should not mention the codes to anyone. Vinny's change of heart would save many, possibly millions, of American lives if the government acted in time. That part was troubling.

Vinny drove north toward Dalton, but the air was still acrid from all the fires. Limbless tree trunks, charcoal-black, stood as monuments to the devastation caused by the two preachers in Jerusalem. He dwelled on his conversation earlier with the cook. A year earlier he certainly would not have bought a complete stranger a meal. His heart had changed, as had his outlook. All because of a man named Jesus.

He was not going to have a Happy Jesus day, unfortunately. Before this day was over he would kill again and probably be killed. The Army of the Christian Soldier would end their reign of terror today.

"BJ," Agent Edgar Allan Poe began, "I have a tremendous trust in you, not only for bringing the codes but from my knowledge of people. You have a good heart. Not all preachers do."

Poe wondered why BJ had not been one of those who disappeared. Maybe God was waiting on him to complete his work. Today was a great help.

"Thank you, Ed. Vinny said that nearly every drone has the same triggering frequency. A drone flies over a bombing device or a chemical dispersing mechanism with electronically controlled valves that have been planted by infiltrators acting as HVAC techs or plumbers. They send out the triggering frequency that activates a time-delay, maybe five minutes, maybe five days. The drones are long-gone before disaster strikes."

Ed and BJ briefly discussed how the United States could use the codes via our own drones to change the frequencies, thereby deactivating the devices. Vinny's list of targeted cities and small towns made it possible to act quickly. They would launch drones, thousands, that would jam the frequencies temporarily until the codes could be programmed into a separate fleet of drones which could deactivate the devices permanently.

Ed told BJ to be careful who he confided in, because all was not as it seemed. Apparently the government had been infiltrated at the highest levels, and the attack the previous day in Missouri was a dry run.

"Looks like there is going to be a drone war," BJ said before leaving. "I am glad I could be a part. I believe the Lord has used me at the end of His miraculous play. I am ready to go home."

On the road again, BJ pulled into a small diner's parking lot and to the drive-thru window. The smell of the two chilidogs soon had his stomach singing opera, and he drove into a deserted campground with a single picnic table intact. A burned out Methodist church sat among burned trees in the background, and he wondered what happened. There had been a lot of church burnings in the mountains.

BJ brushed off the bench with a napkin, took a seat and unwrapped the foiled enclosure insulating the messy dogs. That is when he heard the growl.

Looking up from his meal he scanned the area and was terrified. He was surrounded by at least five large but skinny, brown bears.

Out of starvation or rabies, the white froth dripping from their mouths was not good news. As the bears began to make their moves, he thought for sure his heart would pound out of his chest. There was nothing he could do, the Exxon station across the street was closed, there was no escape.

The bears charged, BJ threw the hotdogs, distracting one and began to pray. He never figured that God would take him this way; and he prepared himself to be eaten alive.

A small, white minivan with a family of four turned off the lonely highway and into the abandoned campground.

"Look, Dad," one of the kids said, pointing out the front windshield.

The four stared in horror as the group of bears leaped on a man standing on top of a picnic table. Then the most amazing thing happened. A bright light emanated from the confused bears, now backing off, and suddenly shot skyward. The man on the table had simply disappeared.

The bears turned and eyed the white van.

✡ ✡ ✡

As the sun lowered quickly in the west, Vinny removed the drones from the back of his rental cargo van. Vinny had visited the training camp on several occasions; and with his photographic memory, he knew the layout and the GPS coordinates.

Using the same technology as self-driving cars, two of Vinny's drones were the highly sophisticated *Agra8* agricultural drone and were self-flying. The craft was preprogrammed and could self-adjust if necessary during flight. Designed as a crop duster, the twenty-two-pound drone could lift a payload of forty-eight pounds. The remaining drones, four in total, would be used as diversions but were also self-flying.

From a mountaintop overlooking the Christian militia's chow hall and barracks, Vinny monitored closely. He watched as folk left the cafeteria and estimated there were about a hundred and twenty people, mostly men. There were no children, and Vinny breathed a sigh of relief.

After setting everything up, he carefully loaded the package of aerosolized anthrax into the two crop dusters' plastic storage containers and extended the arms of the folded spray dispersal units. The other drones substituted a five-pound C4 plastic explosive for the camera that was initially installed.

Vinny climbed in the van to get some sleep before starting his day just before dawn the next morning when the men would fill the chow hall for breakfast and soon, was sleeping soundly. The next thing he remembered was waking up to the faintly beeping alarm at five o'clock and wondering how wakeup time came so quickly. Breakfast was in an hour.

Groggy and depressed about his dreams during the night, it seemed he had gone to sleep only a few minutes earlier; and he recalled the scripture that BJ read that morning, sitting on the lake, fishing, explaining what happened when one died.

"But I do not want you to be ignorant, brethren, concerning those who have fallen asleep, lest you sorrow as others who have no hope. For if we believe that Jesus died and rose again, even so God will bring with Him those who sleep in Jesus."

"Paul said that," BJ explained.

Vinny brushed his teeth like he did every day, spit the residue on the ground and searched for the binoculars. He seemed to always be misplacing things lately, and thoughts of Alzheimer's crossed his mind.

Scoping out the training fields, the chow hall line was forming at the door. Another five minutes, Vinny figured; and the chow hall would be filled to the rim. He sipped his instant coffee and began his day, glad to still be alive. Handling inhalable anthrax with a one-hundred percent fatality rate had been nerve-wracking, but Vinny was a cautious man. A few feet away, a limb cracked.

The chow hall line dwindled; and Jon Travis would be the last to enter. Jon was the Grand Prophet of the militia and founder. He hated Muslims, Jews, fallen away Christians and queers. Especially queers. His own son had been *that* way, and Jon prayed fervently for him that day, before throwing him from the mountaintop overlooking the camp. God had no room for sinners, nor did he.

Vinny slowly pulled his hunting knife, ready for an attack by man or beast. Not many handled a knife like Vinny. His movement was slow and controlled, as though he had never heard the breaking branch. From the sound, there was some weight involved, maybe a bear. Maybe a Christian militiaman.

He turned cautiously toward the sound but the total darkness of the night was a huge disadvantage. He pulled his phone from his pocket, touched the camera icon, aimed and clicked. He closed his eyes tightly as he took the photo, relying on the bright flash to temporarily blind any animal, or anyone, who might be snooping. He counted to five and flashed again.

Vinny opened his eyes; and his pupils remained dilated, absorbing any starlight available. He heard running, but the sound faded as the culprit moved further away. Vinny looked at the image from his camera, and two large, red eyes stared back. A bear. Not good, Vinny said to himself. He had a great fear of dogs or their cousins; but bears, not so much. He would need to work fast.

Jon the Grand Prophet looked up from the entry, glancing as he did every morning at the mountaintop where his young son plunged to his death. The flash of lightning told him a storm approached, and he waited for the thunder. And he waited. The lightning flashed a second time; but again, no thunder. If it was a gunshot, where was the sound that followed the flash? He walked back down the steps and waited.

Vinny launched the four diversionary drones, pre-packed and sealed with C4 and anthrax spores. He waited one minute before launching the two crop dusters. He would need the diversion to mask the sound of the two larger drones. With twelve propellers and twelve electric engines, though not as noisy as the gas-powered drones, they would be detectable in the silence of the night. There was a slight but sporadic breeze. He watched the lone man through the night-vision scope, a man who continued to stare at Vinny. Why is he looking up here, Vinny wondered?

The first diversion exploded with a mighty boom and the night sky lit up like a Roman candle. The barracks below exploded into flame, a few seconds before the two crop dusters began their death dive toward the only entrance or exit at the chow hall, which would prove to be a big mistake on this early morning as militiamen poured out of the building.

The two crop duster drones swept low over the crowd; but the sound twenty-five feet above was drowned by the angry, screaming men below as they rushed toward the barracks. Several militiamen spotted the crop dusters but were perplexed. Everything was happening so fast. Some ran back into the chow hall for cover, but a diversionary drone exploded three feet above the structure, setting it ablaze. Vinny watched from the mountaintop, and human torches ran from the front entrance.

Inhalable anthrax was among the most fearsome biological warfare agents in existence. Though not contagious, those who breathed in the spores would die quickly. With speedy treatment, seventy-five percent would still die; and those who lived would never be the same.

Within thirty short minutes, every building was on fire; and the sweeping drones continued to spray on the crowd below. There was nowhere for them to hide.

The sun slowly peeked above the horizon but was still hidden by mountaintops. Jon Travis held his fist up at one of the sprayers with no idea what was being dispersed, and Vinny hit the DUMP icon. An hour later, Jon would be dead as he drowned in his own fluids after anthrax spores attacked his lung tissue.

Satisfied, Vinny walked to the back of the van to close the cargo doors. He then dialed a number, and Edgar Allan Poe answered.

"I texted you some GPS coordinates. The so-called Christian militia that has been bombing churches and planting Qurans is no more. Absolutely do not come without bio suits. Anthrax spores are everywhere. He disconnected and opened the driver-side door.

He never saw the bear.

Chapter Thirty-Two

<u>July 28, the Seventh of Av</u>

Jeffrey Ross and his family prepared to depart not only their home but also, their country.

"Why aren't Jami and Jenni out here helping?"

"They are not here," Audry said, carrying her backpack to the car. "I don't want to go to Israel, Dad. Mr. Hutz told me it was dangerous."

Samarra walked briskly to the twins' bedrooms, but their beds were unstirred. Panic set in. The country, even Duluth, was not a place to be out all night. Gangs roamed; and there were the animals, rabid and hungry. Jeff's phone rang.

"Hello."

"Mr. Ross?"

"Yes?"

"Mr. Ross, I am the manager at Hands of Mercy Shelter."

Jeff waited without comment.

"I do not want to worry you, but your daughters were on the schedule last night. I do not know if they showed up, but they were always on time."

"They have not returned," Jeff said impatiently.

"Mr. Ross, the shelter was bombed last night. I was not on duty but am now contacting family members of those who were scheduled."

"Survivors?" Jeff asked, holding his breath and trying to control his rapidly beating heart.

Samarra listened as Jeff paced nervously. She mouthed, "What's the matter?"

"There were no survivors, Mr. Ross; and we had a full house. I am sorry. Witnesses said a brown van with no markings was driving around the parking lot for about five minutes. There was a long line outside waiting for tables, and the van stopped in front of the shelter. The driver got out and ran into the woods, and I guess no one paid any attention. Then the van exploded. I am so sorry Mr. Ross.

"The forensic people are trying to identify the bodies, but there are only two of these specialists in the area. It will take a while."

"I will be right there," Jeff said, hanging up and grabbing the key to his silent, silver cycle.

He briefed Samarra in his military sort of way, concerned but controlled. Samarra fell apart. Jeff held her tight, kissed her wet cheeks and strode out the door. Audry held Samarra's hand, trying to comfort her stepmom and hide her own sadness.

Jeff sped down the highway, thankful that traffic was light.

"Wake up, Daddy."

He glanced behind him but knew full well that Audry was not there. It was the second time he heard a wakeup call from his daughter. It was her voice, he was certain; but she sounded much different. Could it be a premonition? Some kind of warning?

He pulled into the strip center where the shelter was located, but the entire strip was smoldering. He spotted the police chief and walked over. He had known the chief for many years.

"Hey Jeff. What are you doing here?"

"Good morning, Chief. Jami and Jenni were scheduled to work at the shelter last night. They never came home. I am hoping… well," Jeff mumbled.

"You want to see the bodies?"

"Yes," Jeff answered.

"Come with me."

Jeff followed the chief of police into a tent structure that was set up for the investigation. The chief grabbed the key to the refrigerated truck parked out back, the hum of the air conditioner disturbing the air. Smoke and ash made the day even more morbid, and Jeff was not looking forward to the next few minutes.

"It's not pretty, Jeff. You sure you want to see this? Hardly any of the bodies are fully intact. Must have been a powerful explosion to do this damage, but why? Why would anyone want to blow up a homeless shelter?"

The chief stopped suddenly, bent over and picked up a burned and shredded copy of a Quran which he promptly put into a plastic evidence bag. He wondered if the book was a plant or was it a reality. The crazy Christian militias were getting as bad as the Islamists.

The chief was right. It was gruesome. Most of the deceased remained clothed, though the clothing was shredded or scorched. Severed limbs and separated body parts were kept in a separate section of the temporary morgue. Jeff held his breath when the chief uncovered the plastic bins of body parts. He was not totally sure of his reaction to seeing only parts of the twins' bodies, but his fears were for naught. They were not with the deceased.

"They aren't here, Chief," Jeff said, relieved for the most part; but where were they? "They both had on red blouses and black jeans."

The two men instinctively ducked at the sound of another propane tank exploding as it shot into the morning sky.

"So where do you think your girls are?" the chief asked.

"Good question," Jeff said. "They were eager to get here. They left home headed this way, then returned because Jami forgot her phone. But then they headed right back to the shelter, at least that was the plan."

The chief's radio crackled to life.

"Go ahead."

"Chief. They done found another body up in the mountains and said this one was eaten by wild animals, maybe some of those starving bears. Over."

"Where?" the chief asked.

"On a mountaintop's all I know. But guess what, Chief?"

The chief and Jeff waited. After about thirty seconds, the chief said, "Go ahead, Vern."

"Down below this mountaintop they found that Christian militia camp. It was on fire, blown to smithereens. Dalton police chief said they got all sort of folk up there in those biohazardous suits, or whatever you call 'em."

"Ask him about the person that was attacked and eaten," Jeff asked, and the chief did.

"I tell ya what chief, I think he mighta been one of them Muslim terrorists."

"Why do you say that, Vern?" the chief asked, rolling his eyes.

"Well, they said he was purty much eaten up, but I guess the bear don't much like the taste of a Bible. He was holding one in his hand. But his name was Aboud. You know what that means. He's a Muskie."

Jeff recognized Vinny's real name but did not flinch. The chief was a friend but would never in a million years understand his relationship to the notorious killer of thousands, probably hundreds of thousands.

"Is that it?" the chief asked.

"Nope, there's one other thing," Vern said.

Jeff and the chief waited in silence, and the chief whispered that Vern sometimes gets lost.

"Are you going to tell me or keep me in suspense?"

"No, no, Chief. I'm gonna tell ya right now. There's been another one of them disappearance things, right over there not too far from the bombing last night. Lady on television just now was having some kinda trouble, a handicapped lady alongside Scales Road. She managed to get out but nobody would stop. 'Course, there weren't much traffic. She said a couple of young ladies pulled over, helped her out; then they disappeared. She sure seemed like she wasn't telling no lie. Said they were there, she blinked; and they had vanished."

Jeff's heartrate nearly doubled, and he felt faint.

"Is there a description of what they were wearing?" Jeff asked the chief.

"Red. They wore something red," Vern said. "Two white ladies who looked exactly alike."

Chapter Thirty-Three

Sai'imi, jubilant over the success of his jihadi brothers in America, was anxious. Jerusalem was decorated in great splendor, awaiting the Grand Opening of the unfinished temple.

"Morsi is a pig!"

Mohammed continued watching the newsfeed. The targeted cities in Missouri, Nebraska, Connecticut and Alabama were doomed in fear and death. The toll at the moment was incredible. Nearly four-thousand were dead, and two thousand were now blind and scarred forever.

"Do not be insulting pigs, Sai'imi," Mohammed laughed.

The Syrian sun scorched the fig trees outside the home of Mohammed's cousin, but the air conditioning managed to maintain a comfortable temperature inside, the upper eighties. Sweat dripped from Mohammed's forehead. Silently he cursed the sun, fearing the heat would make for smaller crowds the next day. He hoped for thousands of Christians and Jews to meet their final fates at the so-called Third Temple.

"Now they are claiming Morsi extinguished a fire in Jerusalem, single-handedly, saving a group of Jewish girls. You want to know what I would have done to those Jewish girls?"

Mohammed did know what Sai'imi would have done. No one hated Jews more than Sai'imi. That is what made him so valuable. It was understandable. The IDF bombed his parents' home in Gaza, killing his mother, father and two sisters.

"I prayed to Allah that there will be many Israel Defense Forces there tomorrow. I hate them," Sai'imi mumbled.

"Sai'imi, do not let your hatred blind the cause of jihad. We will destroy the new temple, conquer Israel and the world. That is the goal; that is the message of the Holy Quran."

The two men sat in silence under the tick-tick-tick of the slowly spinning ceiling fan, and hot air mixed with hotter air in the small confines of the home. The ground again vibrated.

"Do you feel that, Mohammed?"

"How could one not feel it, Sai'imi? The ground shakes all the time. People get used to it and do not feel the vibration."

Sai'imi sipped his luke-warm tea.

"Do you believe the Christian story, Mohammed?"

"Which story? The Christians have many stories."

Sai'imi knew that was true, especially about the end of the world.

"The story about the Jews building a third temple, then the son of darkness claiming to be God. The story about why so many Christians have disappeared. The story…"

"No one has disappeared, Sai'imi. That is another one of their conspiracy theories."

That may be true, Sai'imi thought. Except he had seen that Chuck Hutz guy disappear right on television, in the middle of an interview.

"I saw it with my own eyes, Mohammed. And you were with me."

"Have you ever heard of David Copperfield?"

Sai'imi shook his head in the negative.

"An illusionist. A trickster. He could make things appear different than they really were. He could stand on a table, have the table removed and he appeared to float in the air. Just an illusion. These disappearances are the same."

"What about the earthquake in Jerusalem. My mother had a friend who was Christian. She told my mother that Jerusalem was going to have an earthquake, that hundreds of buildings would be destroyed; but this is the interesting part."

Sai'imi paused to wipe the perspiration off his face.

"What?" Mohammed asked.

"She told my mother that seven thousand people would be killed. Do you know how many were killed?"

Mohammed watched the news when he could, when the reception and internet connections were viable. The cursed sun interfered relentlessly, and communications were usually iffy. He had seen the final tally, a death toll one short of seven thousand.

"A coincidence, my friend. Just a coincidence," but Mohammed had never heard that story. That was the mother of all coincidences.

"Also, Sai'imi, it did not quite make it to seven thousand."

"There is still one Jew in critical condition. She is not expected to live."

Sai'imi let that soak in for a few seconds and continued.

"There are many more stories that have come true? Like all the tidal waves. The wave from the Canary Islands destroyed the East Coast of America. Most of New York City and Boston remain underwater. Miami is no more. This was predicted in the Christian Bible."

Mohammed had never read the New Testament or the Tanach. Most Muslims had not, and he considered the possibility that Sai'imi had.

"I never saw that prediction, Sai'imi. How do you know this?"

"My mother's friend wrote a lot of predictions down for her. My mother would never read the Bible. I still have the list of predictions that would start to come true. I believe this is the end, and our completion is near. Soon we *will* rule the world."

Sai'imi removed the worn piece of paper from his pocket and unfolded the list of predictions. It was a long list.

"Hear it is. This one is a verse in Luke. I guess that Luke must be a chapter in the Bible."

"There will be signs in the sun, moon and stars. On the earth, nations will be in anguish and perplexity at the roaring and tossing of the sea."

Mohammed said nothing, but a slither of anger arose in his heart.

"Sai'imi," he said, curtly, "Do not be deceived by the devil."

Sai'imi sat quietly, pondering the prediction.

"It has come true, Mohammed. The sun is much brighter than it was just a few years ago. And hotter. That could be the sign."

"The sun, according to science, is supposed to start getting hotter, Sai'imi. You know that. Stars get hotter."

Sai'imi did know that. He enjoyed astronomy and spent many nights alone in the desert, staring at the stars and all the meteors. It was a beautiful sight indeed; but at the same time, it was frightening. Mohammed was correct, that science claimed the sun would get hotter and eventually burn out like any furnace. Only that was not to occur for billions of years to come.

"What about the moon? It is red. Is that the sign?"

Mohammed could not deny that truth. He searched the skies the night before, trying to locate the full moon. The search proved fruitless; until finally, he spotted a dark red, perfect circle nearly straight overhead. It was almost invisible.

"Do you ever count the stars at night, Mohammed?"

Mohammed, like many Muslims in desert lands, had made the attempt. It was impossible.

"Of course."

"When I look at the Milky Way through my binoculars, there are not as many stars. Some parts were thick clusters of stars; and now I can count them, at least the stars I can see. Is that a prediction that is coming true before our very eyes?"

Mohammed had noticed. People were talking about it. The stars did seem to be less numerous; but he was certain they were still there. Where could they have gone?

"It is from all the ash and dust in the air. Volcanos are erupting all over the world, and half of Europe is on fire. They have been hidden by all the smoke."

Mohammed was overcome with a brief but violent coughing spasm. His nose began to bleed and he felt faint. The heat was unbearable.

"Are you okay?" Sai'imi asked, genuinely concerned. He whisked some paper napkins from the table and handed them to Mohammed.

It might be true that dust and smoke obscured the stars, Sai'imi considered, except the air was crystal clear. The stars he could see were more visible than ever, as though they were also getting brighter. He shivered at the thought. What if they were all burning out?

"I am fine, thank you," Mohammed said, trying to get his breathing back to normal. He wiped the blood with a dirty napkin. "I need to stop smoking."

Mohammed found himself thinking, oddly, that if he was dying he hoped it was cancer and not Ebola. The coughing and nosebleeds were coming too often, and both were symptoms of Ebola. Mohammed knew the Europeans and Americans were very stupid people to start letting Ebola patients from Africa immigrate to their hospitals. Now it seemed half of Europe had Ebola virus, and sixty percent of those would die. The remaining would wish they were dead. No, he would take the cancer.

"Speaking of smoke, Sai'imi, are the tires in place? Are the blowers in place?"

"Everything is ready. The tires will be ablaze, and we have thousands. There will be so much smoke, Mohammed, the Israelis will never see the drone swarm before it is too late. When the IDF shoots the drones down, acid and anthrax spores will be splattered everywhere."

The plan seemed flawless to Sai'imi, but Mohammed remained skeptical. The Israelis were not stupid people, as much as Sai'imi liked to think they were. Security would be heavy. However, if the swarm could make it over the crowds before the Israelis started firing, the job would be a success. If they were not shot down, their small but deadly payloads would be released on the crowds.

"We have ten tunnels that open as close to the temple as possible. The winds are supposed to be calm, like today. Allah is on our side."

Maybe, Mohammed thought. When things went this smoothly, he was always cautious. The winds were calm, a slight breeze emanating from the north; and that was remarkable. The wind had been the enemy for months, and today it stopped. Maybe, just maybe, Sai'imi was right.

Chapter Thirty-Four

People will flee to caves in the rocks and to holes in the ground from the fearful presence of the LORD and the splendor of his majesty, when he rises to shake the earth.

Isaiah 2:19

"This is not good," Wild Willy commented mostly to himself upon hearing the local news.

"What?" Jeff asked.

Samarra and Audry sat by the earthquake-damaged pool, discussing the possibility that the twins had been raptured. There was, after all, an eyewitness. Instead of sadness, Audry felt relieved. She loved Jami and Jenni, and now they would not have to deal with the rest of the bad stuff that was coming. She said a silent prayer that God would take the rest of them soon.

Samarra walked to the kitchen for a sweet tea and an orange juice for Audry, when the conversation caught her attention. Sinkholes.

"Sinkholes," Will said. "My plane is sitting on a runway at the Gwinnett Airport, and the airport now has several sinkholes that appeared last night. One complete hangar fell into the ground, along with six jets."

Jeff had an interest in sinkholes and the sudden devastation they caused. One swallowed the Corvette Museum in Kentucky a few years back. Not long after that, a man's bedroom in Florida fell into the ground, taking the man with it, never to be found. Port Royal, Jamaica fell into the sea on June 7, 1692, known as the "most wicked" city in the world. Even today it is only a tiny fishing village.

"Maybe you should take it to Warner Robins now. You said you had to land there to fuel up. Is the runway affected?"

That was true, Will knew. The fuel tanks were only partially full. The Gwinnett runway was long enough for the plane to take off, but not with a full load of fuel.

"I need a crew," Will said. "Used to take a crew of twelve to fly a B36J aircraft. Mine is modernized to the hilt, and it can be flown with a crew of two; but an extra would be good."

"There was a sinkhole in Rome last night," Samarra said, walking into the den. "Swallowed the new mosque the pope was building and a lot of the wall around Vatican City. Mobs were overrunning Vatican City the last I heard, and the pope is in hiding."

Jeff reached for the remote and switched to OLNN for *News anytime you want it*! He liked the new motto. The screen pixelated, as usual; and he switched from high-def to standard. A Breaking News alert flashed in bright red at the bottom of the screen, but no Vatican City was in sight.

"What will happen when the Long Valley supervolcano erupts, scientists are now asking about the California volcano after recent activity in the volcano's caldera? The Long Valley Caldera is huge and hides a tremendous amount of magma, about one hundred-forty cubic miles. Until recently, the magma field was thought to be much smaller. Though not as large as the Yellowstone supervolcano, an eruption would be significant.

"Now to Vatican City. The pope has been rescued by President Morsi's security brigade and flown to Jerusalem where Pope Pius will present him with honors at tomorrow's grand opening of Israel's Third Temple. As we have reported, the pope has declared his allegiance to Morsi, saying Morsi is the return of Jesus Christ.

"Part of Vatican City was burned to the ground by religious fanatics last night when sinkholes swallowed much of the city and the protective wall was breached."

The news went to a collage of photos and news clips, and the damage was unwatchable. Samarra turned away and proceeded to the patio with Audry's orange juice. The winds were eerily calm, considering the past few months; and Samarra knew it had to be an omen of something coming, some kind of weather disaster or tsunami. Or maybe something worse. Unprecedented was the new normal.

"Man," Will said after watching another five minutes. "The whole world is breaking apart."

"I know," Jeff replied. "*Entrepreneur Magazine* has an article about a Greek man designing luxurious cave conversions. Some are nicer than million-dollar homes. He's making a fortune."

A lot of good a fortune will do you in this coming mess, Will thought.

"I can't go with you, Wild Willy," Jeff said. "I want Sam and Audry to go but not sure how much help they can be flying the plane. Abe and Condi want to go, and they will be an asset. What about Sarge?"

"Sarge is at Warner Robins, and I have not been able to get through. Too much solar interference. But we can't leave you here."

"I have to stay, Will. The twins…"

"I thought an eyewitness said they vanished like all the others."

Jeff said nothing for a few seconds, contemplating an answer.

"You know, Will. Life is a funny thing. Why would Jenni and Jami, young thirty-somethings who never go to church, be raptured before someone like Sheryl who is always helping people. I know the twins have good and kind hearts, but I never knew their faith in Jesus was so strong. They never talk about religion."

"You hit the nail on the head, Jeff," Will said. "They have good hearts. They were always helping underdogs or people less fortunate. Look how much of your money they have given to *Dine for Dollars* since it reopened."

Will and Jeff had a good laugh.

"Do you ever play what-if with the Bible?" Will asked.

Jeff heard Audry and Samarra giggling outside and wished he was as confident that the twins simply disappeared. He had seen the interview with the lady they helped, over and over and over; and she seemed to be truthful. He had a bad feeling, a premonition, that things would be getting much worse soon.

"What do you mean?"

"I mean, what if something you read in the Bible and have been taught by the preacher, could be taken another way?"

"For instance?"

"Well," Will continued, "I am far from a Bible scholar and am a skeptic about a lot of stuff. My preacher always told us no one would get to heaven if you do not believe that Jesus is the Savior. Like the Jews.

"I know many, many Jews and spend half my life in Israel. There are exceptions, but most all are extremely nice and generous, semi-faithful and have wonderful hearts. The Jews do not believe in Jesus as savior, because they have been told for two-thousand years that he was *not* the predicted messiah.

"Then I learn that Jesus said on Judgment Day he will judge what is in our hearts, because that is where evil and good originate. To me, it sounds like our heart will be judged to see if we make the cut. What do you think? Excuse me, I am going to get a beer."

Jeff listened. He had had what-if moments about certain scripture, at least since he started believing scripture. Maybe everyone had. Wild Willy walked back to his chair, Bible and beer in hand.

"I have really been reading this book a lot lately," Will said, opening the Bible to 1 Samuel and handing it to Jeff. "Read this, the highlighted part. Samuel is preparing to anoint King David."

Jeff studied the highlighted verse and began to read.

But the Lord said to Samuel, "Do not consider his appearance or his height, for I have rejected him. The Lord does not look at the things people look at. People look at the outward appearance, but the Lord looks at the heart."

"You sure are a lot more religious than I ever thought."

"Yeah, I'm more religious than I ever thought," Will said, laughing. "Aludra and I are always reading and discussing. One day she said, 'When I went to the madrassa for school, every day the teacher would teach; and we would believe what he taught. Why would we not? He was the professor. But when I got older and could think for myself, I discovered they were wrong about a lot of things. We believe what we are taught.'"

Will stood up, stretched and turned to leave.

"Going to inspect the plane and will try to get in touch with Sarge. I have a bad feeling that something is about to happen. Something *unprecedented*."

Jeff escorted Will to the front door where his rental car sat in the cracked driveway. The Berkeley Lake quake had a final measurement of 5.2 and managed to crack a lot of the surface of Duluth, Norcross and Peachtree Corners.

The wind was calm for a change, and the weather was strangely mild. Jeff looked up and saw a tiny cloud, white and fluffy, and a daffodil fell out of the sky, landing at his feet. He guessed that was no odder than all the other stuff happening. He leaned over and picked up the flower. He loved daffodils.

"Let me know if it looks like you will be able to take off."

"Ten-four," Will responded. "Just be ready tomorrow at ten o'clock, bright and sunny. Hopefully we will have an eastern wind."

Will worried about taking off in a calm wind. A head wind would provide needed lift. He also worried about his friend.

Jeff closed the door after scanning the yard. There had been trespassers late at night but no attempted break-ins. If anyone tried to enter uninvited, they would have a one-hundred sixty pound, four-legged surprise staring them in the face.

He sat in his recliner and relived Wild Willy's *what-if* conversation. He had a few what-ifs of his own. Within five minutes he was in a deep but uncomforting sleep.

It was a bright, sunny day; and he walked down a path of oak leaves, into the woods that used to be behind his home as a kid. The smell of honeysuckles graced his nostrils; and birds sang above, God's choir.

Get up, Daddy.

He heard it again, but did not turn around this time. The voice from nowhere.

For a minute he thought he was in Heaven. He half-expected Saint Peter to come around the bend to greet him; but this bend was none like Jeff had ever seen, even during Viet Nam. Suddenly he walked through an invisible wall as though it did not exist; and the world became dark and musty, nothing like honeysuckles.

Jeff turned what he felt was one-hundred eighty degrees; but there was no exit, only darkness; then far in the distance, a sunrise began to lighten the early morning with the most beautiful display of vibrant colors he had ever seen, even better than the one time he tried wild mushrooms in high school, that Friday night with his buddies, a night he hoped to never recall.

"Do you enjoy the sunrise, Mistuh Ross?"

Startled, Jeff turned too quickly and a cramp appeared in his aging body, an inch or so below his ribcage. He doubled up in pain. The dark-skinned man walked over, placed his hand on Jeff's back; and instantly, the pain was gone. Jeff stood in relief.

"Thank you. My goodness, what a pain."

"Dat was not a goodness pain, Mistuh Ross. It was a badness pain. Do you mind some comp'ny, Mistuh Ross?"

"No," Jeff said and felt like an automaton. He was pretty sure this was not Saint Peter. He did not even have a white suit.

"I want to show you some tings over dere," he said, pointing toward a small incline covered with dead daffodils. Jeff hesitated.

"It be okay, Mistuh Ross. Do not be afraid."

The two men, assuming the strange man with the Jamaican accent human, briskly made their way to the top of the slight incline; and the dark-skinned man put his arm out, preventing Jeff from going farther than the edge.

"We have to walk slowly from dis point."

The next thing Jeff remembered was walking deep into a dark valley on the other side of the incline, a valley that must be the deepest valley on Earth. Here there was no sunlight or any light, other than that provided by torches, carried by some sort of human-looking creatures. Jeff perspired profusely.

"Who are they?" Jeff asked. "Are they dead?"

The man chuckled.

"Oh no, Mistuh Ross. Dey so wish dey were. Dese people here are waiting and hoping to die, but dey have a long time to live, do you know what I mean?"

Jeff shook his head, and they moved deeper.

"Dese are not zombies, Mistuh Ross. Zombies do not exist. All who are in dis valley are very much alive."

The deeper they went, the darker it became, a darkness he could actually feel brushing his skin; and the intense heat was becoming unbearable.

"I have a bad heart," Jeff said, not expecting that to matter.

"Do you really, Mistuh Ross?"

"Well, I will before this is over."

Then he heard the sounds, moans and groans and crying the likes that he had never witnessed. During the Viet Nam conflict, there had been many blood-curdling screams from instant amputations, but nothing like this. The sounds of complete helplessness hung in the air like the darkness.

"Why are they screaming," Jeff asked.

"Dey are the hungry, Mistuh Ross. Dere bodies are beginning to digest demselves because dey have run out of fat to digest."

"Will they die?"

The moaning, screaming and agonizing cries were more than Jeff could take.

"Oh no," Mistuh Ross. "Dey never die until de end of everyting."

They began their ascent; and with each foot gained, the darkness faded to light. Cresting the valley to the flat ground above, Jeff said a prayer of thanks. Had he just seen Hell?

Laughter in the distance, the laughter of playing children, startled Jeff. What a contrast; agonizing moans to the laughter of children. He looked to the left, and he had never seen so many kids. There must have been hundreds of thousands.

"Who are they?" Jeff asked.

"Dey are de children who will never have a chance to visit dis place of darkness and pain, Mistuh Ross. Dey are de children who will only know happiness and will soon be angels. Dere are more dan a billion of dese children, Mistuh Ross. De aborted. You know de Greeks used to take de unwanted children to de woods and leave dem for de animals to eat. Dese are de innocents. Dey will never visit de Valley of Darkness."

Jeff twisted in his recliner; and in the background the news droned on, something about an invasion of puss caterpillars. Slowly he drifted back toward reality and clarity, leaving the dream behind.

"Who are you?" Jeff asked the dark-skinned man.

"Well, Mistuh Ross, I ain't Saint Peter. I don't even have de white suit."

Chapter Thirty-Five

"There will be signs in the sun, moon and stars. On the earth, nations will be in anguish and perplexity at the roaring and tossing of the sea."

Luke 21:25

Homeland Security Team 1
Warner Robins AFB

S tudying the last of the coding, Ed Poe was now armed with a Doctor of Philosophy in Advanced Cyber-Security Techniques, thank you very much, Purdue University. He had come a long way since living on the streets of Atlanta, thanks to the generosity of Jeff Ross and Jeff's friends.

"What's up, Edgar Allan?"

Sonya Richardson was new to the team, young and vibrant… beautiful inside and out. Her father, fifty-year-old Vice Admiral Joseph Richardson, was head of the Pacific Fleet, at least what was left.

The Ross Ice Shelf wave had been devastating, and eighty percent of Pacific naval assets now lay at the bottom of the deep, blue sea. Thousands of human remains kept the rusting, gray ships company, lying in watery wait for the final rapture when the dead would rise from the sea. From the devastation caused by the Ross Ice Shelf Wave, Sonya developed a keen interest in raging seas, especially tsunami and rogue wave research. She reached for a small, gold-colored box of Godiva truffles lying on the corner of Ed's metal-gray desk.

"May I?"

"Help yourself," Ed said, smiling.

"Why do you have five boxes of Godiva truffles on your desk, Mr. Poe?"

"Well," Ed said, pausing for effect, "This military-gray desk is so ugly, I thought a little gold would brighten it up."

"Good answer, Mr. Poe. I thought you had a box for each lady friend."

Ed laughed and scratched his dwindling crop of gray hair.

"No. If I had five lady-friends, I probably would be in the morgue."

"Or the poor house!"

"Yep. That's for sure. I am working on codes."

"What kind of codes?" Sonya asked, grabbing a second box of chocolates.

"Oh, just your basic codes that prevent bombings, poisonings, anthrax attacks… that kind of stuff."

"Sounds interesting."

"So what kind of espionage are you researching?" Ed asked.

"The Chinese are rumored to have laid a network of thermonuclear bombs parallel to the East Coast with plans to generate a huge tsunami. Then the Cumbre Vieja volcano erupted, the island fell in the ocean and that did the job for the Chinese."

Ed was aware of that fact. A friend's home in Hilton Head, South Carolina, was never found, washed inland twenty-eight miles; with his friend in the house. He was also aware of the growing coalition between Russia, China and Indonesia; though Indonesia was iffy thanks to their ongoing civil war.

"How many bombs?"

"This is conjecture and remains unproven, but the information seems reliable. Twelve to twenty is what we were told. We may soon know. That is why I am meeting with the Pentagon's Warner Robins satellite office."

"What do you mean, 'We may soon know'?" Ed asked.

The first wave had been estimated at fifty feet, followed by a second wave of thirty feet. It had been the third wave that redesigned the East Coast of North and South America, an estimated one-hundred eighty-foot wall of salty sea extending from Newfoundland Island to Rio de Janeiro.

"There is concern that the devices washed inland. Several homes and ships washed in as far as one-hundred kilometers. That's sixty miles. We have a lot of land to cover but any leaking radiation should be simple to detect."

"We better find them before the jihadists do," Ed said. "Or the crazy Christian militias. They have no heart and are perfectly willing to kill women and children."

"Oh, they are not heartless. Their hearts are beating away, one evil beat after another. Some hearts are evil; some hearts are full of goodness. What is interesting is that they all think they are holy. Wonder if these militiamen ever ponder why they weren't raptured?"

"Do you think this could have caused a tsunami?" Ed asked, wondering why he wasn't raptured. Was there a purpose for him to still be hanging around Planet Earth?

"Doubtful. Maybe some small waves but nothing like Cumbre Vieja."

"The seas have roared a lot lately. Used to be tsunamis happened every ten to fifteen years, at least big ones."

"That is an understatement, Dr. Poe. I apologize for calling you 'mister' since you are now a genuine, qualified Ph.D. You may not need these boxes of candy to find a lady friend," she said, picking up yet another golden box of two truffles.

"You know," she continued, "rogue waves were thought to be fantasy a few decades ago, before everyone carried a camera. Finally, one hit an oil rig in the North Sea, about a hundred and twenty feet high; and now everyone is a believer. These giant waves are happening in every ocean and sea. The Caspian Sea, just above Turkey, recorded a wave last year of eighty-eight feet."

"Why?" Ed asked. "What are the reasons for the increase?"

J.L. Robb

Ed did not know enough about climate, tsunamis and asteroids. His specialty, though his undergraduate degree was in biology, was cyber invasion and the prevention thereof. Even without Vinny's considerable help, he would have decoded the schedule of events to come, in time.

"Good question. My theory right now is the numerous earthquakes occurring deep under the sea. Though they are small, when combined it has an effect on the geology. The activity is unprecedented."

"So you don't see it getting any better," Ed said, knowing the answer.

"No, Dr. Poe," Sonya said, looking cautiously to see if anyone was listening, and then she whispered. "God called it a long time ago. When the end times occur, the oceans are going to roar. That's a done-deal. Four luxury cruise ships mysteriously sank since the first of the year. Now everyone is afraid to take planes or ships, and it has killed the traveling industry."

The decoded information that Vinny provided before his terrifying demise was proving to be fruitful, very fruitful as a matter of fact. Twenty-six warehouses had been discovered so far, each loaded with various quantities of drones, some armed with five to twenty-five pound C4 bombs; some armed with biohazards and some supported Teflon canisters of a potent acid. The Missouri drone attacks and a few others slipped through the cracks; but overall, the prevention rate was excellent.

"Is there anything to the guillotine stories?" Sonya asked.

"What guillotine stories?" Ed answered with a question that he already knew the answer to; yes, there was.

Sonya smiled but did not intrude further. She knew the stories to be true, at least for three such places; because the Cumbre Vieja wave washed three large warehouses inland about a mile. For the most part, two of the structures remained intact, floating like large houseboats until hitting higher ground. Those two were filled with jumbled guillotines, and more than four-thousand heads were piled in the corner closest to ground-level.

"You know, the guillotine stories that have gone around for years. The ones where the government rounds up all the people, orders them to pledge allegiance to Allah and get a tattoo or lose their heads. Everyone said that was a conspiracy theory."

"Maybe it is," Ed said. "A conspiracy theory, I mean."

"No. It's not."

Sonya's phone rang, and a few seconds later she disappeared down the hall. Ed was aware of the two warehouses found in eastern South Carolina. It was right out of the Book of Revelation, and Homeland was hot-on-the-trail of the Christian militia residing in the North Georgia mountains. Now it appeared they had been wiped out in a series of strange occurrences. He had a gut-feeling that Vinny probably had something to do with that too, considering where his remains were found.

Ed continued studying Vinny's notes; but he had studied them numerous times, trying to put the scenario together. There were too many drones and they were unlikely to stop all; but the United States provided thousands of electronic jamming drones for the search. Would that be enough?

Sonya reappeared, white as Casper the Friendly Ghost.

"What's the matter?" Ed asked.

Sonya was having trouble talking, out of breath. She fanned her face with her hand.

"The thermonuclear bombs," she said. "They found three. Actually there were five, but two are missing. This is only the first group.

"Investigators followed the drag marks to a dirt roadway. Apparently whoever found them, drug them somehow on wooden tracks. Looks like a lift may have moved them to a truck. That is where the radiation level drifts off. There is a bad leak, so whoever was involved in the theft or driver of the vehicle should be dead in about thirty hours."

Latif, a Yemenite Muslim, remained loyal to Vinny, even though Vinny would have killed him at one time for calling him by his real name, Aboud.

He drove the large cargo truck through the garage door of a non-descript warehouse with a large, red cross. The sign at the entry declared No Trespassing; and anyone driving by would think it was an American Red Cross Distribution Center. It was not.

Latif felt nauseated and light-headed after the arduous and long drive. Only by the blessings of Allah had they found the two Chinese weapons lying in what had been a cotton field about thirty miles west of coastal Beaufort, when Beaufort was coastal. Now it was an island. He was not certain what the weapons were, but they were big. And heavy.

The cargo truck's tires rode low to the ground, trying as best they could to support the five-thousand pound bombs. The drive had been tedious and tiresome as Latif navigated secondary roads, avoiding South Carolina weigh stations.

"Allahu Akbar," came the greeting as Latif opened the driver's door. He stumbled as he stepped down, and the warehouse manager caught him before he collapsed to the stained, concrete floor.

"Are you all right, my friend?"

"Just a little dizzy," Ahmed said. Suddenly he felt hot and tingly all over, as though he was receiving a small, electric jolt.

"It is a blessing you made it, Latif. Our sources said there is a dragon net, or something; and the police are searching. There were more bombs found three miles from these two."

Latif should be upset at himself for missing the other three devices; but the truck could not have handled the load. And he had never felt so bad in his life. Perspiration dropped down his shirt, trying to cool his fever. He rubbed the painful sores on his palms, fearful of what was happening to him. He had worn a facemask and gloves, protecting himself from the devices; but now he considered the possibility that he should have been more cautious.

Within an hour, the heavy-lift crane had transported the two, 25-megaton hydrogen bombs into separate, reinforced cargo vans, olive-brown with no side or back windows. A decal of the fake UPS logo adorned both sides of the cargo vans, along with fake Department of Transportation numbers.

The two vans, driven by Bosnian militants Ismail and Balil, left the distribution center, the doors were closed and the movable shelving motors inside the large building sprang into action. A half-hour later, the facility looked like a Red Cross Distribution Center. Stainless-steel shelves of sterile gauze packs, alcohol swabs, blankets, catheter trays and food-rations lined the walls.

The two vans took secondary roads, and one headed southward toward Warner Robins. The second olive-brown van would do its nasty work in Houston the next day. There had been a plan to destroy the Port of Houston a few years earlier, but the attempt came to a disastrous end when the luxury yacht with the nuke mysteriously sank. Tomorrow, Ismail would change all that.

The effects of the radiation from the bomb that leaked in the fake Red Cross Center would not be noticeable for twenty-four hours or so. That would be fifteen hours after Latif fell to the warehouse floor in the Men's Room, twitching in pain and frothing at the mouth.

Chapter Thirty-Six

<u>July 30, the Ninth of Av</u>

I smail drove the interstates westward toward Houston and made good time, crossing through Georgia, Alabama and Mississippi in the process. The roads were in disarray, and he was certain the secondary roads were in much worse disrepair. A tenth of a mile ahead, a pack of wild dogs or coyotes fought for the freshly killed deer on the side of the highway.

Warned to take backroads, the cargo van, though heavily reinforced, was too small to require a weigh-station stop. He would save much time in his quest on I-10, plus there was the lady in Baton Rouge and *that* rendezvous. The rendezvous was first planned for New Orleans, before New Orleans was under the sea.

Balil continued his journey down the East Coast, where he would eventually shadow Interstate 16 to Macon and then south to Warner Robins.

His van was clean and polished like delivery vans should be, and his perfectly pressed and creased brown uniform and hat completed the picture. Though it was unlikely he could get on the highly guarded base, it did not matter. The hydrogen bomb onboard would take care of business.

He slid the mini-DVD into the player and once again listened to the effects of a 25-Megaton nuclear warhead, detonated over Atlanta.

"Do not be misled into the common belief that a hydrogen bomb and an atomic bomb are the same, only one is larger. They are completely different beasts. While an atomic bomb utilizes the force of a TNT explosion to initiate the fission process; the hydrogen, or thermonuclear bomb, uses a fission device to initiate the explosion. In other words, an atomic bomb uses dynamite to cause the massive

explosion; and a hydrogen bomb basically uses an atomic bomb to initiate explosion."

Balil swerved onto the access ramp of I-16, trying to avoid a pothole that may have been a small sinkhole. The bomb shifted in the back, releasing a small but invisible cloud of lethal radioactivity.

"While the Hiroshima bomb was devastating, there is no comparison to what a 15-megaton device would have wrought if detonated at an altitude of one mile.

"The Hiroshima bomb exploded eighteen-hundred feet above the ground and vaporized anything within a few city blocks. Wooden houses a mile away were knocked down and burned.

"A 15-megaton hydrogen bomb would kill 99% of all life, plants, animals and humans, within a 5-mile radius. Did you get that? People will sustain burns within a 20-mile radius. Folks, that means that people in a 1,256 square mile area will be burned.

"Now let me tell you about Tsar Bomba..."

Balil licked his lips but his tongue was nearly dry, and his eyes began to itch. He opened his last bottle of *Certified Spring Water*, gulping half the bottle. He would take the next exit and buy more, maybe some ice too. That would feel good about now, he thought, a nice cool piece of ice.

"... Bomba had a suspected yield of 50-megatons, weighed 60,000 pounds and blew up one night over an island off the coast of the old Soviet Union in 1961. It was the largest bomb ever built, so large it scared the top physicists in the world; and the program stopped.

"Now, suppose that bomb had detonated right here, two miles over my hometown, Atlanta, Georgia-Go Yellow Jackets. There would be the instantaneous annihilation of millions of folk, from the center of Atlanta to Cumming to Social Circle and Newnan... dead people and dead animals, irradiated water and food. People within five miles would turn into torches, catching on fire, in an instant."

Balil took the exit toward Warner Robins, and the air smelled like dead fish. He was sure he would vomit any second but held himself together. His stomach began to sear, as though someone had crammed a hot iron down his throat; and he went straight to the Men's Room as fast as he could run. He was an hour from the Air Force Base, and the bomb would automatically detonate in three hours. He had plenty of time. He rotated the faucet to wash sweat from his face but fainted when he saw the water. Red as blood, smelling like copper.

In his rush to comfort, Balil did not put the van in PARK and also left the motor running. The olive-brown cargo van began to slowly roll backwards across the convenience store parking lot, when two teenagers saw it and ran to the rescue, only rescue was not on their mind as they jumped in the front seat. It would be thirty-four minutes before anyone visited the Men's Room and found Balil's collapsed body.

"Can you believe it?" one of the teens asked, laughing with glee. "We just found our ride to Piney Oaks Golf Course. What's in the back?"

✡ ✡ ✡

Wild Willy was surprised to see Sarge at Briscoe Field when he arrived to examine the B36J Peacemaker aircraft. Large and small sinkholes covered the grounds; but the new, lengthy runway seemed blemish free. The shiny, silver turboprop-jet, the largest bomber in the U.S. Air Force to never be used on a bombing run, sat stoically on the runway, king of any hill.

"She looks fantastic," Sarge said. "I examined her thoroughly. What's the maximum fuel load for takeoff?"

"We don't need to have more than a half load and really don't need that to get to Warner Robins. About eighteen-thousand gallons. It's a long runway but don't want to risk the plane."

A loud sucking, thump-like sound caught their attention, followed by another; and the men scanned left.

"What's that?" Will asked.

"New sinkholes," Sarge said. "Been out here about two hours and have watched six form. Happens real quick and makes that weird noise. I walked the entire runway, both sides; but the closest holes are about fifty-feet south. We need to drain the fuel. We have about three-thousand gallons too much."

Will did not want to hear that bit of news. Draining and securing three-thousand gallons of fuel would take a few hours. They needed to get the heck out of Dodge. He had a bad feeling in the pit of his stomach. A white Range Rover pulled into the adjacent parking area, and Will motioned the driver to proceed to the runway.

Samarra drove forward, dodging a small sinkhole and parked at the edge, close to the large aircraft. The doors opened, and Will's passenger-crew disembarked. Sheryl and The Admiral would be a great help at Warner Robins should any troubles arise. Condi and Abe, if they could stop looking at each other, would make up part of the flight crew. Samarra, Audry and Chadbo...

"Where is Chadbo?" Will asked.

Samarra said nothing but pointed to the deep, blue morning sky.

"He disappeared," Audry said. "Poof."

"What?" Will asked, searching Samarra's face.

"That is true," Jeff said. "Witnessed by several Goddard Space Center scientists."

Will was stunned by the news, plus he was now short one crew member.

"What happened?"

"He was raptured," Audry said.

Rapture theory was fairly new to Will, and he had some problems with who was disappearing and who was not. Chadbo was a really great guy but not what Will considered to be deeply Christian.

"Mr. Hutz said," Audry continued, "only Jesus decides who vanishes and who does not. And when."

"Jeff, that leaves me one man short. You have to go with us."

Wild Willy did not mourn Chadbo's rapture but was finding himself a little resentful that *any* of them were still around.

Disappearing people had become almost routine over the past few years.

"Hon," Samarra said, looking Jeff in the eyes, "The twins are where we all hope to be one day soon. There were witnesses. There is no reason to stay."

Samarra did not plead often, and Jeff knew she was right. A sucking sound came from somewhere, but he paid no attention.

"How long before takeoff?" Jeff asked.

"About two hours, maybe three. Have to offload some fuel."

Will mentally kicked himself in the butt. As organized as he was, how could he have let the fuel-load slip by? They only needed enough for takeoff and a short trip to Warner Robins. Less weight; shorter runway.

"Tanker trucks should be here anytime," Sarge said.

"I'll be back," Jeff said in his best Arnold Schwarzenegger voice.

"Where are you going?" Samarra asked.

"Going to get Scarlette."

Audry shouted for joy. She was going to miss her doggie, but now the Great Dane would join them on the plane. This was going to be so much fun.

✡ ✡ ✡

"Pull over and let's see what's in the back, bro."

The young, seventeen-year-old driver pulled the olive-brown van into an abandoned parking lot. He looked in the rearview mirror and ran his fingers through his bushy, black hair; as though someone was there to witness his good looks.

The two teens tried and pried for fifteen minutes but could not open the doors to the rear compartment. The hydraulically-locked doors would not budge, controlled by a simple toggle-switch located by the driver's seat.

"Piney Oaks is calling, bro. We need to get there, rent some clubs and warm up."

The two brothers were admittedly, a little out of control; but both were avid golfers, young and foolish. They had some run-ins with the law but nothing serious. This was their first van theft, but they could apologize later. They could not miss the tryouts.

Once a year, Piney Oaks Golf Course had open house for teens aspiring to make the PGA Tour and play as an amateur at the Master's Golf Tournament in Augusta. The two boys knew they would make the cut, would become famous and could buy a set of the latest and greatest golf clubs. No more rentals.

An hour later, the UPS-looking cargo van pulled into the Golf Club parking lot and parked near the loading dock, as though they were making a delivery.

Across Highway 129, twenty-foot-high fences topped with razor wire guarded Warner Robins Air Force Base. The secret package inside the van continued its countdown. Ninety-two minutes until blastoff.

✧ ✧ ✧

Chairman Tseng and Little Nikita met secretly at Baikonur Cosmodrome in Kazakhstan. It was their final meeting before launch.

"Twenty-four hours from now, my friend."

Chairman Tseng shook his head enthusiastically.

"How do you plan to use the Tsar Bomba?"

Little Nikita's anticipation could not be contained as he described the effects of the 100-megaton warheads, thought to be nonexistent. Unlike the 1961 Tsar Bomba test, the new warheads weighed far less than the 60,000-pound original.

"We will launch from submarines, my friend," Little Nikita said, laughing.

The perfection of red mercury catalytic-enhanced nuclear explosives had drastically changed the mass required in early nuclear weapons.

"The warheads have a weight of less than 2,000 pounds and can wipe out any structure in a sixty-mile radius. During the 1961 test, wooden and brick structures forty miles from ground zero were totally destroyed. People located sixty miles away suffered severe burns. The shockwave traveled around the planet at least four times. And that was only a 50-megaton weapon."

Little Nikita was sharing nothing with Chairman Tseng that the chairman did not already know. Chinese intelligence were experts at miniature listening and spying devices, and they had recorded the Tsar Bomba stories many times via the nano-cameras in the LED lights supplied to Russia as a gift.

The meeting was brief, the two leaders shook hands and went their separate ways.

Chairman Tseng loathed Little Nikita and was glad to know the 100-megaton bombs would soon be used on their common enemy. China knew from their spying devices that Russia had an inventory of only five. He was also concerned about the number of missiles that would be fired, that possibly it would be overkill. Four-hundred nukes might overkill the world.

Of course, Little Nikita made a valid point. The United States could probably shoot down or destroy about forty percent of the missiles, but still. The United States would be uninhabitable.

"She will glow in the dark for many years, my friend," were Little Nikita's last words before departing.

✿ ✿ ✿

Jeff drove faster than usual, especially to be as old as he was. He was happy that Chadbo had been raptured, but he missed him and his solar updates. He suddenly found himself lonely. What would he do if all his friends were raptured but he was not? He drifted from those dark thoughts.

He rounded the large fountain in front of his home's entry, ran in the house and was greeted heartily by sweet Scarlette. Ten minutes later, the Great Dane jumped into the back of the Range Rover, happy to be going on a ride; and they headed east toward Briscoe Field.

The car swerved in a sudden gust, and Jeff hoped they could get the plane in the air without being blown off the runway. Scarlette lost her balance and plumped onto the floor.

"Mommy, is Jesus happy?"

The Voice.

Jeff could not help himself and looked in the rearview mirror, knowing full-well that Audry was not in the car.

"What do you mean, honey?"

"You know Mommy, is Jesus happy?"

"Of course he's happy, honey. Why would you ask?"

"Well, I was watching TV; and they were talking about this man on there, you know, named Elton John, who said Jesus was gay. So I got Daddy's old college dictionary and looked it up; and that man was right, except I thought everybody already knew Jesus was happy."

I am absolutely losing my mind, Jeff thought, wondering if hearing voices was an old-age thing. He watched Scarlette's expression in the mirror, but there was no indication she heard the voices. Audry and Melissa.

Jeff wiped a small tear that appeared, trying not to think about the wife who disappeared into the night sky over Jamaica. Ahead, a large hole appeared in Duluth-Lawrenceville Highway; and Jeff maneuvered the Range Rover to the right shoulder.

The Range Rover's radio played softly, and Jeff hummed along with the music...

You are my sunshine, my only sunshine. You make me happy, when skies are gray.

Jeff tapped the dashboard and the windshield darkened. The sun wasn't making anyone happy these days.

Pulling into Briscoe Field, he drove to the extended runway and was pleased to see the six propellers spinning away. At least he knew the engines worked.

"Come on, Jeff!" Samarra yelled and waved, trying to get his attention. She watched the train of sinkholes headed toward the runway. "We have to get out of here."

Jeff, Scarlette and a large suitcase of necessities were soon on the plane, clearance to Warner Robins was verified with the tower; and the behemoth began the takeoff. In the eyes of the crew, he detected much uncertainty. The runway that looked so long, now seemed quite short.

The plane lumbered and lumbered down the fifteen-thousand-foot runway, gathering speed, remarkably, for the hopeful liftoff. Unseen to the crew, a sinkhole swallowed the last section of the runway.

"Does this thing go any faster?" The Admiral yelled to Will in the pilot's seat.

"Watch this," Will said, a devious grin plastered across his face.

Will flipped four toggle switches simultaneously, and the four General Electric J47 jet engines engaged. Will spotted the large sinkhole.

"Oh, Jesus," Will shouted. "Hold on."

The plane shot down the runway and into the air, banking right toward Warner Robins. They would pass over Norcross, and Will remembered how stunned people were when the large plane approached Briscoe Field on the flight from Warner Robins. Even a mile up, the plane looked like it was just above the trees. He loved his big plane.

✿ ✿ ✿

"Man, I ain't never seen a cow *that* red before. Look how red that thang is."

Sarah glanced at the screen, looking up from the latest issue of *Norcross News*. It was definitely red, no doubt; and she wrinkled her nose at the sterile smell of the doctor's office. She nudged her husband, and James glanced at the screen.

"Where is that?" she asked.

"It's over there in Jerusalem. You know today is the day they gonna dedicate that new temple they built. What's wrong with him?" the man asked, nodding his head at James.

For a black man, James was suddenly pale, more pale than Sarah had ever known him to be; and she had known him to be for forty-four years, next month. His eyes were wide open as he watched the newsfeed of the red calf.

"Holy Shmoly," James mumbled. "It's the red heifer."

"The what?" the skinny man with the scraggly beard asked. Sarah thought he looked anorexic.

"The red heifer," Sarah repeated. "It is in the Bible."

She mentioned the Bible without thinking. Scraggly Beard gave her a hard look and then smiled. His two upper-front teeth were missing; and James nearly burst out laughing.

"Do you believe in that book?" he whispered.

"Of course," Sarah said. She would not whisper about the Lord. "Ever'body used to believe in the book just a few years ago."

"I don't know much 'bout it to tell the truth, other than what my cousin tells me. Now it's been banned most places. I was gonna buy one and read it but cain't find none anywhere."

"What do you want to know?" Sarah asked, watching the proceedings on the TV in the doctor's waiting office. There was lots of pomp and circumstance in Jerusalem this day, and the streets were filled in celebration.

"Well," the skinny man finally said. "I don't even know what to ask. How 'bout that-there red cow? What's the story on it?"

"That story is all about the Third Temple," James said.

"The third temple? What's that? And what happened to the first two?"

A nurse, plump with rosy cheeks and dressed in green, opened the waiting room door and apologized for the wait, explaining that the doctor was on his way. Surgery took longer than expected.

Sarah prepared to answer the man, frustrated. How could she explain the temples and red heifer to someone who knew nothing of Israel's history.

"My grandpa was a Jew," Scraggly Beard said. "His name was Abraham."

"Do you know Jewish history?" James asked.

"I tried to read that book by Flavius Josephus but never made it through the dang thang. It is a very long book. You know, the one about the Jews."

"Antiquities of the Jews," James said, though he had never read Josephus' history of the Jewish people.

"Yeah," the skinny man said. "That's the one."

Sarah breathed a sigh of relief.

"There have been two Jewish temples in the past. A guy named King Solomon built the first one. King Solomon's Temple was built for the glory of the God of Abraham and for housing the Ark of the Covenant. The Ark served as the housing for the original Ten Commandments tablets. Are you with me?"

"Yep," the man said, picking at his beard. "I saw the movie. Indiana Jones."

"That's right," James said. "That was a good movie."

Sarah gave both men *the look* and proceeded.

"King Solomon's Temple lasted 367 years before the King of Babylon razed it."

"Nebuchadnezzar," Scraggly Beard said. "The ninth of Av."

"I'm impressed," Sarah replied. "And yes. The date was during the fifth month of the Jewish calendar, the month of Av, on the ninth day."

"Mr. Murphy," the nurse said, entering the room. "Dr. Clayton can see you now."

James rose slowly from his chair and followed the nurse, glancing back at Sarah and giving her a thumbs-up. She was a great Bible storyteller if there ever was one.

"I'll tell ya somethin' else that's kinda in-ter-restin'," the man said. "They come back after bein' freed by King Cyrus and built them another temple. Temple Two," and the man let out a laugh that made Sarah laugh.

"You are funny," Sarah chuckled. "The Second Temple lasted 586 years, approximately. It was destroyed by the Romans in 70 AD."

"On the ninth of Av," the man chimed in. "That there day done proved to be a real dilemma for the Jewish folk."

"I think you know more than you are letting on."

"I do," the odd man replied. "But you gotta be careful in public places, don'tcha know."

"Anyway," Sarah continued, "the Temple cannot be dedicated without the sacrifice of an unblemished red heifer calf..."

"And unyoked," Scraggly Beard said. "Unblemished and unyoked."

"Yes. That is what the Old Testament says," Sarah said, even more impressed.

"Numbers 19," the man said and began to quote the scripture.

"The Lord said to Moses and Aaron: 'This is a requirement of the law that the Lord has commanded: Tell the Israelites to bring you a red heifer without defect or blemish and that has never been under a yoke. Give it to Eleazar the priest; it is to be taken outside the camp and slaughtered in his presence. Then Eleazar the priest is to take some of its blood on his finger and sprinkle it seven times toward the front of the tent of meeting. While he watches, the heifer is to be burned -- its hide, flesh, blood and intestines. The priest is to take some cedar wood, hyssop and scarlet wool and throw them onto the burning heifer. After that, the priest must wash his clothes and bathe himself with water. He may then come into the camp, but he will be ceremonially unclean till evening. The man who burns it

must also wash his clothes and bathe with water, and he too will be unclean till evening'."

"That's amazing," Sarah said, examining the man's face with a new awareness.

"Yeah, the whole thang sounds purty gross to me; but that's what Yahweh said. What's gross to me might be pleasant to the Almighty God."

The man walked over and took a drink from the wall-mounted water fountain.

"Sorry. Mouth got dry. So now the Jews have their unblemished and unyoked red heifer calf," the strange man added. "And the Third Temple is being dedicated today, even though it ain't finished. Coincidence?"

"How did you learn all this?" Sarah asked.

The scraggly bearded, toothless man, smiled and Sarah was certain she saw a twinkle in his eye.

"My cousin's a daggone preacher, don'tcha know. He taught me a lot when we was little. Ya know, it's really strange. Enoch stutters awfully bad, so bad you can barely understand what he's sayin'; but when he preaches in his little, white church with the yeller daffodils, his speech is perfect."

The noise began faintly, a low rumble that rapidly grew toward a roar. The single-story doctor's office began to shake. Doctor Clayton, James and two nurses ran out and through the waiting room, motioning Sarah to hurry. After what happened to Berkeley Lake, everyone was earthquake sensitive.

Sarah followed the group and rushed outside, into the parking lot. She searched skyward for the roar, in anticipation of something; and the sun seemed brighter than ever. Why were they running? Was it a meteor strike? Her heart began to pound.

A dark shadow embraced the parking lot as the giant plane flew directly overhead. None had ever seen a B36J bomber and stared in awe.

"Is it going to crash?" Sarah yelled, trying to be heard.

"No, it is not going to crash," the strange man said; and Sarah's curiosity piqued.

The man was no longer scraggly beard but appeared well groomed. His beard was long but neatly trimmed; and he said *thing* instead of *thang*.

"The plane is a B36J Peacemaker," the newly-groomed man continued. "The largest bomber ever built that never dropped a single bomb in combat."

"What is your name?" Sarah shouted.

The large aircraft slowly moved away, and Sarah realized for the first time that the gigantic plane was not so low. It just looked low.

"Jesus," the man answered and smiled. "My name is Jesus."

His two front teeth were no longer missing.

They returned to the waiting room, and Sarah looked around for the man. Nowhere to be seen.

"Where is the man with the beard?" Sarah asked Dr. Clayton.

Still stunned by the events, a monster plane flying over the building, a plane he had never seen before...

"Dr. Clayton?"

"I'm sorry, Sarah," he finally answered. "Not sure what we just saw."

Dr. Robert Clayton had been around the block but had never seen a plane like that flying over John's Creek and remained shaken. With all the stuff going on in the world and the Berkeley Lake earthquake, a giant plane should not be surprising.

"What man with the beard?" he asked.

Sarah was stunned that he even asked the question.

"The man in the waiting room with no front teeth. And he had a scraggly beard. He had a strange dialect but then..."

"Sally?" Dr. Clayton said to the receptionist who was listening to the exchange. "Did you see this patient that Sarah mentioned?"

"No," she answered.

"I sure saw him," James said. "And Sarah and I own a detective agency. We observe things."

"Well," Sally said. "You may have 'observed' him, but I never saw a toothless man with a beard. Did he tell you his name?"

"Yeah," Sarah said, a look of dismay crossing her face. "He said his name was Jesus. When I looked up, he had vanished."

✿ ✿ ✿

The B36J slowly climbed in altitude; and it seemed that all the people remaining in Norcross, Doraville and Chamblee watched in wonder, some fearful of a plane they had never seen.

Like a giant, cigar-shaped mirror, the sun reflected off the sleek, silver skin of the plane as it made its way to 34,000-feet. Forty minutes later, the plane landed gracefully at Warner Robins; and fuel tankers were at the ready.

"That's the fastest refueling I've ever seen," Sarge said as the B36J lumbered for takeoff, speeding down the long runway.

Jeff looked out one of the round portholes that Wild Willy added to the original and spotted the Piney Oaks Golf Course below. He wondered if he would ever play golf again.

One of the onboard large screens was tuned to *Israeli News*. With the plane on autopilot, most of the group watched the ceremonies, as President Morsi prepared to make his Pre-Dedication speech.

"I am so happy we are going to Israel, Dad," Audry said to Jeff.

"Why is that?" Jeff asked and held her soft hand, a hand that was no longer tiny.

Where had all the years gone? It seemed like only yesterday that he and Melissa had adopted Audry; and now, she was a teenager. A beautiful teenager with glowing red hair.

In an instant, the interior of the plane lit up in the whitest light any of the passengers had ever witnessed, and everyone shielded their eyes out of reflex, most thankful to have their dark-tinted glasses.

Audry nearly fell as the plane shook violently, and Jeff thought surely it must be the wind. Chadbo had warned him of the wind the last time they spoke. Up and down, left to right, the plane was buffeted by something. This was a heck of a wind.

The cockpit filled with near-blinding light, and Sarge feared that the plane would shake apart. He thought that God Himself had grabbed hold of the plane and was shaking it violently.

"What the heck was that?" Wild Willy asked but had an idea. Had to be an asteroid hitting Earth or a nuclear explosion. He activated the two rear-facing cameras and the monitors said it all.

The wide mushroom cloud rose in the west, now higher than the B36J; and the tailwind gusted from the blast wave, increasing the plane's forward speed more than a hundred miles-per-hour. He looked at Sarge, hoping the wings did not rip off.

"This ain't your grandpa's atomic bomb," he said. "I think they just blew up Warner Robins."

Chapter Thirty-Seven

Don't let anyone deceive you in any way, for that day will not come until the rebellion occurs and the man of lawlessness is revealed, the man doomed to destruction. He will oppose and will exalt himself over everything that is called God or is worshiped, so that he sets himself up in God's temple, proclaiming himself to be God.

2 Thessalonians 2:3-4

The Dedication

Temple Mount

Jews and non-Jews gathered for the celebration and the sacred dedication of the Third Temple. Scaffolding still surrounded parts of the building under construction; but there were no workmen on this day, a day the Jews had awaited two-thousand years. It was also a day that Islam said would never happen. Nearly four hundred Jewish workmen had been slain in the process. Armed drones now guarded the grounds.

While Wild Willy and his B36J crew watched the dedication from cruising altitude on a remarkably clear monitor, Sheryl stared out a porthole at the ocean below. She hid her depression but knew she lost many friends at Warner Robins.

"Hard to believe there has been no news so far about whatever happened back there," The Admiral said and held her cold, clammy hand. He wondered if she might be in shock.

"It had to be the base," Sheryl said. "There would be a news blackout. Of course, there are bound to be leaks."

But why hadn't someone called her? Surely they were not all dead.

"What time does this dedication start," he asked, trying to divert her attention.

"About ten minutes, at sunset. All the necessary procedures have been completed. The red heifer has been sacrificed for the cleansing ritual, and those deemed unclean have been sprinkled with the ashes."

"It will be interesting to hear Morsi's big speech," The Admiral said sarcastically.

The Admiral and Sheryl had suspicions that self-proclaimed, World Leader Morsi was a big player in the end-times drama, possibly the anti-Christ, rumored by the ever-decreasing Christian population.

The B36 flew smoothly; and Wild Willy was fully confident that Sarge could handle the plane and walked over to the love seat, occupied by the amorous newlyweds, Abe the Bartender and Condi.

"Looks like this couch was named appropriately. Are you guys going to kiss all the way to Israel?"

"No." Condi answered, standing. "We are going to watch the dedication."

A roar from the crowd gathered around the new temple caught the attention of everyone except Sarge, who maintained his place in the cockpit. The camera panned across the crowd, stopping to focus on some of the celebrants and settled on a small group of four, two couples. They were not celebrating and looks of dismay crossed their faces.

"That's Aludra," Wild Willy said. "Not sure who the other lady is, but the two guys are Ben and Jon. Met them the night Mount Hermon blew up.

"They look pretty glum," Abe said.

"Yeah," Wild Willy commented. "Aludra thinks this is the night that sends the world into darkness, much darker than the world has faced, even darker than the days of Noah. Like the Bible said."

"The Bible said that?" Sarge asked. "Gotta go to the little boy's room."

"Yes," Will answered. "Never knew it until a few months ago when Aludra pointed it out."

"What does it say?" Sarge again prompted and tried to contain his bladder.

"I memorized it," Will said. "Genesis 6."

Sarge waited, uncomfortably for Will to continue.

"Is that it?" Sarge asked. "You aren't gonna tell us?"

Will smiled and began. He figured that his memorization of scripture was quite a surprise.

The Lord saw how great the wickedness of the human race had become on the earth, and that every inclination of the thoughts of the human heart was only evil all the time. The Lord regretted that he had made human beings on the earth, and his heart was deeply troubled. So the Lord said, "I will wipe from the face of the earth the human race I have created--and with them the animals, the birds and the creatures that move along the ground--for I regret that I have made them."

After a brief pause to ponder the wording, Sarge turned and entered the toilet compartment. Before entering he turned and said, "That sounds like Earth today."

✡ ✡ ✡

The Speech

"I would first like to thank the Jewish people for building their Third Temple. My Shi'a brethren in Greater Persia live in anguish because I so heavily endorsed peace with Israel and the rebuilding of their Holy Temple. I can only say to those Muslims who oppose, this was the land of the Jews long before the Muslims invaded and stole it.

"Yes. You heard me correctly. It was King Cyrus II of Persia who rescued and freed the Jews from Babylon and the evil King Nebuchadnezzar. It was this king of Persia who helped the Jews rebuild their Second Temple; and the pagan Romans destroyed it, like the pagan Babylonians destroyed the First Temple."

World Leader Morsi mandated that there would be no drones, armed or unarmed, at the dedication, much to the dismay of the IDF. As darkness set in, Israeli reconnaissance detected a swarm of something, forming to the east of Jerusalem. Soon another appeared to the north.

"Today I declare that I am much, much more than a world leader. Israel will have peace, Islam will have peace, Christians will have peace, for the first time in history since the creation of Adam. Those who rebel against these decrees shall pay a steep price."

"That is interesting," Aludra said.

"What?" asked Hillary and Ben, simultaneously.

"He did not mention the unbelievers or other faiths. I am wondering if they have faith."

"You know what else is interesting?" Ben's wife asked.

Ben waited. Hillary knew a lot about the end-times.

"It is interesting that the World Leader Morsi is protecting believers. In the United States, you can get arrested for public display of a Bible. It is disgusting what is going on in the world's largest Christian community." Morsi continued.

"I will protect the children of God, no matter where they are. The world has turned against the descendants of Abraham, but that is about to change.

"I have control of the armed forces of many nations. Those who I do not control will destroy each other. Even tonight, a Chinese-Russian coalition will attack the Great Satan with the Sword of Allah..."

"Hmmm," Ben said. "That is not good."

Ben had heard his share of blowhards in his life; but this guy took the cake, even better than some recent U.S. presidents. He had followed reports of Morsi's so-called miracles, so why were they not on the internet? He did not believe any of it.

"Israel, for the first time in two-thousand years can continue their Holy and ancient rituals as commanded by Moses."

The Israelites went absolutely crazy; and the crew of the B36J, high above the Atlantic, was glued to the large monitor. Sheryl and Abe exchanged worried glances; because they, more than the others, knew what might come next. Would Morsi declare himself as the Messiah?

"Watch and you will see!" Morsi shouted; and the crowd of mostly Israelis and other Jews from around the world, went wild.

"Messiah! Messiah! Messiah!" the crowd shouted in unison, as though rehearsed; and Morsi pointed to the east and to the north.

Immediately, it seemed to those on the plane watching the monitor, the crowd went silent. Fear rose in their hearts and the hum of a dark swarm of... were they locusts?

Thousands of drones, dark as the night would soon be, flew from the Palestinian territory after exiting the numerous tunnels. Below each was a container of deadly something: acids, microbes, small but powerful explosives.

The IDF responded as best they could, but the drones were like a swarm of flies. There were too many. Loudspeakers outside the new Temple grounds blared for everyone to take cover, but the crowd did not seem to hear a word. It was as though they were in another world. They remained glued to the coming creatures from the dark. Most did not recognize cloud getting ever closer as a drone swarm.

"Do not fear," Morsi said. "I have protected you from harm."

The drones moved forward at a top speed of about sixty miles per hour. As they approached the Third Temple from a quarter mile away, the people waited, anxious in fear. Babies in the crowd wailed; but otherwise there was silence. Then a crash, followed by another crash and another.

World Leader Morsi held his hands high; and one after another, the drones crashed into some kind of invisible barrier or force-field. The crowd stared in disbelief.

Outside the barrier where Israeli Arabs watched angrily from a distance, the deadly drones fell to the ground. Explosions followed by screams of agony as the world's strongest acid dispersed before evaporating, on the people below.

Aludra, Hillary, Ben and Jon could hear nothing but knew they should. One explosion followed another, but their world was one of near-total silence.

"Ever read that book by Stephen King?" Hillary asked quietly.

"The one about the invisible dome that covered a small town?"

No one said anything but watched the hundreds of drones continue to crash into something invisible.

"It is over!" Morsi said to the silent crowd. "It is over."

A colossal cheer rose from the crowd; and the people once again started shouting *Messiah! Messiah!* over-and-over. Inside the dome, or whatever, the sound was deafening.

"From this day forward, I say, I command: Tear down your walls."

As the B36J approached the shores of Western Europe and the sky darkened, Jeff was certain that he spotted a large meteor shower moving east to west toward the United States. He motioned The Admiral.

"I am your savior!" Morsi shouted; and the people screamed, delirious with happiness. "I am the one who was to come. I am the one who the prophets said, 'He will be called God'."

Aludra was amazed and began to cry as she saw the days of Jacob's troubles play out right in front of what had been her Muslim eyes a few years earlier. All the Jewish people accepting this man as the Messiah was prophecy fulfilled but also, disheartening. How could they buy this spiel?

"I AM the Messiah. I AM the Twelfth Imam. I AM God Almighty and have come to live among you."

With those words a giant statue of Morsi was unveiled at the delight of the crowd; and many fell to their knees, bowing to the iron and bronze monument as though it was alive.

While the Haredi Jews, the most orthodox in Israel, celebrated, some suffered discomfort that the Messiah claimed to be God. That was not in the scriptures, only that he would be called God.

To the 144,000 Jews who believed that Jesus was the Messiah; they knew it would not be long. They would soon be beheaded.

Aludra checked her watch. Eight o'clock. Will should be landing just after midnight.

The crew of the B36J watched the dedication end and sat quietly, analyzing the speech. No one said anything, but all were troubled. They all had a good idea of what would come next and then Armageddon and the return of Jesus, greatly anticipated and long awaited.

"I am going to doze for a while," Jeff said to Audry and Samarra, and he laid back in the recliner. Sleep came quickly.

Wake up, Daddy.

Soon Jeff drifted into a familiar world of dreams, dark and depressing.

Abe kissed Condi like she had never been kissed before, as though it was their last; and she knew that God had answered her prayers about the childhood sweetheart she thought she lost.

Chapter Thirty-Eight

The constant drone of the giant bomber and vibration of the reclining sofa solidified the depth of Jeffrey Ross' dreams, except for an occasional *Wake up, Daddy.*

As though sliding down another dark path to a never ending abyss, he began to see things he wished he had not. Front page newspaper headlines spun slowly, like a windmill, showing him things that he hoped would not happen, each newspaper with a progressive date.

Israel Declares Morsi is the Messiah
The Jerusalem Post, August 1, 2020

Yesterday, the Ninth of the month of Av, Israel's long awaited Messiah has finally arrived, and he is a Shi'a Muslim. At the Dedication of the Third Temple yesterday afternoon, World Leader Morsi proclaimed to be not only the Messiah but also Yahweh, the God of Abraham.

The announcement was met with acceptance and jubilee with most in Israel. Though Morsi is a Muslim, the Muslim world has rejected Morsi's claims and say he is an apostate to Islam.

An anonymous call claimed there is a war going on against the Messianic Jewish population in Israel, who have refused to accept Morsi and claim he is the Beast in Revelation.

Ultra-Orthodox Jews chased and captured a group of the Jews who believe in Jesus, stoning thirty to death. The death toll is expected to grow. There are an estimated 144,000 Messianic Jews in Israel, and they have refused to bow to the new Morsi Monument or take his Mark.

Mysteriously, an invisible dome or force-field appears to have protected Jerusalem during the Temple Dedication. There were hundreds of reports of a fleet of drones flying into an invisible, protective barrier. Most of the drones crashed while others maintained flight and crashed into Palestinian territories. Some claim that the invisible Shield of Allah protected the people when Morsi held his arms high in the air, which he did during much of the ceremony.

Burn Baby, Burn: The United States Is On Fire
The London Times, September 9, 2020

Last week the United States was attacked by a coalition from the Far East, including but not limited to, China and Russia. Nuclear missiles were fired from the Gulf of Mexico, the Sea of Cortez and the arctic in the vicinity of the Russian military base, Arkticheskiy Trilistnik.

At this point, sources are inconsistent; but what is consistent is, approximately five-hundred nuclear missiles were fired at the United States. Military.com reports that less than thirty percent were intercepted. An estimated twenty-five percent of the United States is on fire, more than eighty-million are dead and civil war has broken out.

The population of the U.S. has decreased the past five years from a peak of 342-million to an estimated population after the nuclear attack of only 90-million. Millions were killed on the western coast by the Ross Ice Shelf Wave and millions in the east, by the La Palma tsunami.

The revolt against vaccines in America and Europe have resulted in unprecedented spread of smallpox, Black Death, measles, whooping cough, various flus, Ebola and Marburg. The polio outbreak in Europe will only get worse without the vaccine, reports the CDC in Atlanta.

Dr. Edgar Allan Poe from Homeland Security had this to say last week before the attack in an interview on OLNN-London.

"In five years, the world population dropped from eight billion to three billion. One reason is the temperature of the planet. High temps bring drought, fire, famine, crime, disease, war and mean tempers. It has not been war that is killing mankind, at least yet; it is Mama Nature. Wars will be the by-product, and they are coming soon."

Dr. Poe is head of Homeland Bio-Cyber Security and has been warning the world of coming wars for several years

In the meantime, how long will America burn?

Europe Burns as Famine Rages
El País, June 30, 2021

El Pais, Spain's most-read news source, reports that Europe is on fire, primarily a result of arson as Islamic jihadists set fire to forests across the continent.

Eyewitnesses claim that fire rained down from the sky as unprecedented winds spread the conflagration from west to east. Cinders have blown into Norway and Sweden; and much of the Norwegian population that remained have burned to death.

Scientists state that the air is toxic from the decaying carcasses of millions of dead, charred animals. Animals that remain are starving and have targeted small groups of people and other animals for consumption. Most of Europe's animal control infrastructure has been decimated, and one zoologist in Madrid is calling the phenomenon, Animals Gone Wild. That is certainly the case.

Israel Sinks Russian Aircraft Carrier in Mediterranean
World Military News, August 6, 2022

Coincidence? The Ninth of Av has remained a significant date in Jewish history; and once again, a disaster is in the making.

The ten remaining powers in the world have condemned Israel's latest move in the coming war at Armageddon, the sinking of Russia's largest aircraft carrier and shooting down two Chinese J-38 stealth fighters.

World Leader Morsi warned all world leaders to refrain from attacking Israel and has implemented a strictly controlled buy-sell ban to anyone not pledging allegiance to Morsi.

The statue of Morsi that was unveiled at the dedication of the Third Temple has reportedly moved. Several dozen eyewitnesses have posted video on the internet indicating that the statue bowed its head and cried blood.

Pope Pius XIII proclaims that Morsi is the Second Coming of Jesus and suggested that everyone respect and bow to the miraculous, moving monument.

While Morsi may be the Messiah, video footage out of the Holy Land, now comprised of Israel, Egypt, North Africa, Jordan, Saudi and Iran are graphic. Thousands of the remaining Christians are being beheaded daily for not taking the Morsi Mark, and the videos are splattered all over Youtube-Asia showing the executions. Wild birds and other scavengers are fed the remains.

The Orthodox crackdown on all things Christian in Israel continues. Estimates now claim that more than 100,000 of the 144,000 Jesus-believing Jews have been slaughtered, as Israelites continue to defame and mock the message of Christ. Morsi is clearly their man though the Jesus-believing Israelis are quick to point out their existence was foretold in the Bible:

"Do not harm the land or the sea or the trees until we put a seal on the foreheads of the servants of our God. Then I heard the number of those who were sealed: 144,000 from all the tribes of Israel."

It is reported that Morsi has control of large parts of the world's military and is responsible for the recent solar storms that have derailed power grids in Russia, China and what remains of charred Europe and the U.S.

The military buildup surrounding the Holy Land continues as the Morsi Alliance begins to unravel. Egypt is the first to rebel and has stationed troops in the Sinai.

Indonesia's large Islamic Army of Allah has moved by sea instead of the land routes once planned through India and Pakistan. The Hindu-Islamic War continues to rage throughout the intensely irradiated countries.

Jeff stirred as the plane was buffeted by strong winds and looked out the porthole by the recliner. With the moon virtually invisible now and so many stars missing, he expected to see nothing below except pinpoints of light in areas that remained with electric power. That was not the case. Far below the plane, Spain and Portugal were aflame; and Jeff thought it possible that the entire countries were burning.

Wake up, Daddy.

"I am awake, Audry," Jeff answered and reached for her hand. She was not there. He fell back to sleep, wondering what the next headline would be. Could it get worse?

He now sat alone in a dreamland Starbucks with a latte in hand. Dreams were so weird. He picked up the new *Jerusalem Post Holy Land News* and began to read. CHRISTIANS PURGED was the headline, an article about the slaughter of the remaining Coptic Christians in North Africa at the hands of jihadists who considered the Christians as infidels, worthy only of slaughter.

Jeff looked around the coffee shop, and it resembled the one in Dunwoody, the one he went to every morning until it was bombed that day. Wow, he thought. How time flies.

In the twinkling of an eye, an absolute instant, Jeff seemed to be suspended in a world of darkness and the pungent odor of sulfur and organic decay replaced the sweet aroma of his Starbucks latte.

Brightness burst out of the darkness, orange and hot; and there were thousands of people running in fear, some dressed and some not, clothing ripped and shredded and charred.

"Run! Run!" a disheveled man shouted, his skin dark gray from soot. "Yellowstone blew up. You need to hurry. Ash is falling! Ash is falling everywhere!"

For the first time, Jeff realized that the smothering darkness would not go away for years. In his strange vision, everywhere he looked, there were volcanos erupting; and large plumes of smoke and ash assaulted the environment with volumes of greenhouse gases from God, not mankind. Or maybe it was Satan, the ruler of the earth. Knowing this was not reality but only a dream, Jeff ran anyway, as fast as his old, tired legs could carry him; and he fell off a cliff.

Falling, he controlled his emotions, telling himself it was only a dream. With a soft thump, he landed in a bed of leaves, surrounded by the sounds of the sick... moaning, groaning and the stench of incontinence and death.

He scanned his surroundings, expecting Missy T and Kipper T to show up any minute; and everywhere he looked was paralysis.

"What is this place?" he asked a dark-haired girl, maybe twenty-something, in a blue Medline wheelchair next to the pile of leaves. Remarkably, the wheelchair looked unscathed.

"It's a polio camp, dum-dum. What do you think it is?" she snapped, stooped and unmoving except for her lips. Her breathing was heavy and appeared difficult as she gulped in as much smoke-filled air as possible. "I hate this place."

Jeff tried to do a quick count but there were too many.

"Why do so many have polio?" he asked.

"They destroyed the vaccine, that's why. Are you stupid or somethin'?"

Jeff did not answer. He could not blame the poor girl, so young and confined. No wonder she was so ticked off.

"I will pray for you," Jeff said and gently held her paralyzed hand.

"Who you goin' to pray to? The god who put me in this chair? The god that let the vaccine get destroyed? The god who infected millions with smallpox? The god who brought us AIDS?"

She sobbed.

"No thank you, sir. Not interested in your kinda god."

He left the girl, pretty but twisted and walked down the sloping terrain. Moonlight brightened the night, and he smiled. This was what he loved about dreams and thanked God for the full moon, no longer red, at least in this world.

He walked cautiously, fearing another cliff; but that did not happen. Instead he was sitting by a pool at a South Florida resort, the luxurious Cheeca Lodge on Islamorada Key. The ocean lapped at the sandy seashore; and a mint julip and vase of bright yellow daffodils graced his small table. He picked up the newspaper.

World War III Breaks Out on Plains of Megiddo, Israel
Omega Letter News Network-Istanbul, July 20, 2023

Is this the War of Armageddon?

Israel and Messiah Morsi are celebrating what they are calling a 'fulfillment of prophecy' that will lead to Morsi's takeover of the world. Pope Pius XIII was seen dancing in the streets when Turkish and Russian soldiers invaded from the north and overwhelmed Israeli troops.

Jeff paused, thinking about what he just read. Why would the so-called Jewish messiah be celebrating at the capture and death of Israeli troops? That did not make sense. He read on.

The Israeli troops were overwhelmed and slaughtered by the troops from the North when they refused to fight for Morsi, claiming he is a false messiah.

Some of the few remaining Christians in Israel, the ones who have not been hunted and slaughtered like pigs, are claiming the takeover will be Islamic, not Jewish. These are the Jewish Christians who have refused to take the Morsi Mark and apparently have their own mark on their foreheads that only they can see.

The headline rotated and faded, only to be replaced by another, and another. The dream was intense, more intense than usual; and he never felt the turbulence as the B36J flew through the flame-driven wind from the burning forests below. Unbeknownst to Jeff, the plane had become a sauna.

Blip Is Back and Brighter Than Ever
Omega Letter News Network-Jerusalem, July 24, 2023

The mysterious, bright light that has appeared several times over the past 10 years, has reappeared and astronomers claim it has been moving through space at an extreme rate, several times faster than the speed of light, which is impossible according to Einstein.

The light was spotted using the Chinese Space Explorer Telescope a week ago and is now located directly above Israel, height unknown. Mechanized fighting in the Plains of Megiddo has ceased due to equipment malfunction. GPS communication satellites have been mysteriously knocked out of service. There has been little solar electromagnetic activity directed at Earth, and many are blaming the loss of communication on Blip.

The warring forces have been seen in hand-to-hand combat and on horses and camels, fighting with swords. Temperatures in the Plains are well above record highs.

As the world's powers brutally battle, using large cavalries to replace tanks, rivers of blood have appeared in battle areas, some as deep as two and three feet.

The light continues to hover, somewhat like a UFO; and the fighting continues. Radiation levels are deadly in areas, and death estimates have topped 50,000,000. That is fifty-million, folks. Environmental scientists are warning about total global collapse.

Hailstorms reported throughout the Holy Land with 100-pound hailstones have destroyed complete cities and killed tens of thousands of people and millions livestock. The stench is reported to be unbearable.

The plane remained airborne, encountering turbulence that should have torn it apart. The inside temperature climbed to one-twenty, and Jeff's clothing clung to his sweat-ridden body.

JESUS CHRIST RETURNS
Omega Letter News Network-Jerusalem, July 27, 2023

It is the Ninth of Av in Israel, a day with a tragic history for Jewish people; but today is like no other.

The few remaining Messianic Jews being held for slaughter in Guillotine Houses across the Holy Land disappeared yesterday as the extremely white light over Israel began to intensify exponentially. There were many eyewitnesses.

There has not been darkness in the Holy Land since the light arrived three days ago, and reports from the Plains of Megiddo claim that a Heavenly Army emerged from the light and wiped out all the enemies of Israel. Jewish Defense Forces are gathering the weapons of war to be melted and recycled as instruments of peace and goodness.

It was these events that led to the widespread mourning as Jews around Israel and other parts of the world realized that Morsi was the predicted hoax, not the savior; and that they had been wrong for 2,000 years, searching fruitlessly for a messiah that had already come and been crucified.

The B36J was sweltering, and Jeff's clothing was drenched. The huge plane rocked like a storm-struck sailing yacht.

Wake up, Daddy.

Slowly, Jeff returned to reality, and reality was quite hot. An orange glow from the ground below lit the interior of the plane with a hell-like glow. Buffeting winds wreaked havoc and the plane rocked from side-to-side. *Where was everyone?*

Jeff looked but saw no one in the plane. He seemed to be alone. He made his way to the cramped cockpit, opened the door and there sat Kipper T and Missy T, pilot and copilot.

"Well, hello there," Missy T said. "Kind of hot, isn't it?"

"Where is Audry?" Jeff asked.

The plane suddenly dove, and Missy T let out a "WHOA" and grabbed the control stick. The plane leveled but still swayed side-to-side.

"Everyone is gone, my friend."

Jeff stared through the front windshield; and small, white wisps moved upward toward the sky.

"Those are spirits of the dead who were killed for believing in the Christ, Jeffrey. Resurrected to the Army of God for the Great Battle of Megiddo," Kipper T explained. "Just like it plainly said in the Lord's Book."

Jeff felt alone and the plane rocked like a bull in a rodeo. How was this plane staying in one piece?

"It's not in one piece, Jeff," Kipper T said, a note of seriousness to his tone. "We lost three of the engines."

"The whole world looks on fire," Jeff said glumly.

"It is for the most part," Kipper T said. "It is the Lake of Fire."

"The one where Satan will be thrown in?" Jeff asked.

"You got it," Missy T said.

In an instant the orange glow of the Lake of Fire vanished and Jeff saw nothing except beauty and splendor. Animals were everywhere, lingering among the people, lions with lambs living in peace. There was no war, no fighting, no disease, no automobile accidents because there were no automobiles or trucks. The air was crystal clear and the plane quickly cooled. It was the most beautiful place he had ever witnessed.

"What is this place?" Jeff asked but knew the answer.

"This is the kingdom of God, a renewed Garden of Eden," Missy T explained. "Just like Isaiah said:

"The wolf will live with the lamb, the leopard will lie down with the goat, the calf and the lion and the yearling together; and a little child will lead them. The cow will feed with the bear, their young will lie down together, and the lion will eat straw like the ox."

Jeff hoped the plane would land in this beautiful and peaceful land, but the plane abruptly did a one-eighty, heading back over the Lake of Fire. The plane fell and began to slowly circle, and Jeff looked out one of the portholes. Every engine had been torn from the wings, and the flaming lake rushed toward the plane.

"Do you know how to fly this thing?" Jeff shouted.

No answer. Missy T and Kipper T had vanished. The plane spun out of control and fell at a steep angle. Jeff wept.

✡ ✡ ✡

Beep… beep… beep… beep…

Jeff lay supine with his head supported by a sterile, hospital-smelling pillow. He felt oblivious and drained as he slowly stirred.

Wake up, Daddy.

Had they landed?

Silence.

Nothing but silence. No low rumble of the B36J, cruising over a Lake of Fire. Only the quiet but annoying beep-beep-beep.

His depression was deep. He had seen death, destruction and disease that no man should ever witness; and the haunting cries of the suffering would never leave him. Where was he?

"They didn't make it," he mumbled.

"Mr. Ross? Mr. Ross?"

The nurse, shocked at the sudden turn of events, hit the red, emergency call button.

"Who did not make it, Mr. Ross?" she asked.

Jeff began to cry.

"The dead," he sobbed. "The dead who will never really die. They will suffer in death. I don't want to go with them."

Jeff ran his hand through his hair, puzzled that his gray and thinning crop was much longer than normal. He tried to open his eyes, but the light was blinding.

"Where am I?" he asked, now noting the pain of the IV in his arm, dislodged by his sudden movement. He dozed off and began to snore.

Three nurses and a doctor entered the room, dressed in green scrubs. They had not expected him to survive.

"Never heard him snore before," the head nurse said. "Has anyone called his wife?"

"All vital signs are normal," someone said, and the chart was duly noted.

"He woke up," the attending nurse explained. "Out of the blue. He said something about someone not making it."

Jeff dreamed of smoke and the lurid odor of the *unclean*. He gagged at the smell, and the nursing staff briefly paused. A technician prepared to suction if necessary, but it was not.

"Do you think he will wake up again?" a young nurse in training asked.

"Most likely," Doctor Khular said. "Comatose patients do not snore, as a rule. This is a good sign."

The staff was jubilant, almost giddy. They had hoped and prayed that Jeffrey Ross would make a full recovery; and when he began to mention names in his sleep, they were encouraged.

"What is he saying?" Dr. Khular asked.

"He keeps mentioning names. The Admiral, Abe the Bartender and someone he called Wild Willy."

A ruckus at the door of the hospital suite announced the arrival of Jeff's wife; and she flew through the door, out of breath.

"I got here as fast as I could," she said. "Is Jeffrey still awake?"

"He is dozing at the moment, Mrs. Ross and is talking in his sleep. He keeps mentioning people."

"Turn on the news," she said. "That might jar him. He loves the news."

The head-nurse grabbed the remote and activated the monitor, appeasing Jeff's wife and also curious to see if the news would be a stimulus. Her eyes teared as she watched Mrs. Ross tenderly hold her husband's hand, like she had done every day since the stroke; and she paused to listen to the President speak.

"… present course indicates that a collision with Earth looks imminent. At its current speed, the anticipated impact date is next January 16 to 18, 2012. I know that December 21, 2012, at least according to Mayan predictions, has been portrayed on numerous news and cable programs as the date of the end of days. Several other apocalyptic writings seem to indicate that 2012 will be the last year of life as we know it."

Jeff stirred and squeezed… someone's hand, soft and familiar. The smell. Something about the smell. Gardenias. Melissa always smelled like gardenias. He drifted into darkness, but this dream had a bright light at the end of the very dark tunnel. *Blip.*

Jami, Jenni and Audry entered the medical suite, cautious but optimistic. They had been praying all the way to the Medical Center of Duluth, and eight-year-old Audry was especially excited.

"Bombs have detonated all over the United States, France and England. Manhattan had an earthquake, and now there's this terrible news of an asteroid or some other large Near-Earth Object heading our way."

Jeff moaned, drifting again toward consciousness, trying to focus on the news report in the background.

"It's the Dark Comet," Jeff mumbled as he drifted in-and-out of sleep.

Why were they still reporting on the Mayan Apocalypse that never happened? Someone kissed him on his forehead, and he slowly managed to open his eyes.

Beep, beep, beep, beep, beep…

Jeff's heart raced and the staff went into action, moving everyone away from the bed. A defibrillator kit was at the ready when, as quickly as the Afib started, it stopped.

"Jeff, you will one day see Melissa again."

Beep… beep… beep… beep.

"Am I dreaming," he asked, looking up into a face, a beautiful, loving, concerned face; and he began to cry. If this was a dream, he wanted to stay here.

Melissa squeezed his hand and tears streamed down her face. She ran her fingers through his long, graying hair, and mouthed *I love you.*

"Welcome back."

Chapter Thirty-Nine

For God so loved the world that he gave his one and only Son, that whoever believes in him shall not perish but have eternal life.

John 3:16

"Where have I been?"

Groggy and weak, Jeff's brain had not quite registered what was happening. Was he dreaming or was this reality?

The medical staff stepped out of the hospital room, joyful for the family and for themselves. They had all grown fond of the family during the months-long drama, and many specialists doubted that he would emerge from the coma. His brain and heart activity had been all over the scale.

Melissa, also stunned with the rapidity of the day's events and the sudden return of Jeff's faculties, did not know where to begin.

"You had a stroke Tuesday night, sixty-four days ago."

Jeff had no recollection of anything and remained unsure if he was or was not dreaming. Seemed like he had done a lot of dreaming lately.

"You were in Villa Rica at Moon Mountain Observatory, exploring the heavens with your new telescope. A fellow astronomer saw you collapse and called 911.

"What happened? I didn't have any heart problems did I?"

He did not recall anything in his life that led him to fear stroke or heart problems.

"Jeffrey," Melissa said, "That is the strange part. The doctors have found absolutely nothing. You have no paralysis of any kind. As a matter of fact, the nurses say you jerked a lot during the coma."

"Coma?" he mumbled. "How long?"

"Sixty-four days," she repeated.

Jeff elevated the back of the bed and saw a newspaper on the bedside table. The bold headline startled him.

MAYA MADNESS AND THE COMING APOCALYPSE
Gwinnett Gazette, December 12, 2011

"What year is it?"

A neurologist entered the room; and hearing the question, asked Jeff, "What year do you think it is?"

The doctor held out his hand, "Dr. Khular. Chief of Neurology."

"I'm not really sure, doc. I'm not sure that I'm not dreaming, actually."

"Do you feel like you are dreaming?"

"I have no idea," Jeff answered after a pause.

He mentally scanned his memories, the Mayan fiasco, the comet hitting the moon, the flu, the beginning of nuclear war... Samarra.

"Maybe 2019 or 2020. I've lost touch with time I guess."

"Interesting," the doctor said. "It should come back. The memory, I mean."

The neurologist explained that Jeff was in remarkably good health, considering his age and medical issues. It would not be unusual to have twisted or confused memories, including lapses in time.

"So what year is it?" Jeff asked.

"It is 2011, Mr. Ross. Did you have many dreams?"

"Man, did I ever?" he answered after a pause. "I think I am dreaming now."

He squeezed Melissa's hand again, looking at her closely.

"But I sure hope not."

"You are not dreaming, Mr. Ross," the doctor reassured. "What was your last memory before awakening. Do you remember?"

Jeff concentrated, trying to recall and confusing thoughts surrounded his spinning head. The thought of going crazy crossed his mind.

"I think I must be insane."

"No. No. No," the doctor laughed. "You are fine. Jeffrey, do you remember what you were dreaming? When the nurse called me, she said you were groaning and sweating profusely, like you were frightened."

Jeff's heart raced and the blood pressure monitor alarmed.

"No more questions," Dr. Khular said. "You rest, and we will talk later."

The doctor walked toward the door but paused at Jeff's comment, turned and asked, "What did you say?"

"I was on a B36 over Israel I think."

"You mean a B36 bomber?"

"Yeah," Jeff replied, surprised. "You know of that plane?"

"Yep. My grandpa flew one. Unbelievable piece of workmanship."

"Well," Jeff said, "This one crashed. That is my last dream memory."

"Would love to hear that story sometime," the doctor laughed and exited the suite.

Jeff and Melissa listened as Dr. Khular told the head nurse that Jeff could go home the next morning if the examination was successful. Melissa's happiness at the turn of events resonated within, but... with caution. What happened during the two-month coma? Who were the people he would occasionally mention? What has he forgotten about me?

"Did I talk in my sleep?" Jeff asked.

Had he talked about Samarra? Was Samarra real or unreal? His head ached.

"Not really," Melissa said. "You mentioned some names from time to time, especially someone named Abe. I thought it must be the astronomy student that called 911 when you collapsed that night. His name was Abe."

Chapter Forty

Melissa was amazed at Jeff's speedy recovery and thanked God often for bringing him back. The thoughts of divorce no longer fluttered through her mind. If Jeffrey did not want to go to church, she would drop it. Maybe Jesus would show him the way.

She had never been able to generate any interest in believing the reality of God, nor had his mother, even though she prayed every day that Jeff would have a Jesus-moment. That prayer was never answered.

Then God almost took him. She prayed and God brought him out of the darkness and back to her arms. She would never let him go. This time her prayers were answered. Maybe the experience would have a positive effect, because he was actually talking about Jesus.

"It has only been a month, and I think you have all your muscle-strength back. And you have your energy back."

"I feel great. Still confused a bit about the dreams I experienced. They were so real."

"You know," Melissa said, "Jesus told his apostles that when you die it is like going to sleep. He did not say it was going to sleep, only that it is like going to sleep. You have no real memory. Like a dream. Then you wake up and are resurrected for judgment. It seems like you were alive and well the day before, and then it is suddenly Judgment Day. Dreams really mess with time. Was that what the coma was like?"

Jeff considered the question. He remembered everything, at least he thought he did.

"Not really," he said. "I do remember the dreams, they are vivid. I think God was guiding me."

Jeff genuinely felt that was true. He shared as many of his experiences with Melissa during his recovery as he remembered.

"Look at this."

Melissa handed him a postcard advertising a new church opening in downtown Duluth. Once serving as the Masonic Lodge, the church had been restored to original condition.

The small, white church sat in a field behind City Hall, completely surrounded with daffodils.

"This is the church you described to me, the church in your dreams."

Jeff examined the postcard and could not believe his eyes. It was identical to the seven white churches; and memories of Enoch the stutterer, Kipper T and Missy T flooded his consciousness. He missed them and was saddened.

"Wow," Jeff mumbled. "It's identical."

His mood swings were not intolerable but were plenty unpleasant. The dreams had been so life-like, the people had become his friends.

"They are opening the doors Saturday, and I was planning to attend. They are supposed to have a great preacher. I mean, in case you would like to go with me."

"You know, Melissa. I really miss my friends, the ones in my dream."

Melissa listened to Jeff's stories about The Admiral, Abe the Bartender, Chadbo, Sheryl, Wild Willy, Edgar Allan Poe and Condi. The way Jeff explained them and their stories was sometimes humorous but mostly not. They had shared one tragedy after another. And then there were his guardian angels, Missy T and Kipper T, and a preacher named Enoch.

"Okay," he finally said. "I would like to go to the new church with you."

Saturday afternoon, preparing for the opening of the newest little church in town, Jeff grabbed his small backpack off the closet floor and tossed it to the bed. Then he heard a thump.

He walked to the far side of the bed and picked up the book that had fallen out of his backpack and to the floor. It looked familiar and he immediately knew why. It was the Gideon Bible that kept appearing in his dreams. It had to be. Life is odd, he thought and grabbed the key-pod for the Mercedes SUV.

They arrived early and were greeted by an elderly, black woman with gray hair.

"Welcome to de Seven Churches. Please fill out dis nametag if you do not mind."

"Jamaica?" Jeff asked, loving the accent.

"Yes, my deah. How do you know?"

"It's a long story," Jeff said and smiled at the old woman. Very grandmotherly he thought.

The church was exactly like those in his dreams. It had a yellowish glow from the thousands of daffodils sharing their tint, and the small marquis stated: You Better Slow That Cadillac Down!

Melissa, Jami, Jenni and Audry entered, and Jeff brought up the rear. As he ascended the front steps of the church, a short man with dark hair drew his attention. The man looked familiar as did the gentleman he was talking to, tall and distinguished.

"Did you see the short guy outside?" Melissa asked, squeezing his hand. "He was talking with a tall man with silver hair."

"I did," Jeff answered. "Why?"

"The short guy gave me a huge smile like he knew me, that's all."

"Did you see his nametag?" Jeff asked.

"Yep. His name is Vinny. I do not recognize him though."

Jeff did a one-eighty and walked out the door. The short guy was nowhere to be seen, but the tall man with silver hair made his way to the portico and held his hand out.

"Good afternoon," he said. "And welcome. My name is Justin."

Jeff examined Justin's nametag and knew immediately why he recognized the man. His nametag read THE ADMIRAL. A gust of wind blew a yellow daffodil that fell at Jeff's feet.

"Jeffrey Ross," he said, and the wheels of his mind spun. "Have we met before?"

"Yes," The Admiral said. "I think we have. Let us go inside. I understand the new preacher is out of this world." He winked.

Jeff took a seat alongside Melissa and the kids wondering what exactly was happening. A couple sat beside them, Darrell and Tacy Edwards; and she was certain Jeff mentioned them, from his odd dream.

"Gggood mmmorning," the height-impaired preacher said after walking to the pulpit. "Mmmy nname is Enoch; and I ssstutter, don'tcha know."

Melissa gave Jeff a what-in-the-world-is-going-on look, confused and bewildered. Jeff had mentioned the stuttering Enoch from his dreams.

"I ddo nnot ssstutter wwhen I ppreach ttthough. To-dddays' ssermon is cccalled *What if?*"

"What if we speed through life, doin' this and that, goin' here and there and forget the glory of Jesus the Christ; because we're goin' too fast? We got football to watch, and ballet recitals. Next thing you know, life is over and you realize… I could've spent more time lovin' God, don'tcha know."

"When my momma died, I sat back one day in my recliner chair, thinkin' 'bout some of the things I said to her when she was alive. What if I had told her I loved her more often? It would've made her feel good, don'tcha know.

"Well, there ya go. Don't go through life so fast you forget to let The Almighty and His Son know how much you love them; 'cause when you die, you discover the glory and the reality of God.

"Jesus is gonna return, don'tcha know; and when he does, it will bring tears to the eyes of the folk who rejected him and called him a liar and a fraud. It's gonna bring tears to the eyes of Christians who have been convinced that Jesus is okay with sinnin'. He ain't."

An hour later, the sermon was over and the Ross family made their exit. Melissa noted the various nametags, now curious; and there they were: Chadbo, Wild Willy, Sheryl, The Admiral, Condi, Hutz the Putz. Where was Abe and Edgar Allan?

Jeff drove the family back to their Sugarloaf home, keeping his feelings to himself. He felt strangely troubled, when he thought he should be rejoicing.

"You're quiet," Melissa said.

"Just thinking," Jeff answered.

"Did you recognize the beautiful woman standing at the front door of the church when we left?"

"Nope," Jeff answered. "You are the only beautiful woman that I notice."

"That's good, Mr. Ross. You still have your charm. She was gorgeous though and acted like she recognized me."

"What was her name?"

"Not sure," Melissa said. "It looked like Samantha or Samarra."

Nothing really shocked him on this day. He had never mentioned Samarra from his dreams and wished he had seen her. Arriving home, the three girls disappeared in a flash. Jenni and Jami were going to a Mayan Apocalypse Party. Melissa and Audry headed to Avalon to shop for a birthday present; so he planned to hang out and contemplate. He was doing a lot of contemplating lately.

As the afternoon wound down, Jeff drove to Perimeter Mall and past the Starbucks he stopped at every day, or did he? Was that just a part of his dream? The front windows were shattered, and yellow police tape surrounded the building.

He listened to the *Breaking News* report on the SUV's audio system as he steered into Park Place Shopping Center. He wanted to check to see if Park Place Café still existed. A brown van similar to a UPS van entered behind him and turned left, circling the parking lot.

"An entire family disappeared today in Puerto Rico. Witnesses said Pastor Rob Mariner and his family were singing gospel hymns outside The Cathedral of San Juan Bautista when asked to leave by police. Apparently there was another bomb scare.

"According to police and eyewitness reports, the family did as ordered. While walking down Old San Juan Street, they vanished 'into thin air' according to Father Pedro. We are trying to verify this story, which seems preposterous.

"Another Muslim group is taking credit for the daycare center bombings that killed twenty-six children and three teachers yesterday in Atlanta."

Jeff carried his backpack and Gideon Bible with him and entered the small café and bar. Park Place was exactly like he remembered, and he was glad it was not a dream. He loved their music and the menu was excellent.

"Pssst, Jeff."

He turned left to see who called his name; and there she was, sitting alone in a large, spacious booth, Missy T. She was identical to the Missy T in his dreams. Jet black hair, short skirt, blue eyes and beautiful, pale skin. He pinched himself.

"This is not a dream, Jeffrey. Have a seat."

He slid across the booth and looked straight into her eyes. She looked real enough. He reached over and touched her hand.

"You're real," he said.

Even more confused, he thought to himself: *What the hell is going on in my life.*

"Yes, I am real; and that is exactly what God has done for you."

"What?" he queried.

"Saved you from Hell, Jeffrey. Two months ago, you had a stroke and God spoke to you. You were an atheist at that time, if you remember. I think you called the Bible 'hogwash'. Remember?"

He did remember and was shamed by the memories, shamed by things he said, shamed and embarrassed.

"Would you two like to order?"

Jeff looked at the menu but knew it by memory… unless it had changed.

"He will have the Park Place Southern Walnut Salad, and a glass of house merlot."

How did she know that was his favorite salad?

"We have a Merlot Special, if you are interested," the waiter replied, waiting patiently.

"That will be fine," Missy T said.

"How about you, young lady?"

"Diet Coke and a slice of your angel food cake," she said and winked at Jeff.

"What is going on in my life, Missy T?" he asked as the waiter walked away. "You're right. My last memory about God was a girl holding a protest sign, 'God is coming and she's mad as hell.' I can't remember the sequence of events; but about the same time as I saw the girl, I saw a really, really bright light."

"Blip," she said.

"Yeah… Blip."

Outside, the front doors of the brown van opened and two men dressed as clowns, exited, leaving the van parked in the handicapped parking space by the lobby of Dunwoody Senior's Center.

"Melissa is going on in your life, Jeffrey. She believed; you did not. So she prayed, diligently. Every day she prayed for your very lost soul. She knew your good heart and loved your heart, but she did not love your belief system. She prayed you would find the God of Abraham, Isaac and Jacob and not some new age liberal god. She spent 25 years hoping you would become a strong Christian who at least tried not to sin; but you did not.

"God listened to Melissa's incessant praying and answered her. He intervened in your life, in the heart of an atheist… think about that. Even an atheist can be changed in an instant, at least an instant to God. He loves you or what happened to you would not have happened. Had that been the case, you would have played and spent money in this life, having a great time; but after this test, you would spend eternity in a very dark, dank place. Total darkness except for the fire."

"What about Samarra, she seemed so real? And The Admiral and all my friends..."

Jeff's thoughts drifted to the friends in his dream. He missed them.

"All of you were at the little, white church yesterday. Do all of you really exist?"

"Of course we do, Jeffrey. God has so many angels in His tool box. He has tools that mankind can't even imagine, some good and some, not. God's heavenly host is magnanimous, and we serve Yahweh at His pleasure. It was Yahweh's pleasure to save your eternal life. That is what we did."

The waiter balanced the tray carefully as he approached the table with a bottle of wine and the house specialty salad. There was no angel food cake or Diet Coke.

"Is Abe the Bartender an angel?" Jeff asked, suddenly depressed; but Missy T was nowhere to be found. She had simply vanished, like she always did.

The waiter sat the bottle of wine and salad on the table.

"Did you see the lady that was sitting here a few minutes ago?" Jeff asked, noticing the lack of angel food cake.

"No sir, I did not."

Jeff didn't look at the waiter but stared instead at the bottle of Duckhorn Merlot and smiled.

"Do you remember me, Mr. Ross?" the waiter asked.

Jeff examined the younger man's face but with no recognition.

"I can't say that I do," Jeff replied, "but I do like your wine selection. You are an excellent waiter."

"Oh," the man said, "I am not the waiter. I was in Villa Rica looking through my new scope that night you collapsed, and I called 911. You did not regain consciousness so did not think you would remember. It is great to see you back to normal."

"Thank you for saving my life," Jeff said, astonished. "Are you the manager here?"

The two-hundred-pound fertilizer-diesel bomb exploded with such impact that the entire front of the Senior Center facility became an instant mishmash of crushed glass, steel and aluminum. Smoke billowed from the fires set by the bomb, and the front door of Park Place Café blew off the hinges. Jeff and the waiter crawled under the table for cover, but there were no follow up explosions.

"We have to stop meeting like this," Jeff said with a nervous laugh.

The waiter stuck out his hand.

"No, I'm not the manager. My name is Abraham, and my friends call me Abe the Bartender."

CPSIA information can be obtained
at www.ICGtesting.com
Printed in the USA
LVHW092340081021
699971LV00002B/71

9 781532 394065